DEATH IN THE C

A MEDIEVAL MYSTERY

DEATH IN THE CLOSE
A MEDIEVAL MYSTERY

ANDY BOUCHER   LUKE CRADDOCK-BENNETT   TEGAN DALY

INVESTIGATIONS BY

ALEKSANDRA BOLCZYK, LISE BREKMOE, LUKE CRADDOCK-BENNETT, KATH CROOKS, TEGAN DALY,
JOZEF DORAN, DAVID DOYLE, TOM ELLIOT, LIAM FOGARTY, MARIUSZ GORNIAK, JANE GREEN,
KATIE KEEFE, TIM LEWIS, SIMON MAYES, JASON MURPHY, ANNIE PARTRIDGE, BEN RAFFIELD,
DALE ROUSE, GREG SHEPHERD, DAN STONE, SANDRA THOMAS, BENEDIKTE WARD

WITH SPECIALIST CONTRIBUTIONS BY

KATH CROOKS, JANE EVANS, JULIE FRANKLIN, BROOKE GARRETT, SHEILA HAMILTON-DYER,
SARAH-JANE HASTON, NICHOLAS HOLMES, ANGELA LAMB, JULIE LOCHRIE, FIONA MCGIBBON,
JANET MONTGOMERY, RICHARD K MORRISS, JASON MURPHY, GEOFF NOWELL, ROBERT THOMPSON,
SCOTT TIMPANY, CARMELITA TROY, RACHEL TYSON, WAIKATO UNIVERSITY

ILLUSTRATIONS BY

JULIA BASTEK-MICHALSKA

EDINBURGH 2015

Cover photo by Headland Archaeology (UK) Ltd © Headland Archaeology (UK) Ltd

Published in 2015 by Headland Archaeology (UK) Ltd

Headland Archaeology (UK) Ltd
13 Jane Street
Edinburgh EH6 5HE
T 0131 467 7705
E publications@headlandarchaeology.com
W www.headlandarchaeology.com

Headland Archaeology (UK) Ltd is a registered company SC342945

British Library Cataloguing-in-Publication Data
A catalogue record for this book is available from the British Library

ISBN 978-0-9556419-2-3 (Paperback edition)
ISBN 978-0-9556419-3-0 (Hardback edition)

This publication was supported by the Marc Fitch Fund and Hereford Cathedral Perpetual Trust.

HEREFORD CATHEDRAL
Perpetual Trust

Design, typesetting and production by Julia Bastek-Michalska, Andy Boucher, Julie Franklin and
Caroline Norrman; Headland Archaeology (UK) Ltd

Manufactured in Poland by LF Book Services

PREFACE

In September 2009 work began on a £5m project to restore the Cathedral Close as a suitable setting for the Cathedral and more attractive public space. The project involved intrusive ground works for the laying of services and rearrangement of paths and parking areas. Due to the historical importance of the site and the presence of archaeological remains immediately below the surface, the main contactors, C J Bayliss, were assisted on the project by a team of professional archaeologists from Headland Archaeology.

The scheme itself was designed to minimise impact upon important archaeological deposits, and where possible to preserve remains in situ. Wherever possible the ground surface of the Close was built up to accommodate the higher curbs on the new and replacement paths. Any works that broke ground were monitored by archaeologists, and where archaeological deposits were revealed that could not be left in place, the archaeologists were afforded the time to remove the deposits and create a full record of their existence.

The renovation of the Close provided a unique opportunity to study the archaeology of a large area of land right at the centre of Saxon Hereford. It was the largest excavation to be carried out in Hereford for 50 years and turned out to be one of the largest medieval/post-medieval burial ground excavations undertaken in Britain.

Andy Boucher
Director, Headland Archaeology (UK) Ltd

VOLUNTEERS

In line with the Heritage Lottery funded nature of the project, we would like to thank the following who gave their time to help process the finds and human remains: Danielle Adams, Franka Addyman, Charlotte Alexander, Tony Bevan, Julie Bowen, Vicki Collins, Robert Edwards, Catherine Flower, Linda Friedman, Tina Friedman, Abigail Green, Isobel Griffith, Charlotte Handley, Sandi Harriss, Ami Hartland, Fran Jones, Sian Jones, Phil Kelly, Angela Olsen, Alex Martin, Hillary Mee, Greg Miller, Daniel Mills, Gerry Moore, Ian Moore, Matthew Payne, Elizabeth Roberts, Sam Robertson, Gwen Settlefield, Ben Sheen , Rob Sherwood, Val Siddal, Owen Sleet, Sylvie Smith, Graham Spencer, Jacqueline Spicer, Emma Spurling, Susanne Tarp, Emma Tomlinson, Alice Trowell, Derek Trumper, Linda Ward, Callum Whithall, Danielle Wildgoose, Gwyn Williams, Isaac Williams, Oliver Wren

ACKNOWLEDGEMENTS

A large number of individuals were involved in the archaeological aspect of the project. These include both the current cathedral archaeologist Richard K Morriss as well as his predecessor Ron Shoesmith who were involved in the delivery and planning of the work. On the cathedral side Robert Kilgour the Cathedral Architect, alongside Adrian Stenning, kept track of the progress of the project and assisted in resolving the many issues that arose throughout, with Andrew Eames (the then chapter clerk) providing occasional helpful guidance.

We are also indebted to the input of Julian Cotton and Dr Keith Ray from Herefordshire Archaeology regarding the management of the planning requirements and Simon Mays of English Heritage for useful discussions regarding the approach to the osteological work at the inception of the project and Tony Fleming (Ancient Monuments Inspector) and Lisa Moffatt (English Heritage Science Advisor) for their continued support and advice throughout.

Regarding the conduct of the site work much of the progress made on site would not have been achieved without the co-operation of local contractor C J Bayliss Ltd, and in particular Russell Davies who liaised with management and staff through the project to ensure that both the archaeological and landscaping aspects of the work were completed successfully.

The Hereford Cathedral Close Project was supported by the National Lottery through the Heritage Lottery Fund, together with The Jordan Foundation, Albert and Monique Heijn, Historic England, Herefordshire Council, Garfield Weston Foundation, Hereford City Council, Mark and Elaine Ellis, Lawrence and Elizabeth Banks, Bob and Bea Tabor, The Rowlands Trust and The Headley Trust, in partnership with the Chapter of Hereford Cathedral, The Friends of Hereford Cathedral, the Mappa Mundi Trust and the Hereford Cathedral Perpetual Trust.

The Hereford Cathedral Perpetual Trust was founded in 1995 as the fundraising and development arm of the cathedral. We help to fund repairs to the building, and support the cathedral choir and education programmes through our work. We need to continue our fundraising through gifts, events and legacies. For further information, please contact Hereford Cathedral Perpetual Trust, email perpetualtrust@herefordcathedral.org, or telephone 01432 374261. Charity number 1051168.

The authors would like to thank David Whitehead and Richard K Morriss for their comments and feedback on the early versions of the text.

CONTENTS

LIST OF ILLUSTRATIONS

LIST OF TABLES

LIST OF CONTRIBUTORS

JULIA BASTEK-MICHALSKA	illustrations, finds photography, cover design
ANDY BOUCHER	project manager
LUKE CRADDOCK-BENNETT	site director
KATH CROOKS	pottery, metalworking waste, ceramic building material
TEGAN DALY	human bone
JANE EVANS	isotope analysis, British Geological Survey
JULIE FRANKLIN	metalwork, stone and bone finds, clay pipes, bottle and vessel glass
BROOKE GARRETT	isotope analysis, Durham University
SHEILA HAMILTON-DYER	animal bone
SARAH-JANE HASTON	environmental
NICHOLAS HOLMES	coins
ANGELA LAMB	isotope analysis, British Geological Survey
JULIE LOCHRIE	lithics
FIONA MCGIBBON	lithological identifications for stone finds
JANET MONTGOMERY	isotope analysis, Durham University (Table 59 and Illus 125)
RICHARD K MORRISS	architectural stone
JASON MURPHY	osteological assistant
CAROLINE NORRMAN	typesetting, page design and layout
GEOFF NOWELL	isotope analysis, Durham University
ROBERT THOMPSON	Hereford trade token
DR SCOTT TIMPANY	environmental
CARMELITA TROY	osteological consultant
DR RACHEL TYSON	window glass
WAIKATO UNIVERSITY	C14 dating

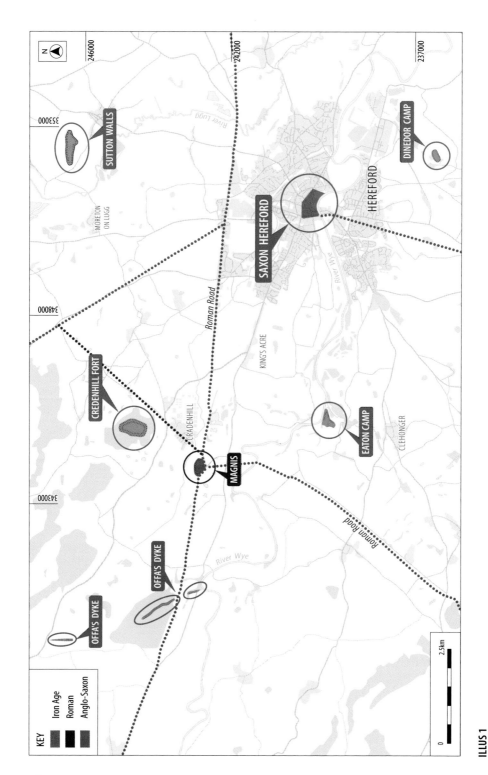

ILLUS 1

Map of Hereford and surrounding area showing key sites from Iron Age, Roman and Saxon periods

CHRONICLES UN-CHAINED

Hereford would appear to be a prime location for settlement, situated on a well drained river terrace, with natural springs and a fording place across the River Wye (Illus 1). Chance finds of stone tools (eg Illus 2) confirm there was human activity on the site of the later city during the prehistoric period, but so far no evidence for settlement has been discovered[1].

Archaeologists have long looked in vain for definitive proof of Roman occupation of the site. Rarely a major excavation takes place without a few sherds of Roman pottery or building material being found, but as yet there has not been the long anticipated major discovery of Roman occupation.

The place-name 'Hereford' derives from the Old English for 'army ford', and shows the importance that the natural crossing place

0   2.5cm

ILLUS 2
Flint arrowhead recovered from the West
End, early Bronze Age (SF2013)

over the River Wye had in establishing the settlement. The ford is believed to be located to the south of the Bishop's Palace gardens on a continuation of the line of Broad Street and the northern part of Gwynne Street. It has been suggested that the use of this ford may date back to the Roman period when the river crossing is thought to have formed part of the 'Watling Street' as it passed between Leintwardine and Monmouth[2].

In 1920 Alfred Watkins further defined an early defensive enclosure identified in the late 19th century with the cathedral at its centre[3]. Rectangular in plan, the enclosure was bounded by the King's ditch in the west (following the line of Aubrey Street down towards the River Wye), and what we now know to be the Saxon defensive ditch to the north roughly

1   Thomas & Boucher 2002, 3

2   Wood 1903, 188
3   Watkins 1920

following the line of East Street and West Street. From the junction of Offa Street and St John Street the line of the ditch was traced southwards to Castle Hill. Watkins was content to leave this early defensive work as undated. George Marshall, however, used Watkins' model so suggest a Roman origin for the town[4]. Marshall suggested that the layout of Roman Leintwardine (Bravonium) could be superimposed onto this early urban centre with the central street at Leintwardine falling on the line of Church Street and the fort's rounded corner corresponded to the junction of Offa Street and St John Street.

To date, no definitive evidence has been found to support Marshall's theory. Excavations by Shoesmith on the northern ditch and Heys and Norwood on the line of the King's ditch have produced no Roman material[5], and a Saxon origin (certainly for the northern defensive work) is generally accepted. Shoesmith does however record that the ditches had clearly been re-cut a number of times and this could have removed all trace of their potential Roman origin.

Along with the almost commonplace recovery of stray sherds of Roman ceramics, a number of Romano-British coins have been discovered in Tupsley, Kings Acre and Newton Farm and a hoard of eight coins was discovered in a garden in Hunderton in the 1950s. Whilst these artefacts could have been deposited by people on the move, a number of larger stone objects discovered in the city suggest a more purposeful Roman presence. Two Roman altars were reused in the construction of two 7th or 8th century grain-drying ovens found close to Victoria Street, and a further altar was found near St John Street. During the extension to the former Woolworths store on Eign Street in 1962, a quern stone dating to the Iron Age or Romano-British period was recovered.

Without the discovery of a building or defensive work dating to the Roman period there is a tendency to explain away stray finds within the city as having been imported from the nearest Roman settlement of Kenchester (Magnis), four miles to the north-west of Hereford. It is not uncommon for Roman masonry to be reused in later buildings, indeed Leland, writing in the early 16th century, speaks of the people of Hereford pulling down the ruined buildings of Kenchester and using the best stone for their own buildings[6]. Leland's direct reference to the re-use of material from Kenchester by the people of Hereford, provides a convenient explanation for the presence of Roman architectural material within the city. At present, the latest piece of evidence was the discovery of opus signinum in a rubble layer sealed in sequence by a Norman surface and late Saxon soil layer in Broad Street. It is currently thought that this could relate to a riverside shrine. The volume of evidence is currently not there to support anything other than a Saxon origin to settlement in Hereford. Leland considered that 'of the decaye of Kenchestre Herford rose and florishyd'.

THE SAXON PERIOD

At the decline of the Roman empire and subsequent abandonment of Britain in the early 5th century, petty princedoms emerged to fill the power vacuum. In many parts of Britain, this vacuum was filled by Germanic settlers, but there is evidence to suggest that the Herefordshire region remained largely British. In the land between the Wye and the Severn, covering much of modern Herefordshire, the

---

4   Marshall 1940, 68

5   Shoesmith 1982, 89

6   Shoesmith 1992, 3

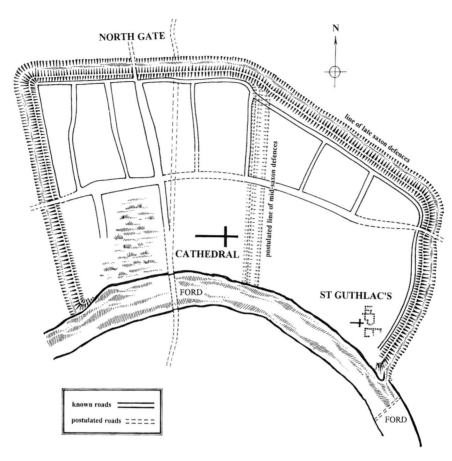

NORTH GATE

N

line of late saxon defences

postulated line of mid-saxon defences

CATHEDRAL

FORD

ST GUTHLAC'S

FORD

known roads
postulated roads

ILLUS 3
Plan of Saxon Hereford (after Stone & Appleton-Fox 1996)

kingdom of the Magonsaete was established, and the southern part of the modern county, known as Ergyng, was ruled by Welsh kings throughout the 6th and 7th centuries[7]. The Old English term '-saete' may indicate people of a British origin, and indeed the first king of the Magonsaete adopted the name Merewalh, which means illustrious Welshman.

In the West Midlands, smaller petty kingdoms were coalescing into more stable kingdoms by the 7th century, with the kingdom of

Mercia emerging as the dominant power in the region. By the 8th century, Mercia's sphere of influence extended westwards to the present border with Wales, and by AD 800 the sub-kingdom of the Magonsaete had been subsumed.

The documentary evidence for the foundation of Hereford is sparse, obscure, often contradictory and largely concerned with the religious foundation of the city. It has traditionally been held that the foundation of the diocese of Hereford dates to AD 676 when Seaxwulf, the Mercian bishop at

7   Hooke 2006, 43

Lichfield granted a church and land to Putta. Unfortunately Bede, in his Ecclesiastical History of the English People, does not specify the location of Putta's church, however, an episcopal list dating to the early 9th century records Putta as the first bishop of the western Hecani (later known as the Magonsaetan) who are thought to have occupied an area broadly equating to the Hereford diocese. Some historians now question Putta's involvement in the foundation of the diocese[8] and suggest that the Episcopal lists were fabricated to lend credibility to the rule of Offa and his desire to hand the kingship down to his son. Because Bede had not specified the location of Putta's church, Offa was able to fabricate the episcopal lists to place Putta at the head of the Hereford diocese and therefore create the illusion of a well established Mercian diocese dating back to the late 7th century. The purpose of this was to emphasise the extent of the Mercian see to demonstrate the need for an archbishop. The pope agreed and an agreeable archbishop was appointed, with the power to consecrate Offa's son, Ecgfrith as king. The plan worked, and even if the foundation of the see does date to the late 7th century persuasive arguments have been made for the seat of the Bishop being at Lydbury North, Ledbury or Leominster rather than Hereford[9].

Christianity seems to have been well established in the Welsh borderland by the 6th century and it seems probable that the western Hecani were already Christian prior to the conversion of the Mercians, the religion having been established during the Roman period. The organised, politicised Christianity of the Mercians was being inserted into a pre-existing Celtic Christian landscape. Current archaeological evidence points to the Castle Green area of Hereford as the location for a religious establishment with its roots in Celtic Christianity. Excavations on the site in 1960 and 1973 demonstrated the existence of religious buildings, with associated burials dating from the 7th to 11th centuries[10]. On the balance of probability, the site, later dedicated to St Guthlac, may have existed throughout its life as a religious establishment separate and distinct from the later cathedral on the close and the wider diocese of Hereford, having its origins in the Celtic rather than the Roman church.

If there was a Bishop of the Magonsaete located elsewhere within the diocese, two pieces of evidence suggest that it had been moved to Hereford by the end of the 8th century. The more convincing of these is a document of AD 803 in which Wulfheard describes himself as Bishop of the Church of Hereford. The second and slightly more fanciful evidence comes from the Anglo-Saxon Chronicle where it is recorded that in AD 794 King Offa of Mercia had Ethelbert, king of the East Angles beheaded. Apparently the young Ethelbert had come to the royal estate at Sutton in Herefordshire in order to obtain the hand of Offa's daughter Elfthryth in marriage. On the instructions of either Offa or his queen, Cwenthryth, the young king was murdered and thrown into the marshes by the River Lugg. The location of the body was miraculously revealed to friends of Ethelbert by a great beam of light and the appearance of a spring. A vision of Ethelbert appeared to a nobleman and instructed him to take his body to Hereford. During the journey, Ethelbert's head fell off the cart and was found by a blind man, who was miraculously restored to sight[11]. Approaching Hereford the group delivering the body stopped to rest and another spring miraculously appeared at the site of St Ethelberts well, located on Castle Hill, to the east of present day Quay Street.

8   Hillaby 2001
9   Blair 2001, 11

10   Shoesmith 2000, 293
11   Shoesmith 2000, 293

The church which was originally dedicated to St Mary, was by the end of the 10th century dedicated additionally to Ethelbert. From a modern perspective, it is difficult to draw too much historical fact from the tale of Ethelbert's demise. The importance of the tale is perhaps in the way it draws a key protagonist, King Offa of Mercia (AD 757–96) into the story of Hereford.

Hereford's location on the frontier between the Welsh and the Anglo-Saxon kingdoms clearly made it vulnerable. The Life of St Guthlac, written before AD 749, records that at the beginning of the 8th century 'the Britons were troubling the English with their attacks, their pillaging and their devastations of the people'. In AD 743 Ethelbald, the king of Mercia, and Cuthred of Wessex campaigned together against the Welsh. The Book of Llandaff records the 'plunderings' of the 'treacherous Saxon nation', and makes specific reference to this happening 'on the borders of Wales and England towards Hereford'. The culmination of these hostilities may have been the battle of Hereford in AD 760 which is recorded in several Welsh sources[12]. The extent of Offa's involvement in the battle is unrecorded, however, having come to the throne after the death of Ethelbald in AD 757, Offa certainly continued hostilities with the Welsh and completed the settlement of the land beyond the River Severn, defining its western boundary by the construction of the great dyke that bears his name.

There is a strong possibility that the construction of the dyke was part of a wider reorganisation of the political and religious landscape of western Mercia, which led to the development of Hereford under Offa[13]. Archaeological excavations have indicated that a planned grid system of streets and houses was laid out in the west of the city at some time between the mid 8th and mid 9th centuries[14]. Extrapolating this evidence eastwards it was surmised that Broad Street formed the central north-south thoroughfare and an east-west road joining Castle Street to King Street was believed to have crossed through the area now occupied by the cathedral. Shoesmith also suggests that the remains of the grid system are fossilised in the modern day Berrington Street, Aubrey Street, Church Street and St John Street. No. archaeological evidence has been found to support this other than the excavations around Berrington Street[15].

The reorganisation of Hereford as a planned settlement may have afforded the opportunity for the creation of a religious precinct at its heart. The documentary evidence for the cathedral church being established in Hereford at the beginning of the 9th century (rather than the late 7th century) would appear to fit with developments elsewhere within the city and wider region. A gravel rampart excavated on Victoria Street is believed to be the earliest phase of defences for the city and is dated to the mid 9th century[16]. During the period between AD 800 and AD 850 the religious, political and strategic importance of the settlement rises to the fore, and it is perhaps to this period more than any other that we can date the emergence of modern Hereford.

Little is recorded about the early development of the cathedral close. The antiquarian John Duncomb, writing in the early 19th century, speculated that the cathedral church during the time of Offa was constructed of wood. His assumption is based on the description

---

12   Whitehead 1982, 13
13   Blair 2005, 288

14   Shoesmith 2000, 293
15   Shoesmith 1982, 91–2
16   Shoesmith 1982, 74

of the church that replaced this structure, given by 16th century historian Vergil, as being of a 'marked distinction from that which preceded it'. The replacement, built of stone, was constructed by Milfrid around AD 825[17].

Following a resurgence in warfare with the Welsh during the first half of the 9th century, Alfred emerged as the dominant Saxon king of the latter part of the century and adopted a more conciliatory approach to the Welsh. It is during this period that Mercian supremacy passed to the West Saxons[18] and Herefordshire comes into being as a tribute area for the town itself. The territory of the region, however, does not extend beyond the River Wye and Hereford finds itself right on the border of the West Saxon state. In truth, both the Saxons and the Welsh had a common enemy during this period so some degree of co-operation was inevitable – it was now Danish raiders who became the predominant threat to the stability of the region. In AD 893 Ethelred of Mercia called out the King's thegns 'from every fortress (burh) east of the Parret both west and east of Selwood, and also north of the Thames and west of the Severn together with a section of the Welsh'[19] and defeated the Danes at Buttington in Montgomeryshire. Hereford was almost certainly the only Saxon 'burh' west of the Severn and it would seem that by this date the place not only had defences but was an integral part of the West Saxon defensive system[20].

0   1cm

ILLUS 4
Silver penny of King Cnut (1016–35) recovered from St John's Quad, 1024–30 (SF0818)

Danish raids continued into the 10th century and the men of Hereford are specifically mentioned in AD 914 when, alongside the men of Gloucester they inflicted a heavy defeat upon the 'great pirate host' which had been marauding in Archenfield and had captured the bishop of that region. Local Historian David Whitehead[21] suggests that during the early 10th century, Hereford may have been used as a base for the Saxon rulers to launch attacks into Welsh territory. Alfred's daughter Aethelflaed, Lady of the Mercians, oversaw the creation of a series of defended settlements during the late 9th and early 10th centuries, and the defences of Hereford may have been strengthened or extended during this period. Certainly, the town must have been of some prominence, when in c 930 King Aethelstan met the Welsh Princes in Hereford for talks.

Dumcumb speculates that the turmoil of the period led to the deterioration of Milfred's cathedral:

'. . . if the Danes did not offer positive violence to the fabric, the state of continual warfare or alarm must have occasioned a neglect of the common means necessary to its preservation. Perhaps to this cause it may be assigned, that the lapidea structura (stone structure) decayed within the short period of two hundred years. . .'[22]

Bishop Aethelstan (c 1015–56) emerges as a key figure in the history of Hereford cathedral in the early 11th century, at a time when the

17   Duncomb 1804, 521
18   Whitehead 1982, 14
19   Garmonsway 1953, 87
20   Whitehead 1982, 14

21   Whitehead 2007, 21
22   Duncumb 1804, 522

English crown passed into Danish hands. Victory over the English at Assandum and the subsequent death of King Edmund II led to Cnut (1016–35) (Illus 4) assuming the throne and the settlement of the southern part of the west midlands, including Herefordshire, by Danish incomers[23].

Aethelstan is variously recorded as either rebuilding the cathedral during his incumbency or 'constructing his minster from its foundations'. It is unclear whether Aethelstan built an entirely new cathedral at this time or simply carried out repairs to Milfred's 9th century structure. In either case, the documentary references suggest that his works were extensive. Although the exact dates are unrecorded, it seems likely that Aethelstan embarked on the project c 1020–40.

Little is known about the form of the late Saxon Cathedral and various suggestions have been made for its former location within the close. In their comprehensive assessment of surviving Anglo-Saxon architecture, H M and J Taylor[24] record that the surviving northern wall of Bishop Robert's 1079–95 chapel, now incorporated into the southern wall of the later Bishop's cloister, in turn incorporated the northern wall of an earlier building. The Taylors believe that two double-splayed, round-headed windows are Saxon in date. If this is the case, the natural conclusion would be that they formed part of Aethelstan's minster.

Unfortunately the construction of Aethelstan's great minster coincided with a resurgence of Welsh nationalism under Gruffydd ap Llewelyn. It has been suggested that the Welsh perhaps regarded themselves

as the rightful rulers of Herefordshire, and Llewelyn's attacks on Leominster in 1052 and Hereford in 1055 were part of a deliberate plan of reconquest. The political situation was favourable to Llewelyn, the rule of Herefordshire during this period being divided between the English house of Godwin and a Norman faction led by Ralf, the nephew of Edward the Confessor.

Llewelyn attacked Hereford on the 24th or 25th of October 1055, with the help of Elfgar, a disgruntled Mercian nobleman outlawed by Edward the Confessor who was under pressure from the House of Godwin. The Welsh forces confronted Earl Ralph 'the timid' and an army comprised of both English and Normans two miles distant from the town. Under the control of Ralph, the English soldiers, apparently unused to mounted combat were routed. Florence of Worcester records the events;

'Before any spear had been thrown the English army fled because they were on horseback, and many were killed there – about four or five hundred men – and they killed none in return. And then they went back to the town and burnt it with the glorious minster which Athelstan the venerable bishop had built. They stripped and robbed it of relics and vestments and everything, and killed the people and some they carried off.'

The extent to which the cathedral was damaged is not entirely clear. Certainly the attack was violent – Canon Eilmar, four of his sons, and two further canons were murdered while defending the doors of the cathedral. The building did however survive to some degree. Aethelstan died the following year and is recorded as being 'buried in the church which he himself had constructed from the foundations'. This would suggest that the cathedral was still standing and in a suitable state to receive the body of a bishop.

23   Keynes 2000, 16
24   Taylor & Taylor 1965, 295

The cathedral standing in Hereford today is not that of Aethelstan. The earliest parts of the current building are Norman and date to the early 12th century, which raises the question of the whereabouts of the great minster of the 11th century, and indeed, the one or possibly two churches before it. Even if the sacking of Hereford did not destroy the Saxon Cathedral, it seems almost certain that it destroyed any contemporary documentary evidence to indicate its location. Other than the Hereford Gospels and Bishop Aethelstan's evangeliary, which pre-date the sacking, the existing record of Hereford's cathedral church starts in the 1050s.

Clues as to the location of Aethelstan's cathedral exist. The possible Saxon masonry identified in the southern wall of the Bishop's cloister would place the cathedral to the south of the current cathedral in the area between the northern end of the Bishop's Palace and the College of Vicars' Choral. Duncumb records the tantalising tale of 'excavations' undertaken in the 17th century, which also suggests a location to begin the search.

> 'Its position is uncertain, but about 1650 Silas Taylor found, 'beyond the lines of the present building, and particularly towards the east, near the cloisters of the college, such stupendous foundations, such capitals and pedestals, such well-wrought bases for arches, and such rare engravings, and mouldings of friezes' as left little doubt in his mind that they were the foundations of the cathedral destroyed by Alfgar and Griffin'[25].

If Silas Taylor was correct in his belief that he had found Athelstans' cathedral then it is clear that the Norman cathedral was not built on the same site, but to the north

of its Saxon predecessor. According to his description, St John's Quad would appear to be a possible location for Taylor's excavations and potentially the Saxon Cathedral.

The sacking of Hereford in 1055 brought about a renewed focus on the defence of the town. After pursuing the Welsh raiders, Harold Godwinson (later to become King Harold II) embarked upon a program of extensive works. Florence of Worcester records that Harold dug a broad deep ditch around the town and fortified it with gates and bars. The documentary sources do not make it clear whether Harold constructed entirely new defences at this time or whether he repaired and refortified an existing defence.

The earliest Saxon defences of Hereford are believed to date to the 9th century. Originally they were formed from a turf and clay rampart with a timber face and exterior ditch[26]. In the early to mid 10th century, the timber was replaced with a stone wall. By the late 12th century, due to the expansion of the city, the defences were extended to enclose a larger area, which is traceable in the city today as the medieval stone wall added to the defences in the first half of the 13th century. To the east and west, the Saxon defences occupy the same line as the later 13th century wall. The northern line of the Saxon defences lies approximately along the route of East Street and West Street, ie the northern ditch identified by Alfred Watkins. Harold's contribution to the line of the original defences is becoming clearer with evidence for wholesale recutting of the existing northern defences now dated to around his time at Eign Gate.

What we can now confidently attribute to Harold is the creation of a defended

25   Duncumb 1804, 523

26   Shoesmith 1982

area to the south of the River Wye. Recent archaeological work on the defensive circuit to the south of the river known as the King's ditch has returned carbon dates suggesting that this earthwork was part of Harold's refortification, and indeed a concentration of works to the south of the river would seem sensible considering the Welsh threat. Based on the existing evidence, it would appear that Harold repaired, or even remodelled, the existing defences to the north of the river and created additional defences to its south.

THE MEDIEVAL PERIOD

With the consecration of Bishop Robert of Lorraine in 1079 the fortunes of the diocese and of the cathedral revived[27]. Robert came from Lotharingia (a region equivalent to modern day eastern France, western Germany and western Switzerland), and had been trained at the cathedral school in Liege. The new bishop came to an arrangement with William FitzOsbern, the Norman overlord of the Marches, whereby Robert gained the manor of Eaton Bishop in exchange for an area of land beyond the northern Saxon defences[28]. Fitz Osbern used the newly acquired land to create a Norman suburb and market place and in doing so shifted the commercial heart of the town from the area around the cathedral to the part of Hereford today known as High Town. This shifting of the commercial area could be seen as the first step towards creating the space necessary to rebuild the cathedral on a grand scale. In practice Robert did not get to realise that dream. His contribution to the development of the cathedral was the construction of the Losinga Chapel, a square, two-storey building dedicated to St Katherine and St Mary Magdalene.

(Illus 5) A large part of the building was demolished in the 18th century, but the north wall of the building is still standing and is incorporated into the south wall of the south-west cloister. Perhaps due to the presence of potential Saxon masonry within the surviving wall of the Losinga Chapel, it has been suggested that the most likely location for Bishop Aethelstan's 'glorious minster' was in the region between Robert's chapel and the Romanesque cathedral to the north. However, the 'Saxon' masonry appears to relate to the northern wall of a former building[29] suggesting that the Saxon building extended to the south of the suggested location. Shoesmith suggests that the reality of a functioning Saxon Cathedral sandwiched between the Losinga Chapel and a construction site to the north is unlikely, and in line with Silas Taylor's observations proposes the area of the College of the Vicars Choral as an alternative location. David Whitehead suggests a location closer to the river[30]. The present Cathedral Archaeologist Richard Morris makes the observation that we should keep an open mind regarding the location of the Saxon Cathedral and entertain the probability that more than one church or chapel existed in the complex, as at pre-conquest Worcester and Winchester[31].

What existed on the site in the years prior to the construction of the Romanesque cathedral is not entirely clear. The sweeping away of the Saxon in favour of the Norman was an experience common to almost all English cathedrals of the late 11th and early 12th century, but there presumably must have been a period when both the Saxon Cathedral and the emerging Norman cathedral co-existed on the site. There are no documentary references to a new cathedral building being

27 Barrow 2000, 23
28 Whitehead 1982, 17
29 Taylor & Taylor 1965
30 Whitehead 2007, 23
31 Morris 2000, 204

constructed between the sacking of the Saxon minster in 1055 and the construction of the Norman cathedral at the start of the 12th century.

ILLUS 5

Engraving of Losinga Chapel

The Norman impact on the layout of the town should not be underestimated. Prior to the conquest it seems likely that the area now occupied by the quiet and tranquil Close was the centre of a busy, crowded Saxon town. The main east-west thoroughfare is thought to have passed beneath what is now the northern side of the Norman cathedral. The area was likely to have been filled with trade, industry, housing and religion – both the spiritual heart and the secular heart of the town existing side by side. The creation of a new market place to the north may have allowed for the centre of the Saxon town to be swept away, to be replaced by a dedicated ecclesiastical complex on a far grander scale than had existed before. In practice, it would appear that trade, play and even occupation of the Close occurred throughout the medieval period and the dream of a spiritual haven was not entirely realised.

The core of the current cathedral's plan and structure is made up of the Romanesque cathedral built between about 1107 and 1148[32]. Bishop Reinhelm, elected in 1100 but only consecrated in 1107, was described in the cathedral obit book as fundatoris ecclesiae or founder of the church (Illus 6). Conflicting sources have resulted in debate as to whether Reinhelm or his predecessor Robert actually begun the work, but it seems likely that Reinhelm oversaw the greater part of the project.

Although Aethelstan's cathedral was clearly damaged in the Welsh attack, references to Aethelstan being buried within the building would suggest that the cathedral was serviceable at the time of his death. What is not clear, is when the structure was finally removed from the site. Did Aethelstan's cathedral continue to perform the functions of a cathedral church until the Norman cathedral was completed, or was the Losinga Chapel built for this purpose, heralding the end of the Saxon structure even before the foundations of the Romanesque structure had been laid?

In about 1144, coincidentally around the time of the consecration of the new Romanesque cathedral, St Guthlac's Priory moved to a new site on the edge of town where the present day County Hospital and Bus Station are situated. This religious community had lost most of its land holdings after the conquest and become encircled by the castle. The arrangement is unlikely to have been satisfactory and things appear to have come to a head during the war of succession between King Stephen and the Empress Matilda between 1135 and 1153. In 1140, in an attempt to gain control of the castle, Matilda's forces took control of the newly built cathedral and established a siege engine on the tower to hurl missiles at the castle. New earthworks were thrown up to attack the king's forces which involved the exhumation of a number of recently buried corpses, much to the horror of the townsfolk. David Whitehead[33] identifies the site of the exhumations as the burial ground attached to St Guthlac's on Castle Green. However, considering that the Close is

---

32   Morris 2000, 204

33   Whitehead 1980, 5

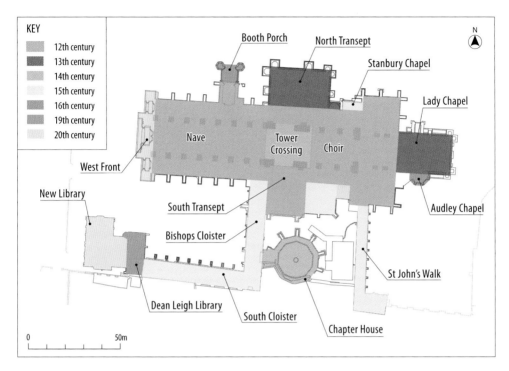

KEY

- 12th century
- 13th century
- 14th century
- 15th century
- 16th century
- 19th century
- 20th century

N

Booth Porch

North Transept

Stanbury Chapel

Lady Chapel

Nave

Tower Crossing

Choir

West Front

New Library

South Transept

Audley Chapel

Bishops Cloister

St John's Walk

Dean Leigh Library

South Cloister

Chapter House

0   50m

ILLUS 6
Development of the current cathedral

more likely to be the receiver of recently buried corpses at this date, and that Matilda's forces were apparently attacking from the west, it would seem that the Cathedral Close has an equal, if not greater claim to be the location for the earthworks.

HISTORY OF BURIAL AT THE CLOSE

The earliest burial ground for the city was almost certainly at St Guthlac's in the present Castle Green area, where burials dating from the 7th to the 12th centuries have been found. The point at which the cathedral replaced St Guthlac's as the main burial place for the people of Hereford is not known, but a date in the 11th or early 12th century seems likely. When St Guthlac's Priory relocated in 1144, the cathedral was not only claiming exclusive burial rights over the parishes of the city but

also several outlying ones. Once the cathedral had achieved a monopoly on burial it fought hard to maintain it – burial fees and legacies were a valuable source of revenue.

Disputes over burial rights did occur. In 1288 when Hampton Bishop made a bid for burial autonomy, an agreement was struck with the cathedral related to the status of the person to be buried. It was agreed that any parishioner whose goods at the time of his death exceeded 6s. in value should be brought to the cathedral cemetery for interment, whilst women and those of lesser means should be buried at home. Allensmore attempted a similar break for burial independence in the 14th century. The cathedral, once again determined to maintain control over the high value burials permitted local burial of children and paupers, but no others[34]. Not to be defeated, the parishioners of Allensmore 'accidentally' buried some of their wealthier dead and no doubt received their burial fees. An agreement of 1348 allowing general burial, provided that the funeral profits went to the cathedral rather than the local church, must be seen as a victory for the cathedral. Not only was the cathedral maintaining a valuable string of income, but it was reducing pressure on what must have been a rather crowded burial ground.

The first documentary reference which specifically mentions the 'Close' dates from 1389 when a royal licence was given to the dean and chapter to enclose the cemetery and to keep the gates locked after curfew. The reason behind the enclosure was, amongst others, the mischief done by swine and other animals that dragged the dead bodies from their resting places in the ground. Whilst painting a very graphic image of the realities of a medieval urban graveyard, it also suggests that burials were incredibly shallow.

Bishop Spofford's register records that in 1434 he wrote to the dean and chapter that 'he grieved to say that the beauty of our cathedral has long been marred by unseemly trading, and the cemetery desecrated by animals overturning the bodies...and by other servile and unseemly works, so that it more resembles a highway or open ground than a cemetery and holy place dedicated to God.'

The problem of burial crowding got worse through time. The level of the Close prior to landscaping in the 19th century was much higher than today, a result of centuries of burial within a confined area. Various old

---

34   Swanson & Lepine 2000, 79

deeds speak of the ascent to the Close from different sides. Church Street was described as the lane which leads from the cemetery steps, and Speede's 1606 draft map of Hereford clearly shows steps entering the Close from Broad Street and Castle Street (Illus 7). The English antiquary John Aubrey alludes to the pressure on the graveyard in his descriptions of the Cathedral's crypt:

'Under the cathedral-church at Hereford is the greatest charnel-house for bones that ever I saw in England. In 1650 there lived amongst those bones a poor old woman that, to help out her fire, did use to mix the deadmen's bones: this was thrift and poverty: but cunning alewives putt the Ashes of these bones in their Ale to make it intoxicating.'

In addition to conjuring up a macabre image of 17th century poverty, Aubrey's description highlights the pressure on burial space and the disturbance caused to earlier burials by later ones.

By the late 18th century the problem of overcrowding had clearly reached a level where it even outweighed concerns over lost burial revenue. On 11th September 1790 the dean and chapter wrote to the several parishes in the city and suburbs...

The Dean and Chapter...having very seriously considered the present state of the Minster churchyard and that of the Lady-Arbour (the only places of interment in this populous City) how greatly crowded they are, and have long been with Bodies... how great reason there is to apprehend that some contagious Distemper may arise to the endangering the Health and even the Lives of the Inhabitants have found it absolutely necessary to declare, That from and after the 25th day of March 1791 no bodies can be admitted for Sepulture here, except of

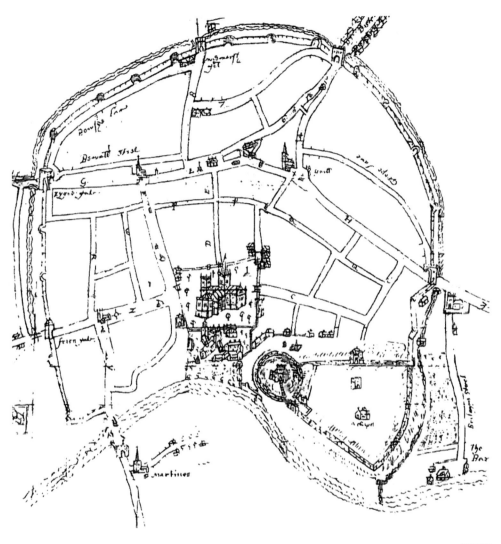

ILLUS 7
John Speede's draft of the map of Hereford (1606)

those who shall happen to die within the Precincts…'[35]

If the term 'precinct' refers to the boundaries of the Close and associated cathedral buildings then it must be assumed that the number of burials post-dating 1791 was very few indeed and largely limited to the clergy. Alternatively, it may be that the parishioners of St John's were still allowed to be buried within the Close, as the Cathedral housed their parish church[36]. In recalling the Hereford of the early 19th century, F E Gretton remembers:

---

35   Morgan 1976, 17

36   Hoverd 1998, HAS359

'The Minster Yard was an untidy and uncared-for place, with pathways made ad libitum in all directions, while the earth was so accumulated round the walls that only an inch or two at the top of the crypt windows…remained, just enough for our marbles to slip through.'[37]

Cathedral records indicate that the Close was cleared of grave-stones in 1796 and the ground level was lowered in 1850–1. The reduction in ground level was clearly quite significant in places as subsequent excavations on the Close have encountered burials immediately below the surface. How much soil was removed during the landscaping can be judged by comparison of the present level with that shown in topographical drawings made prior to the landscaping. Buckler's print of 1816 shows that the soil level against the north transept was just below the chamfers on the plinth, indicating that the soil level in this area was later lowered by about 0.7m. There is also agreement in early 19th century prints about the soil level around the Lady Chapel, a print from Britton's Hereford Cathedral dated 1831 indicating a similar reduction in ground level. It seems probable that the level of the Close had already been lowered to some degree prior to the landscaping of 1850–1. The topographical prints show a dearth of headstones within the area of the cemetery, implying that work of some sort had been carried out previously.

THE BUILDINGS OF THE CLOSE

It is easy to think of the history of the Close as being about the history of burial. This is not, however, the complete story. A quick look at existing maps of the site shows buildings appearing and disappearing during the last 400 years and there is no reason to believe

that this was not the case for the preceding 500 years.

Excavations in and around the Close have so far failed to identify evidence for the canonical properties, that would have been a key feature of the Norman and medieval precinct. Shoesmith[38] believes that the current buildings forming the northern edge of the Close may well respect the positions of the original Canon's dwellings but suggests that the grounds of the original buildings extended further to the south, meaning that historically the Close covered a smaller area than it does today.

Up until the end of the 12th century references to canons' houses suggest that they were built of flimsy materials[39] and that they were somewhat temporary in nature. A document of 1180–6 records the Bishop ordering the removal of a house built upon the cathedral graveyard by a former Archdeacon. This implies a certain pressure on available space, and can be considered another sound reason for the enclosure of the site in 1389. We can be fairly confident that historically the Close was a more crowded space. The evidence from Taylor's map of 1757 suggests that the edges of the Close were more rigidly defined by buildings than they are today (Illus 8). The present row of properties on the eastern side of Broad Street previously continued further to the south and encroached onto the north-west corner of the Close. Buildings are indicated in this position on Speede's 1606 draft of the map of Hereford, and are more accurately plotted on Taylor's 1757 map of the city. The buildings were demolished following a fire in 1935, but photographs taken prior to their demolition show street level hatches suggesting that they were cellared.

37   Gretton 1889

38   Shoesmith 2000, 300
39   Barrow 2000, 39

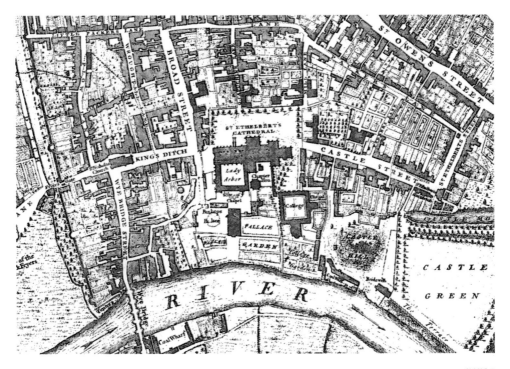

ILLUS 8
Isaac Taylor's map of Hereford (1757)

The north-west corner of the Close has also been suggested as the original location for St Ethelbert's hospital prior to its relocation to Castle Street in the 16th century[40]. In *c* 1225 a house for the poor is recorded as being founded on lands next to the cemetery of St Ethelbert. Some light is thrown upon the location of the hospital in 1406 when the mayor of Hereford gave permission for the custodians to make a stone or wooden step measuring 4ft in width 'in the street called Brodestrete to aid divine worship in the chapel of the almshouse.'

Buildings also encroached upon the eastern side of the Close, Taylor's map shows a building extending northwards from what is currently 'School House', directly to the east

of the Lady Chapel. The additional buildings to the east and west would have narrowed the entry points to the Close, creating a far more enclosed area than today.

The cathedral buildings themselves have of course been altered, modified and added to since the original construction of the Norman building. Certainly the most dramatic event that brought about changes to the original fabric was the structural failure of the west end on Easter Monday 1786 (Illus 9). The western range of the Bishop's cloister which had abutted the west end had been demolished in 1762 to make way for a new school room. The effect of this has subsequently been blamed by some[41] for weakening the foundations of the

---

40   Whitehead 1986, 416

41   Roberts 2001, 147

ILLUS 9
The collapse of the west end (1786)

Romanesque structure and causing the loss of the façade and half of the original nave and aisles. A report of the incident in the Hereford Journal captures the outrage and horror felt by the journalist at what must have been one of the most memorable events in 18th century Hereford:

> 'the ruins though awful, afford a pleasing view, especially to behold the statues of kings and bishops resting one upon another.'

The rebuilding of the west end was entrusted to James Wyatt, who curtailed the nave by one bay and created a bland, much maligned facade that was eventually rebuilt to the design of John Oldrid Scott between 1904 and 1908. By and large, the third and latest incarnation of the west end is tolerated

as a slight improvement on Wyatt's attempt but far short of the artistry of the original.

The collapse of the west end seems to have been the catalyst for a change of attitude towards the Close. James Wyatt, in his report into the collapse of the west end, had observed that the gradual raising of the churchyard's level over the centuries, had prevented proper drainage and resulted in the weakening of the foundations. The decision to halt burial occurred within five years of the collapse and the busy crowded space of the medieval and early post-medieval period appears to have given way to a more peaceful, respectful environment culminating in the landscaping and removal of remaining grave stones in 1850–1. Since that time, aside from the removal of properties abutting the

Close on Broad Street and Castle Street, the only changes of note have been variations to paths, railings and tree plantings. In essence the renovation works of 2009–11 have not dramatically altered the open appearance of the Close in the present, but they have had far reaching consequences for understanding what it looked like in the past.

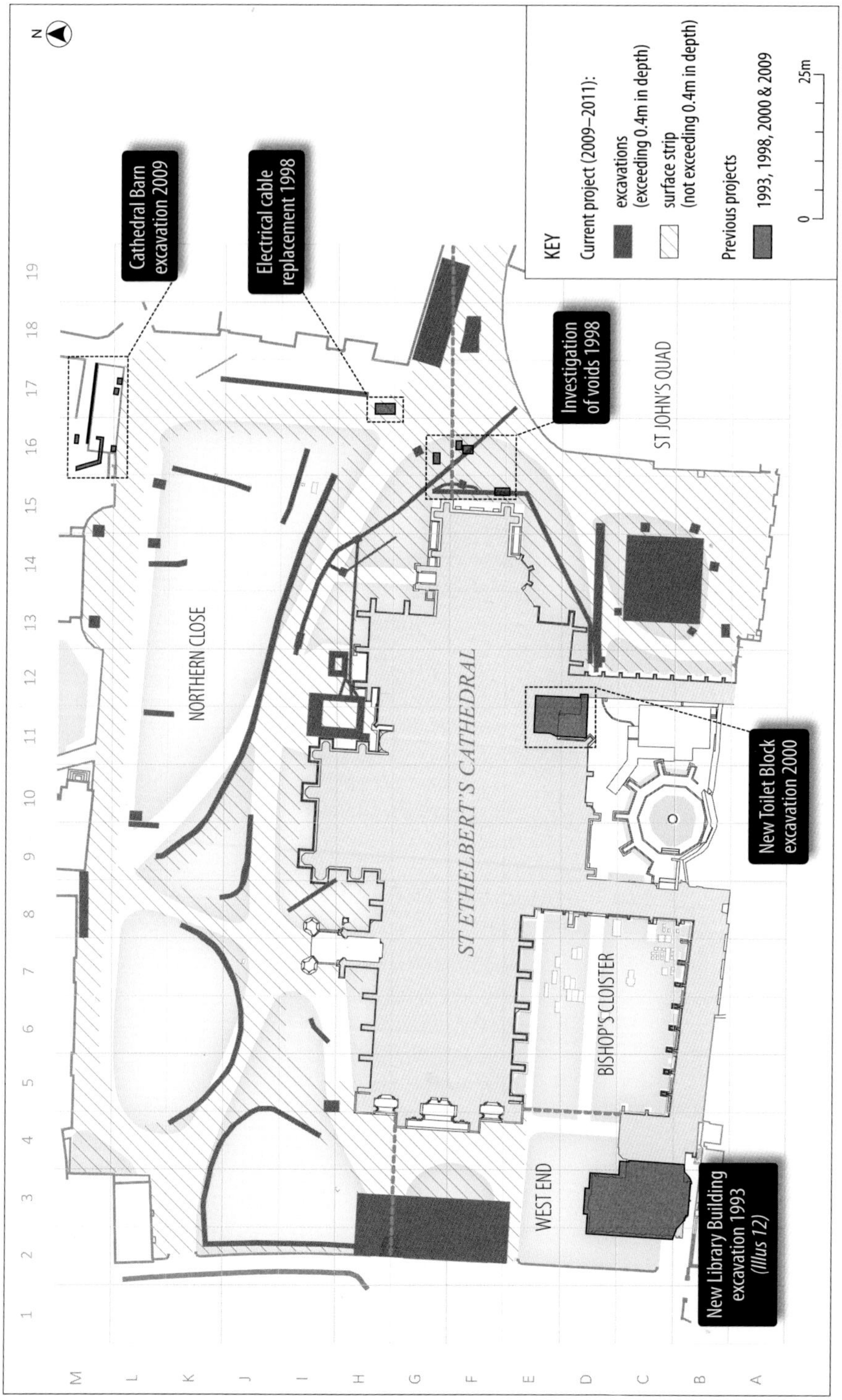

KEY

Current project (2009–2011):

excavations
(exceeding 0.4m in depth)

surface strip
(not exceeding 0.4m in depth)

Previous projects

1993, 1998, 2000 & 2009

0   25m

Cathedral Barn
excavation 2009

Electrical cable
replacement 1998

Investigation
of voids 1998

ST JOHN'S QUAD

NORTHERN CLOSE

ST ETHELBERT'S CATHEDRAL

New Toilet Block
excavation 2000

BISHOP'S CLOISTER

WEST END

New Library Building
excavation 1993
(Illus 12)

ILLUS 10
Archaeological excavations (2009–11) and location of previous excavations

2

SIFTING THE SANDS OF TIME

So what do we know so far about the development of the area within the close on the basis of archaeological evidence? There have been a number of excavations undertaken over the past few decades to which the works undertaken between 2009 and 2011 have added (Illus 10).

As mentioned in the previous chapter the earliest ecclesiastical occupation in the city is documented as having been located on what is now Castle Green. The site, which is believed to have been dedicated to St Guthlac in the late 9th century, is first mentioned in AD 975. Excavations carried out in 1960 and 1973 however, show that it was being used as a graveyard as early as the late 7th century[1] (Illus 11). Burial continued on the site until it was relocated to the Bye Street suburb of Hereford in the mid 12th century. Between the mid 11th and mid 12th centuries, St Guthlac's was confined within the outer bailey of the Norman castle. A geophysical survey on the site undertaken in 2008 further highlighted the confused co-existence of priory and castle structures.

In all 85 burials were excavated on the Castle Green site although density calculations suggest that between 7,000 and 15,000 individuals were buried there prior to the construction of the castle in the mid 11th century. The earliest burials, dating to the 7th and 8th centuries, were all termed simple burials (ie no evidence for coffin fittings, stone lining, shroud pins etc.), and associated with an earth platform on which a timber building stood. The elevated position, the relationship with the burials and the eventual replacement of this structure with a stone church suggests that the timber building was originally constructed as a church. The stone church being the latest in a succession of religious buildings and survived until the end of the 17th century.

A further building to the south of the timber platform church was believed to have been a mortuary chapel. Crop marks show the building to be rectangular, approximately 8m wide and 20m in length. Burials dating to the 9th or 10th centuries were excavated within it.

A complex building was revealed in parch marks occupying the land between the timber

---

1   Shoesmith 1980

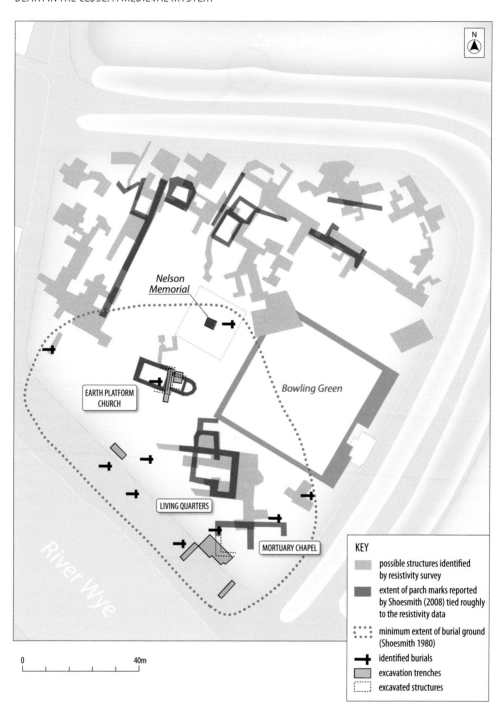

ILLUS 11
Archaeological surveys on Castle Green

platform church and the mortuary chapel. It has an east-west orientation and apparently consists of several small rooms surrounding one or two larger ones. It is possible that the remains represent the domestic buildings or communal living quarters associated with the religious settlement.

Thirteen 'charcoal' burials were identified where large oak timbers appear to have been burnt and the resulting charcoal used to line the grave. The purpose was not clear, but Shoesmith suggests that it was possibly done to soak up decomposing body fluids and control smells. The charcoal burials were dated to between the 9th and 11th centuries. Some of these burials were 'simple' (ie without coffins), over half were within coffins. Though coffined charcoal burials were seemingly later than simple charcoal burials, there was no clear chronological distinction in the broader site between simple and coffin burials.

Simple burials dating from between the mid 10th and mid 12th centuries were the most frequently encountered (33). There were very few Cist burials, three found during the laying of a main sewer pipe through Castle Green in 1886 and one during the subsequent excavations dated to the late 11th to mid 12th centuries.

The latest burials on the site were nearly all infants or very small children. Some were buried with care but many were in small, shallow graves dug without regular spacing or consistent orientation. Shoesmith suggests that the 24 infant interments may have been a late use of a consecrated piece of ground for the burial of unbaptised children.

The largest excavation in the Close itself prior to the current phase of work occurred in 1993 prior to the construction of a new library building (Illus 12, 13).

A light brown silt loam overlay the natural gravels of the river terrace. Cut into this deposit were a number of stake-holes and shallow pit features, some containing Roman tile. The largest feature identified was a 2m wide ditch passing through the excavated area on a north-south alignment. Further Roman tile was recovered from this feature.

Twenty-one early burials were excavated in the east of the site, all in clearly defined rows. The level of intercutting between burials was suggestive of three generations of burial (approximately 90 years). Two of the graves contained patches of black staining possibly indicating the presence of a coffin and one burial had 'pillow stones' to hold the head in place in the grave. Iron barrel padlocks were found in the pelvic region of two of the burials and it is on the basis of these that a late Saxon date was initially assigned to these, although the artefact type continues into the medieval period, and is more common during that period. To the west of this early burial ground, and contemporaneous with it, was a multi-layered metalled road. The surface ran broadly parallel to the modern day Broad Street although on a slightly different angle. A drain on the eastern edge of the road separated it from a stone built cellar measuring 5.1m by 2.75m internally and surviving to a height of 2.85m. Although the construction date of the basement could not be ascertained, the pottery evidence suggests that it was certainly in use during the 11th century. Cess deposits had filled up the lower part of the basement and a Saxon sword was found within these deposits. It is possible that the basement related to a high status structure, one possibility being an early Bishop's Palace, pre-dating the 12th century structure in existence today, or a canon's house.

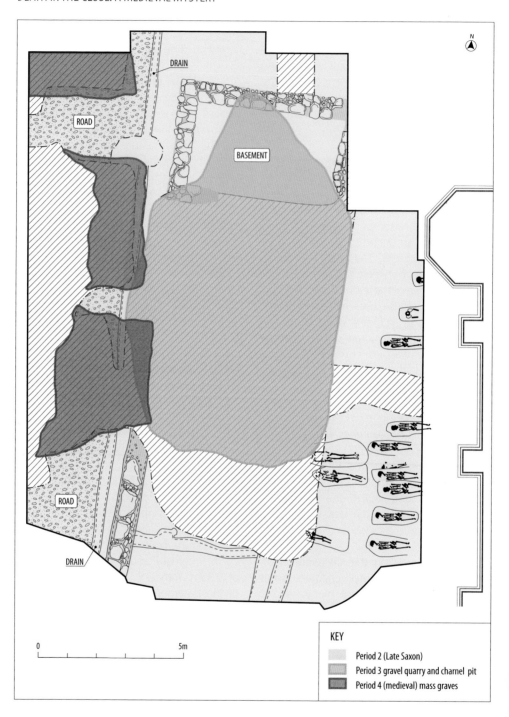

ILLUS 12
New Library Building excavations, plan of main elements

ILLUS 13
New Toilet Block excavation

Despite those features mentioned above there was no conclusive evidence for Saxon occupation in the area of the excavation. In fact the only other indication of Saxon features from the close (since Silas Taylor's observations in the 17th century) (see Chapter 1) came during the replacement of electrical cables in 1998 immediately to the west of the Old Deanery. Here a small pit contained animal bone and a single sherd of pottery dated to the 10th or 11th century; no burials were observed.

Interestingly the road and basement on the New Library site were both on the same alignment as the 12th century Bishop's Palace (see Illus 122) implying contemporaneity. The only other medieval surface (again made of gravel) known from the Close came from an investigation of a hole that opened up east of the Lady Chapel. This included a stone

slab sealing a void whose decay had caused the collapse. The use of a hand auger here established that natural gravels were present at a depth of 54.77mOD.

Subsequent to the earlier features mentioned above on the site of the New Library Building a massive pit measuring 11m by 7m in plan and continuing to a depth of 5.5m was excavated through the road, basement and cemetery. The pit was filled with mainly disarticulated remains of approximately 5,000 people. The disarticulated nature of the remains suggests that they were not originally interred in the pit but had been moved there as part of a mass clearance of burials from another area.

After the deposition of the disarticulated material, the pit and rest of the excavation area were sealed with a substantial layer of

0   5cm

ILLUS 14
Mortuary chalice and paten from New Toilet Block excavation

came from an excavation for the New Toilet Block in January 2000, subsequently featured as part of a BBC Meet the Ancestors Special.[2]

The 12 burials uncovered were thought to predate the 16th century treasury extension. The earliest burials were buried in stone lined cists and occurred at a depth of *c* 56m OD and were associated with pottery dated to the 13th and 14th centuries. Three of the burials excavated each contained a mortuary chalice and paten, indicative of a priest's burial (Illus 14). Mortuary chalices of lead alloy are recorded in the cemeteries of several towns, the burials dating from the late 13th century onwards. In 1229 the bishop of Worcester ordered that churches should have two chalices, a consecrated one of silver for use during Mass, and an unconsecrated one of pewter, to be used for the burial of the priest.

The implication is that stone Cist burials on the Close could date from between the 12th and early 14th centuries. The remaining burials were likely to have been interred in shrouds as no material other than the skeleton was present.

In the New Library Building excavation all of the burials followed the Christian tradition of being buried in the stretched out (supine) position, and all but two were buried on an east-west alignment with their heads to the west. A variation of burial orientation of up to 30° from true east-west was noted amongst the burials, a result perhaps of aligning burials to buildings or pathways present on the site at the time of burial. Chronological variations in arm position were also noted. The earliest burials had their hands placed on their pelvis or arms laid at the side of the torso. On later burials the forearms were placed across the chest or across the stomach.

soil, although the pit needed re-levelling on a couple of occasions following this. Eleven hundred bodies were interred, dating to between the late 12th and mid 16th centuries across the whole of the excavated area. The first burials were encountered within 0.1m of the 1993 ground level, with the earliest burials being revealed at a depth of 1m.

Several of the earliest burials were in stone lined graves and the presence of decorated stone with some of the burials indicated that stone was being re-used from elsewhere to line the graves. The few burials of this type observed during excavations on Castle Green imply that they start in the early 12th century. The largest cluster of such burials identified prior to the current piece of work

---

2   Crooks 2000

ILLUS 15
Wall beneath Cathedral Barn

In terms of the medieval cemetery, perhaps the most interesting discovery beneath the New Library Building were three large pits arranged in a row, containing the remains of approximately 200 bodies. Burials from the pits have been radiocarbon dated to the mid 14th century and in all probability relate to the Black Death of 1348–49. Layers of burials were separated by layers of clay, suggesting that groups of bodies were regularly sealed. After the mass graves had been completely filled, this area of the Close ceased to be used as part of the cemetery although burials continued in the remainder of the excavated area well into the 16th century.

An increased understanding of the layout of the Close in the medieval period was provided by work allied to the 2009–11 Cathedral Close project during the restoration of the Cathedral Barn in the north-east corner of the Close[3].

Excavations beneath the barn identified a substantial faced stone wall with its associated footing (Illus 15). Predating the foundations of this were deposits containing metalworking waste and 12th to early 13th-century pottery. Following the construction of the wall a 0.4m deep sequence of alternating compacted surfaces and occupation deposits built up alongside it until around the 16th or 17th century. Pottery found within the surface contemporary with the construction of the wall dated from between the 13th and 15th centuries.

Previously it was believed that the building was a much altered, but in situ, 13th-

---

3   Shoesmith 2011

century aisled timber-framed structure. Dendrochronological samples provided a date range of 1253–88 for the earliest phase of the barn, with a date for what was clearly a later roof of 1491–2.

John Speede's 1606 map of Hereford shows what appears to be a wall surrounding the Close, and yet no building in its north-east corner in the vicinity of the location of the barn. Whilst it is difficult to rely fully on the accuracy of structures depicted in his survey, this rather temptingly fits the archaeological evidence. The wall appears to have been demolished in the 17th century on the basis of pottery associated with the ground level at the time. Clearly the barn which is built from above this level cannot be in situ and appears to have been constructed on the site in the 17th century using the central portion of a 13th-century aisled building (not reassembled in order) and the roof from a late 15th century building. The function of the earlier medieval wall was not fully understood from the small interventions undertaken, however, it could be either a stone building or possibly part of a precinct wall, adapted and altered at a later date. Either way there is documentary and archaeological evidence implying that the Close was enclosed, and the 1389 date referred to in Chapter 1 seems to fit with all the other available evidence.

This would mean that the large gravel extraction pits identified within later features and deposits on the New Library site occurred after the enclosure of the Close. It seems that from the mid 16th century onwards this area was used as a garden.

The latest evidence for use of the Close as a burial ground came from a small intervention at the West End of the cathedral in 1998. Here an undisturbed lead coffin was discovered with a depositum plate recording the remains of Mrs Mary Powell who died on 2nd February 1823, aged 92 years. It is notable because it post-dates the late 18th century when burial officially ceased within the close.

The New Library Building excavation of 1993 was probably the most important for informing the current phase of work in 2009–11. It showed the extent and survival of pre-burial archaeology below the Close, and the importance of it for understanding the formation of the city. Overlying this was a densely packed post-conquest cemetery, the extent of which was confirmed by the excavation of a trial pit in 1998 immediately adjacent to the Lady Chapel where densely packed articulated skeletons were also revealed. Clearly any future development works at the Close needed to involve a greater appreciation of the level of archaeological material present and the need for planning and co-operation between cathedral, contractor and archaeologist.

IN SEARCH OF CLUES

As archaeologists faced with the prospect of an extensive and prolonged investigation into the Cathedral Close then it would be wrong to state that that holy grail of Hereford's archaeology, the whereabouts of the Saxon Cathedral, had not at least fleetingly crossed the minds of those involved in the project. With little control over the location and extent of the investigation, which could only react to areas of intervention by the main contractor, any such discovery was always going to be serendipitous.

From the 12th century onwards, the Close had been almost completely turned over to use as a burial ground, and evidence for activity unrelated to burial during this period was scarce. The burials, which will be discussed later, were tightly packed and intercutting, forming a layer of human remains approximately 0.6m deep. In the north of the Close, where the ground is visibly higher, graveyard earth covered the burials to a depth of approximately 1.2m. In the south of the site, burials were present within 0.1m of the surface.

The ground-works, which had been designed to cause minimum disturbance to the archaeology rarely impacted below 0.4m

and therefore opportunities to investigate the pre-cemetery archaeology were limited. However, these opportunities did arise, and when they did the story that unfolded was intriguing at the very least.

The site was originally divided into five excavation areas that matched the progress of the main contract works. For the purpose of the following discussion these have been grouped into three distinct zones based on the amount and coherence of archaeological features identified within them. The largest and deepest excavation was in St John's Quad; with a slightly shallower, but still extensive, excavation at the west end of the cathedral; and more sporadic deep interventions across the northern part of the close. No. archaeology was observed in the Bishop's Cloister.

ST JOHN'S QUAD

EARLIEST ACTIVITY
To allow for the root growth of two trees due to be planted in the centre of a new parking area, a Silva Cell suspended pavement was proposed. The system, which also allows for the dissipation of storm water, entailed

ILLUS 16
St John's Quad, deep excavation in progress

the excavation of an area measuring approximately 16m by 16m to a depth of c 0.8m below the existing ground level (Illus 16–17). This was not sufficient to enable the full excavation of the site to the level of natural gravels which were present at a depth of approximately 1.2m below the modern ground level (55m OD). The earliest deposit encountered was a layer of light brown silty clay. Hand augering showed this deposit to be 0.5m deep, but excavation only impacted upon its upper 0.1m. It contained a low density of finds comprising a small amount of animal bone and traces of metal working residues. A prehistoric flint knife or scraper was also recovered along with three sherds of pottery of a type commonly made in the 10th and 11th centuries.

A similar deposit has been frequently recorded as overlying the natural gravels across the city, and has variously been interpreted as a topsoil deposit pre-dating human activity or build-up of periglacial silts just after the last ice age. Either way it is likely to be a naturally formed deposit, its upper surface defining a long standing ground level spanning through prehistory into late Saxon times.

A part finished quern was found in an early layer, predating activity on site, however, the presence of 10th or 11th century pottery in the same deposit suggests a certain amount of disturbance and it may be contemporary with these finds. Rotary querns were used for grinding cereals and other foodstuffs from

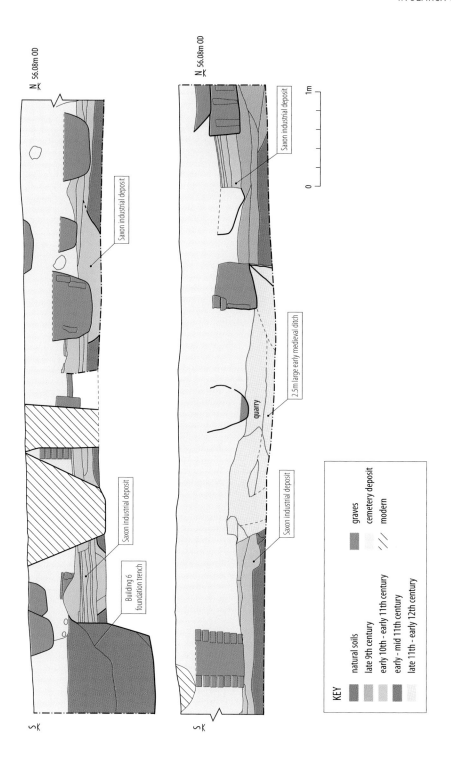

ILLUS 17
St John's Quad, east facing section of deep excavation area

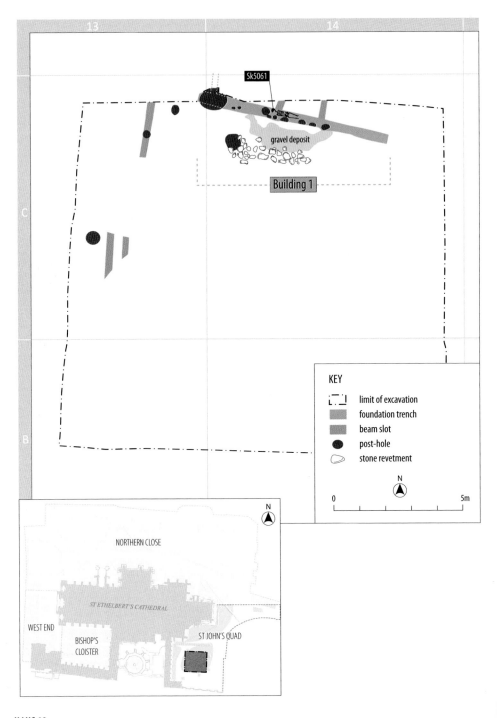

ILLUS 18
Late 9th-century features

the Iron Age through to the medieval periods. Their use began to decline from the 12th century onwards as prohibitions began on home milling for reasons of taxation[1]. It was made from locally available sandstone and could indicate pre-Saxon activity in the area.

Five sherds of pottery dating to the Roman period were recovered from St John's Quad and the West End. All were of Severn Valley type wares. All were residual in later contexts. Two of these have been worked into spindle whorls.

LATE 9TH CENTURY

The late 9th century coincides with the period when it is now believed that the main phase of Saxon defences were constructed, clearly a significant point in Hereford's past.

The earliest archaeological features on the site related to the remains of what must have been a very large structure represented by a foundation trench and post-holes (Building 1). The main part of the structure was located on a slightly embanked area in the far north of the deep excavation area (Illus 18–19, 22).

Whilst the true scale of the structure cannot be determined with most of the building lying outside and to the north of the trench, some indication as to its size was evident. A 7.5m length of foundation trench was recorded and was clearly from a substantial structure as it had a width of between 0.4 and 0.5m and depth of 0.3m. It was orientated approximately 14° askew of true east-west. An indication as to the method of the building's construction was provided by a line of post-holes mid-way along the foundation trench. Rather than being erected in the middle of the trench the posts were set tight against its

ILLUS 19
Foundation trench, Building 1

southern face, impressions of the posts were in fact still visible in the side of the feature.

The above clearly formed the southern wall of a building as no other associated structural features lay to its south. In addition internal structural evidence in the form of two shallow beam-slots lay at right angles to it, continuing northwards out of the excavation. A compacted area of lime residue possibly indicated the presence of a mortar floor between these internal beam-slots. The shallow north-south beam-slots either represent the positions of internal partitions within the building, or could have been floor joists supporting a raised wooden floor. The latter implies two phases of internal floor, the mortared floor being replaced by a later wooden one.

However, the scale of the building exposed here was only truly realised when a 1m

---

1   Ottaway & Rogers 2002, 2799

diameter and 1.9m deep post-pit was discovered at the west end of the south wall foundation. From the soft, dark fill it appeared that the post had decomposed in situ. To better understand this feature, and attempt retrieval of dating evidence, the excavated area was extended slightly to the north exposing the end of another internal north-south beam-slot and indicating that the south wall also continued beyond this large post setting to the west. Lining the base of the main east-west foundation trench and continuing down the eastern side of the large post-pit was an intermittent lens of soil with a high charcoal content. Beyond the presence of charcoal there was no evidence for in situ burning and it seems likely that the lens represents a preservation technique of charring wooden structural elements before placing them in the ground. It appears that the posts had been left to rot in situ as the soil filling both the post-pit and the post-holes within the foundation trench was incredibly loosely compacted and dark in colour.

There was evidence that the contemporary ground surface survived to the south of the building. At this point the ground dropped away by approximately 0.2m over a distance of 2m. Set into the slope was a deposit of flat irregular stones, loosely forming an east-west paved revetment to a deposit of gravel between the stones and the building.

Some indication for other less substantial structures contemporary with this large building, possibly even adjoining or extending it, came from three segments of beam-slot on a similar orientation to Building 1 as well as a post-hole. These all lay to its west and were heavily disturbed by later features.

If the discovery of such a large early structure wasn't enough then what was subsequently uncovered proved to be even more enigmatic. In the base of the foundation for the building's south wall a small grave containing an 8–10 year old child[2] was unearthed (Illus 20). The orientation of the grave matched that of the foundation trench and no grave cut was visible in overlying deposits filling the foundation. One might expect that finding one more burial towards the end of excavating the best part of 1,200 inhumations from an area was all in a day's work. But this one seemed different. It appeared to be stratigraphically removed by a considerable number of deposits from the early Norman cemetery. The building was clearly earlier than the cemetery and had the burial been cut from the cemetery levels it is unlikely it would have so neatly occupied the centre of the foundation trench. Also there appeared to be some damage to the skeleton that coincided with the position of posts set in the trench. Therefore even at the time of the discovery it seemed that either the body had been intentionally buried in the base of the southern foundation of the structure, or it pre-dated the structure and was part of an earlier, phase of activity beyond the limit of the excavation work.

Given the potential significance of the above discoveries two radiocarbon dates were obtained to try and date them. The first of these was from a piece of charred emmer wheat seed[3] found in the soft, organic fill of the post-pit at the western end of the foundation trench. The second came from a sample of bone[4] taken from the burial in the base of the foundation. These measurements can be calibrated to provide a most likely date between c AD 850–950 for the construction of the building.

---

2   Sk5061
3   WK-34563 1156±27 BP
4   WK-34568 1148±28 BP

ILLUS 20
The 'foundation trench burial', Sk5061

The presence of post impressions within a foundation trench suggests that the building was of post-in-trench construction. In this method a continuous trench is dug for the closely set posts rather than individual holes. The posts can either be set in the centre of the trench, or to one side as was the case with Building 1. Normally load-bearing, the spaces between the posts were filled with planks or other material such as wattle panels. Most of the known examples of this type of construction belong to the late Saxon period and are from urban or aristocratic contexts, although there are earlier examples in rural contexts eg Maxey (Cambridgeshire) and Chalton (Hampshire).

Building 1 shares a number of characteristics with a long hall excavated at Cheddar in Somerset. The hall believed to pre-date AD 930 forms part of a royal palace complex and is of post-in-trench construction, with the posts set to the side of the trench to take advantage of the additional stability offered by the surrounding soil deposits. Measuring

approximately 23m by 5m, the hall was demolished in the 10th century and a new hall built on the site.

The diameter of the Building 1 post-pit and width of the foundation trench suggest a structure on a massive scale. Post-pits like the one here have distinctive sloping sides because the timbers they supported were too large to be dropped vertically into a post-hole. It was instead necessary to excavate a hole larger than the post, with sloping sides to ease the task of levering the timber into an upright position. Post-pits are used where the posts need to be founded deeply. They are also necessary to give maneuvering space for the erection of uprights which may often have exceeded 10 metres in length[5]. Anglo-Saxon post-pits exceeding 1m in depth are incredibly rare. Where they have previously been identified at sites in Yeavering and Cheddar they have been part

---

5   Rahtz 1976, 85

33

of royal halls[6]. Practical experiment at West Stow Anglo-Saxon village, where a number of Saxon buildings have been reconstructed from archaeological evidence, has shown that a 0.2m square oak post has no structural value after c 20 years[7]. It is probable that the larger sectional area of the post which occupied the post-pit would translate into a potential lifespan far exceeding this.

So what was the building? Due to the limited amount of the structure excavated and the distinct lack of clues as to its purpose, a myriad of possibilities exist, all with some merit. The most attractive proposition is that it is one of the former cathedrals known to have been on the site. On first impression, Building 1 would appear to fit the criteria for an early cathedral church. As excavated, the long axis is on an approximate east-west alignment, and the substantial post-pit could represent the corner of a tower. The north-south aligned beam-slot emerging from the section to the west of the post-pit, possibly being the foundation of a porticus.

Although there was certainly a cathedral church on the site during the late 9th and early 10th century, Duncomb in his interpretation of the accounts of the 16th century historian Vergil is convinced that the existing structure at this time was the stone cathedral (lapidea structura) built by Milfrid in c AD 825.

Duncumb's belief that the cathedral of the 9th century was built in stone rather than wood is not grounds to discount the possibility that Building 1 is a former cathedral. It must be remembered, however that like today a cathedral is a complex of many buildings, and in the case of Saxon Worcester and Alfred's Winchester, more than one church. The proportion of the building uncovered by excavation means that it is simply not possible to determine the use of the building. Due to the current setting of the remains in the cathedral grounds, there is a tendency to view the excavated foundation trench as the southern wall of a building on an east-west alignment. There is however nothing to prevent the trench relating to the shorter southern wall of a north-south orientated building, more in keeping with the 12th century Bishop's Palace than the cathedral. Certainly, the existence of a bishop's palace pre-dating the 12th century is probable. Fenn and Sinclair[8] suggest that a palace is likely to have been present on the site of the present cathedral and palace since the creation of the Saxon burgh in the 8th or 9th century.

A further, intriguing possibility exists – that Building 1 is a royal palace. The similarities in construction and date with the potential royal palace excavated at Cheddar have already been noted. The establishment of the cathedral, the re-organisation of the town and the creation of the defensive circuit through the intervention of the Mercian Kings in the 9th century[9] all suggest that Hereford was a royal centre. The case for an administrative building, or at least a place where king or his officers could expect hospitality is strong. Whitehead suggests Castle Green as a likely location for such a building, but the centre of a newly planned town seems logical, and it is not common for ecclesiastical and manorial sites to co-exist.

It is acknowledged that Aetheflaed embarked on a scheme of burgh building and war against the Welsh during the early

---

6   Ibid
7   West 2001, 25

8   Fenn & Sinclair1990, 1
9   Whitehead 2007, 14

10th century and it seems likely that she would have used Hereford as a base from which to launch her attacks into Welsh territory. The radiocarbon dating of Building 1 does not discount the possibility that it is connected to this period and could potentially be the building where Aetheflaed's nephew, King Aethelstan signed a treaty with the Welsh princes in *c* AD 930.

Given the apparent contemporary nature of the burial and construction of the building there is perhaps some clue that can be gleaned from this as to the nature of the structure discovered here. In the pre-Christian Saxon period, burial of infants in pits, ditches and the floors of buildings was not uncommon, but the burial of a child within the foundation trench of an ecclesiastical building has, as far as can be determined, never been recorded.

0   2.5cm

ILLUS 21
Iron 'spatulate tool' (SF0899)

of the medieval building at Westbury was not established, and it was not clear why it alone amongst the buildings excavated received a foundation burial.

Segregation between the burial of adults and sub-adults has been observed at a number of Saxon sites. At the Saxon settlement of Flixborough, a group of burials were found along the internal wall of a structure within an otherwise domestic setting. Of the six burials, five were aged between three and twelve years and showed signs of dietary deficiencies. The only adult burial was of a female in her 20s with a foetus buried at her feet. The small inhumation cemetery associated with the site by contrast, contained no burials under the age of 17[11].

A similar pattern of segregation was found on the ecclesiastical site of Whithorn, Dumfries and Galloway, dating to the 8th and 9th centuries[12]. This development included a church, a burial chapel into which four adult burials were inserted, and a burial ground abutting the east wall of the burial chapel containing the graves of about 56 children.

There is clearly a pattern of segregation of adult and non-adult burial within an

Foundation burial has been observed in non-Saxon contexts. Excavations at the deserted settlement of Westbury, Buckinghamshire, uncovered a baby buried under the southern wall of a 13th century building. The excavator commented that the appearance of the burial being deliberate, intentional and even purposeful was so strong that it is certainly possible that it represented some sort of foundation deposit[10]. The function

10   Ivens et al 1995, 145

11   Crawford 2008, 201
12   Hill 1997, 557

ILLUS 22
Dig team marking out Buildings 1 and 2

Anglo-Saxon context and also an element of liminality in the burial of children. Burial of children adjacent to the church walls is widespread in the Saxon period and the wall of the church (and other buildings) appears to represent both a physical and spiritual barrier.

The examples given above of Saxon burials associated with buildings, provide possible explanations for the 'foundation trench burial' but none are entirely satisfactory. As the only Saxon burial revealed during the excavation it is not possible to assess whether the location of the burial was down to segregation. Even if segregation was part of the answer, it is not the whole. The 13th century child burial from Westbury appears to be a closer parallel than the Saxon examples.

Assessment of the animal bone assemblage recovered from these early deposits revealed an unusual dominance of pig bone over cattle and sheep bones. In other Hereford assemblages cattle dominate in all but the smallest and statistically unreliable groups of bone. The bone of an eagle was also identified and is an incredibly rare find and tends to be associated with high status sites. A shallow trench associated with the construction of the cobbled surface contained an odd looking tool[13] (Illus 21). Similar tools are known from other Anglo-Saxon sites[14] and from contemporary sites in Ireland[15]. Their function is a mystery. Suggestions have included tools for knife sharpening or strike-a-lights for making

13 SF0899
14 Ottaway et al 2009, 218
15 Hencken 1950, 118

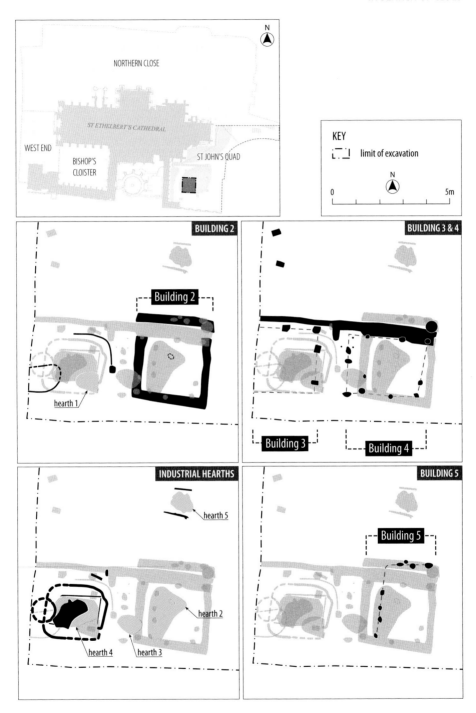

ILLUS 23
Early 10th to early 11th century industrial phase and associated features

ILLUS 24
Building 2 partially excavated with post-holes from Building 4

fire[16]. Both these suggestions assume that the pointed end was a tang for a handle and the slotted end was used. However, the round section of the 'tang' would not have worked well as a tang, allowing the tool to swivel in its handle. Instead it may have been held by the slotted end and used as a pointed tool, though if so, then the function of the slotted end is unclear. The copper alloy bead fitted to the tang of this example is unusual, if not unique. It is fitted at the point the square sectioned shaft of the tool changes into the round sectioned 'tang'. It is a simple form of decoration but does lift this above the more rudimentary of tools. Unfortunately it gets us no closer to an explanation of its use.

16   Ottaway et al 2009, 218

AN EARLY 10TH TO EARLY 11TH CENTURY INDUSTRIAL COMPLEX

Towards the lower levels of the excavation, considerable spreads of burnt material became evident and it could well have been these that Silas Taylor observed and reported as the burning associated with the destruction of the cathedral in 1055. In fact this appears to be an intense phase of industrial activity to the south of Building 1. The archaeological evidence suggests that the building was still standing as although industrial activity is intense elsewhere, none was taking place within the vicinity of the structure.

A second rectangular structure (Building 2) measuring 3.2m by 2.9m was identified in the south of the excavation area defined by beam-slots (Illus 22–24). In the middle of the building was a small scooped feature measuring 0.25m in diameter containing a range of animal bone (including bird, salmon, perch, cow, pig and sheep), the broken remains of a knife and a single sherd of pottery dated to the 10th or 11th century. A flat stone had been placed over the material before it was backfilled. It could be this was simply a post setting later replaced with a pad stone.

The knife[17] had an angle-backed blade (Illus 25). These are known from Roman and Saxon times and continue in common use through to the 11th century, though later examples are known[18]. Knives are usually the most common tool found on medieval sites. They were regularly carried by both men and women and used for dining, self-defence and other general purposes[19].

On the west side of the building was a 3m by 3m, sub-circular, shallow depression containing features associated with industrial activity. In the centre was a hearth (Hearth 1) (Illus 23) surrounded a compacted deposit containing pig and roe deer bone that appeared to represent a heavily trampled working area. The baked clay

17 SF0902
18 Ottaway 1992, 562–4
19 Cowgill et al 1987, 51–7

0   5cm

ILLUS 25
Iron knife, early 10th to early
11th century (SF0902)

0   2.5cm

ILLUS 26
Glass bead, early 10th to early
11th century (SF0909)

and ash of Hearth 1 only contained a small trace of metalworking residue as well as traces of waste products from glass making, whilst the remains of a sub-rectangular pit to the west of this hearth contained smithing slag and vitrified clay, the earliest indication for smithing in the near vicinity.

After it had fallen out of use a linear gulley was dug through the footprint of the square Building 1. The final filling of this feature contained material suggestive of both domestic and industrial waste including large quantities of glass-making waste, burnt and unburnt animal bone alongside some hammerscale and smithing slag lumps. Animal bone species represented included bird, cow, fowl, goose, pig, sheep/goat, red and roe deer. Only two sherds of pottery were recovered from the feature, both of which dated to the 10th or 11th centuries. Two decorative beads were also recovered, one made of antler tine[20] and apparently unfinished when it was lost or discarded, presumably by the maker, and a second made of blue-green translucent glass[21] (Illus 26). The latter is of a type produced from the Roman right through to the medieval periods, but most commonly found during the Saxon era.

20 SF0908
21 SF0909

ILLUS 27
Industrial deposits cut by later graves

The gulley appears to have been associated with a post built structure as immediately to its south were a series of post-holes appearing to form a north-eastern corner. As this was constructed on the same orientation and very similar footprint to Building 2 it was possibly built to replace it. Alternatively it may have been constructed adjacent to Building 2 and later extended to the east across the earlier building's footprint. The construction of the foundation for Building 6 on the south side of this and edge of excavation to the west mean that Building 3 was only represented by 4 post-holes forming a right angle and a slot or gulley to their north. It probably measured about 3m in width with a length greater than this. The later eastern extension (Building 4) measured 3.5m by 2.3m in plan with its northern line of post-holes continuing on the line of those associated with Building 3 and overlapping the southern edge of the extended gulley and its fill. The gulley is wider where it runs adjacent to Building 4 (Illus 23). The post-holes associated with this structure contain 10th or 11th century pottery as well as residues indicative of metalworking and glass working.

A series of deposits indicative of high temperature processes typified by their multi-coloured appearance overlay the structures described above (Illus 27). These contained more concentrated areas of burning which appear to be hearth bases. The nature of the deposits implies close association between domestic and industrial activity as they contained both animal bone and metalworking residues. The burning indicates industrial activity at this location the animal bone on the other hand could be either waste brought from elsewhere or derived from shared middens implying adjacent occupation.

Above a grey silty clay layer containing mammal, fish, and bird bones plus the occasional piece of hammerscale lay Hearth 2. Deposits associated with its abandonment contained large quantities of animal bone from a wide range of species including cattle, pig, sheep, domestic fowl and salmon. The significant amounts of hammerscale and smithing slag found within the hearth deposits along with a fragment of horseshoe[22] and a small whetstone[23] strongly suggest the presence of a blacksmith's forge dated to the 10th or 11th century on the basis of a sherd of pot in soot from its upper layer.

The whetstone is a miniature one, well made with a perforation for suspension from a belt (Illus 28). At 44mm long it is almost too small for practical use, and in another context would be assumed to be a personal whetstone for sharpening small blades while on the move. Though here it seems likely that it was used in the smithy. It was probably dropped near the

0   2.5cm

ILLUS 28
Stone whetstone, early 10th to early 11th century (SF0906)

hearth and being nearly black in colour was lost in the soot.

Another nearby hearth (Hearth 3) (Illus 23) was constructed in a circular bowl-shaped depression which in common with the other hearth deposits contained material relating to both domestic and industrial activity. Moderate amounts of smithing residue were present along with unburnt mammal bones, nutshells and charred cereal grain.

The latest hearths that survived as part of this 10th/11th century industrial activity demonstrated more advanced construction methods. Hearth 4 contained large amounts of smithing slag and a smithing hearth base with the charred remains of lengths of timber set into the clay forming an open rectangle measuring 2m by 1.3m around it (Illus 23, 29). The timber rectangle enclosed an area of the clay floor

ILLUS 29
Wood-lined Hearth 4

---

22   SF2160
23   SF0906

set with large rounded and sub-rounded cobble stones. The stone surface showed evidence for burning, and the timbers had clearly been burnt in situ. At its western end a sandstone sill appeared to complete the rectangle and enclose the cobbles. A similarly constructed wood-lined feature (Hearth 5) was found to the north-east of this. Here a smaller hearth deposit was flanked to the north and south by straight timbers which appeared to enclose the burnt material (Illus 23). The feature was dated through pottery to the 10th or 11th centuries and the hearth material also contained large amounts of smithing slag.

Another small structure (Building 5) defined by a group of closely set post-holes forming its north-west corner on the site of the earlier buildings described above post-dates Hearth 2 (Illus 23). Its post-holes contained 10 or 11th century pottery, iron slag and burnt mammal bone as well as glassmaking waste.

The evidence from the above quite clearly underlines intense and prolonged industrial activity, the presence of animal bone and plant remains being associated with general waste stored near the area. Two radiocarbon dates were obtained coinciding with the end of this activity[24], these being AD 987–1021 from oat seeds in material raked from Hearth 4, and AD 992–1023 from a cereal grain in Hearth 3. In all probability the latest date for this activity is 1040.

The two wood-lined hearths imply some technological development over the course of this industrial phase. Wood-lined industrial hearths have previously been recorded within Saxon contexts. A reconstructed

smithing hearth at West Stow is built from a square wooden box set into the ground and standing to approximately waist height. The box is lined with clay to contain the embers and to prevent the wood from burning. The remaining wood of Hearth 4 had been burnt in situ illustrating the potential risk of using wood in hearth construction. If the activity is smithing then these features would need to be covered by some sort of structure, the darkness enabling the smith to see key changes in colour in the heated metal so that it could be properly worked. It may be that the earlier structures served part of this function, but there is no evidence from the period of use of the later smithy hearths for any associated shelter.

The waste associated with the industrial deposits illustrates other types of manufacturing activity taking place here. Several tools point towards textile working in the form of three spindle whorls[25] (Illus 120), used in spinning thread, and a flat pin-beater[26] (Illus 121), a type of weaving tool. The pin-beater was of a type in use between the late 9th and 14th centuries[27]. Two of the whorls were of stone and their asymmetrical shape is the predominant form from the 7th to 10th centuries, declining in favour of more symmetrical profiled whorls over the course of the 11th century[28]. One of the whorls was made from the proximal end of a cattle femur, a type most common between the 10th and 12th century[29]. Thus all were consistent with textile manufacture taking place here in the 10th or early 11th centuries.

24 WK34566 and WK34567 dates are calibrated and quoted respectively to 68.2% probability

25 SF0855A, SF0855B, SF883
26 SF1050
27 Rogers 1997, 1755
28 Rogers 2007, 24
29 Rogers 2007, 25–6

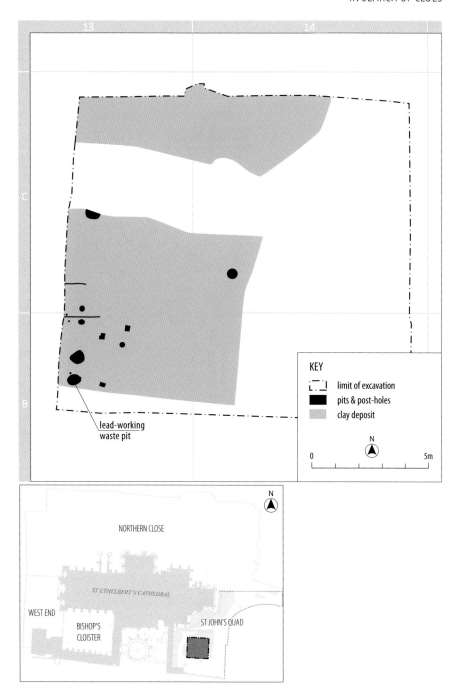

KEY

- – · limit of excavation
- ■ pits & post-holes
- clay deposit

lead-working
waste pit

NORTHERN CLOSE

ST ETHELBERT'S CATHEDRAL

WEST END

BISHOP'S
CLOISTER

ST JOHN'S QUAD

0   N   5m

ILLUS 30
Early to mid 11th-century features

43

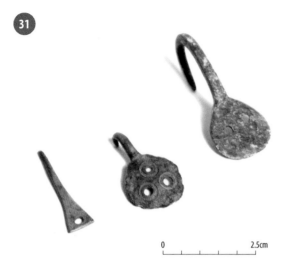

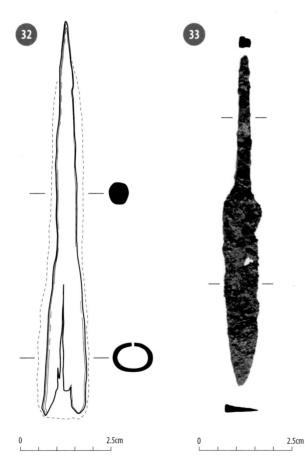

ILLUS 31
Copper alloy hooked tags, 7th to 11th century (left to right SF0903, SF1045, SF0596)

ILLUS 32
Iron arrowhead, early to mid 11th century (SF2143)

ILLUS 33
Iron knife, early to mid 11th century (SF0880)

THE EARLY TO MID 11TH CENTURY

All the industrial activity and any remains of the earliest structure Building 1 were buried beneath a c 0.1m thick mid brown silty clay which covered the excavated area (Illus 30). Nineteen of the 21 pieces of pottery found within this are 11th century in date, the remaining two 12th to 15th century sherds being intrusive, probably related to the later burials cutting this deposit. As in the previous phase, activity in this period is largely confined to the south of the excavated area.

The artefacts recovered from the layer point more to general rather than specific activity in the area. Items recovered include a 'hooked tag'[30], the exact purpose of which is unknown, but believed to be a dress fastening (Illus 31, left). The use of these tags was dated in Winchester to between the 7th and 11th centuries, and seems to have died out around the time of the Norman conquest. An arrowhead[31] and a very small knife[32] were also recovered (Illus 32, 33).

30	SF0903
31	SF2143
32	SF0880

It is clear from the mixed dating of the pottery as mentioned above and the presence of a horseshoe dated 1270 to 1350 in deposits associated with this phase of activity that features and deposits further up the archaeological profile begin to be more and more affected by mixing and removal as a result of later grave digging. However, equally evident is the continued presence of pre-funerary archaeology. Later grave digging renders this almost uninterpretable and thus our glimpse of 11th century activity in this part of the site seems to comprise evidence for lead working due to the presence of large amounts of lead working waste in a 0.6m diameter pit towards the south; redeposited midden deposits (on the basis that animal bone and pottery within it shows signs of wear and abrasion) in a shallow ditch to the north; and a number of small post-holes.

Further soil deposits seal this brief resurgence in activity. Moderate amounts of smithing slag, fragments of furnace lining and a wide variety of animal bone was present within the deposit. Regarding the bone, three worked pieces are notable: a salmon vertebrae modified and used as a bead[33] (Illus 34); a sheep/goat tibia sharpened into a crude pointed implement[34];

0   2cm

ILLUS 34
Bone bead made from modified salmon vertebra, early to mid 11th century (SF2246)

0   2.5cm

ILLUS 35
Bone pin made from a pig fibula, early to mid 11th century (SF2003)

and a pig fibula fashioned into a perforated pin[35] (Illus 35). Though all are fairly rudimentary in their manufacture, the association of these finds might suggest that bone working was being undertaken in this area.

In the south of the excavated area the straight sided, regular foundation trench for Building 6 is respected by the rather mixed soil layers referred to above (Illus 36, 37). Initial thoughts were that it post-dated these. However, on further consideration it seems more likely that the soil layers built up alongside the structure, the resultant relationship being between its subsequent removal and robbing and those soil layers that surrounded it at the time.

Frustratingly, and in common with Building 1, this fragment of foundation continued beyond the limits of the excavation to both the west and south. To the east the feature was truncated by later activity. In all, a 7m long section was available within the excavation measuring 1m at its widest point.

The fill of the foundation contained sandy gravel with frequent mortar inclusions. Tip lines were clearly visible in section. In the uppermost fill, two substantial blocks of worked sandstone were present along with large pieces of mortar (Illus

---

33   SF2246
34   SF2242

---

35   SF2003

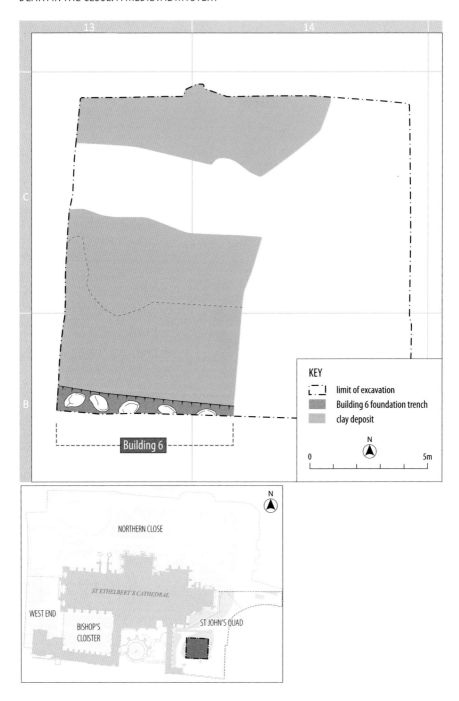

ILLUS 36
Building 6

ILLUS 37
Foundation cut for Building 6

ILLUS 38
Worked masonry within the Building 6 foundation cut

38). The largest of the stones had a curved, worked face with both diagonal linear and chevron tool marks. It appeared to have formed part of a circular column. The second block of masonry did not form a distinctive shape, but was faced on one side with visible tool marks.

It is difficult to resist drawing a parallel with the description of Silas Taylor's excavations in the 17th century:

> 'Its position is uncertain, but about 1650 Silas Taylor found, 'beyond the lines of the present building, and particularly towards the east, near the cloisters of the college, such stupendous foundations, such capitals and pedestals, such well-wrought bases for arches, and such rare engravings, and mouldings of friezes' as left little doubt in his mind that they were the foundations of the cathedral destroyed by Algar and Griffin'.[36]

Whilst our 21st century discoveries are apparently not as extensive or varied as Taylor's, we must allow for a little poetic licence on his part.

The evidence for the foundation trench relating to Aethelstan's Cathedral is compelling. The location matches Taylor's description perfectly. It is difficult to date solidly on archaeological grounds but accepting the adjacent soil layer developed during its use would imply that it was standing during the 11th century. The trench cuts deposits dated to the late 9th or early 10th centuries, and the fills of the trench are in turn cut by a Cist burial – a tradition known to date to the 11th to 13th centuries in Hereford.

The orientation of the foundation is also of note. If the line of the trench is projected through the Close, the orientation matches, not the 12th century Romanesque Cathedral, but the 11th century Losinga Chapel, which is believed to have been built whilst Aethelstan's Cathedral was still in existence.

---

36 Dumcumb 1804, 523

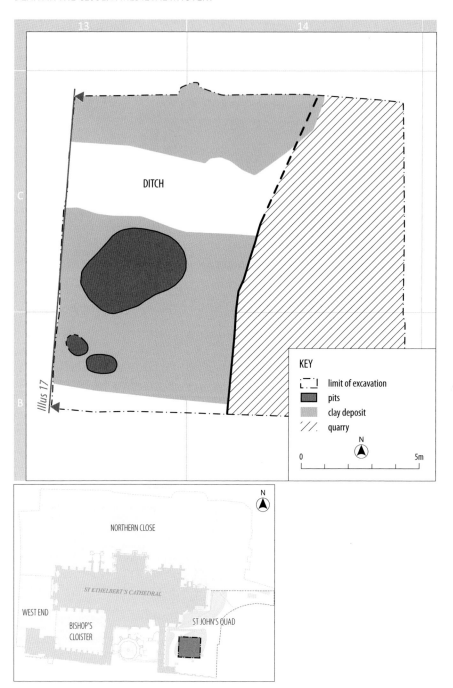

ILLUS 39
Late 11th- to early 12th-century features

LATE 11TH TO EARLY 12TH CENTURY

At this point in time the archaeology is characterised by the excavation of large features across the site, which have undoubtedly destroyed much of the evidence for pre-11th century activity (Illus 39).

Little is known about the nature of the features as the required excavation level was reached before definite conclusions could be drawn regarding their purpose.

A very large feature cut through the east end of Building 6 and appeared to be present for the full north-south extent of the excavated area. The western edge of the feature lay about 7m from the east boundary of the excavated area. Three fills were visible in plan, the boundaries between the fills presumably representing tip lines sloping down towards the east. The upper c 0.2m of the feature was hand-excavated and pottery dating from the 12th century was recovered. Below this the archaeology was to be left in situ. However, hand-augering established natural gravel at 55.03m OD just outside its west edge (the accepted level of undisturbed natural gravels in this part of the Close). A bore hole 2.4m to the east of this, and into the feature itself, hit natural gravels at 52.71m giving the feature a depth of 2.67m another adjacent to the eastern boundary of the excavation hit natural gravels at 54.05m OD giving it a depth of 1.27m even here. Bone was recovered from the head of the auger at depths of 54.92m OD and 54.52m OD, unfortunately it was too fragmentary to determine whether or not it was human.

An east-west ditch also contained multiple fills from which 12th century pottery was recovered. The auger survey revealed the ditch to be far shallower than the north-south feature with its base being encountered at 54.9m OD giving the ditch a depth of c 0.5m.

A large pit measuring 4.5m by 3m was present to the south of the east-west ditch. The upper deposits were hand excavated and found to contain pottery dated to the 11th and 12th centuries. A dark brown stoney silt continued down to a level of 54.45m OD. Beneath this a white mortar deposit was present for a depth of 0.05m. A further deposit of dark clayey silt with a high water content continued to a level of 53.7m OD at which point natural gravels were encountered. The total depth of the feature was 1.8m.

Two small hearth features containing both iron and lead slag were present during this phase of activity. The pottery recovered dated the features to the 11th or 12th centuries.

The scale of the features during this phase of activity is in stark contrast to previous activity on the site. Concentrated, intense land use is superseded by large destructive features that pay no respect to what has gone before.

The activity of this phase has strong parallels with the gravel quarry and charnel pit phase identified in 1993 during the excavation for the New Library Building at the west end of the cathedral. The 1993 quarry pit was similar in scale to the large feature on the east side of the excavations here and equally destructive to the late Saxon structures and deposits. It was also the final phase of activity before the west end was turned over to cemetery use – a situation mirrored here.

The New Library Building excavation quarry pit was reused as a mass charnel pit. There is no evidence for this occurring in St Johns Quad to the extent of the remains of 5,000 individuals contained within the 1993 pit although bone was indeed present, suggesting that the fills of the feature were not archaeologically sterile.

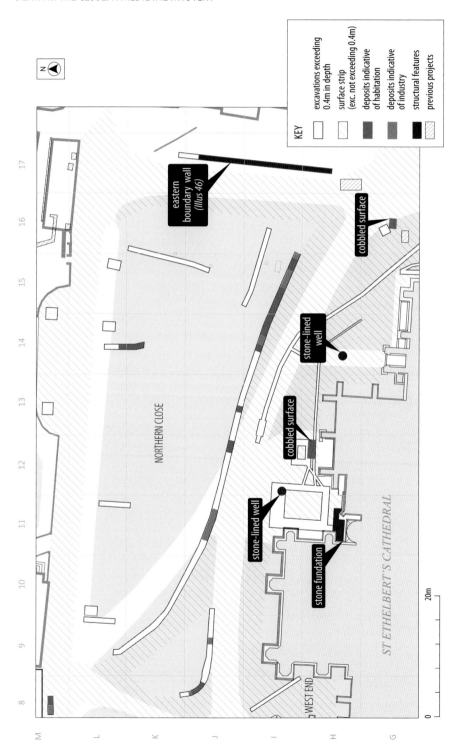

KEY

excavations exceeding
0.4m in depth

surface strip
(exc. not exceeding 0.4m)

deposits indicative
of habitation

deposits indicative
of industry

structural features

previous projects

eastern
boundary wall
(Illus 46)

cobbled surface

stone-lined
well

cobbled surface

stone-lined well

stone fundation

NORTHERN CLOSE

ST ETHELBERT'S CATHEDRAL

WEST END

0   20m

ILLUS 40
Plan of features to the north of the Cathedral

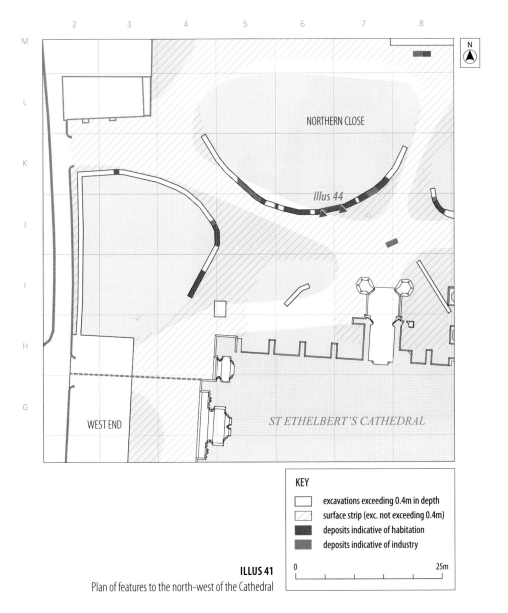

ILLUS 41
Plan of features to the north-west of the Cathedral

KEY

☐ excavations exceeding 0.4m in depth
▨ surface strip (exc. not exceeding 0.4m)
▨ deposits indicative of habitation
▨ deposits indicative of industry

0   25m

Even when considered in isolation from the results and interpretations of the 1993 excavation, quarrying does seem to be the only activity that could sensibly explain such large features being excavated at this time. The activity post-dates what is believed to be the early 11th-century cathedral church and predates the cemetery from which the earliest radiocarbon dates fall sometime between the mid 11th and mid 12th centuries. This places the features both physically and date-wise in the early Norman period just before the current cathedral building started, and indeed when there was reorganisation of much of Hereford, a time when gravel for building and surfacing must have been in high demand.

ILLUS 42
Soakaway excavation

ground surface), was almost wholly concerned with the removal of human remains and it was only at the very bottom of these trenches that pre-burial ground deposits were encountered.

Although the excavated areas were not conducive to gaining a complex understanding of the pre-burial archaeology, enough was seen to describe the basic nature of the deposits to the north of the cathedral. In addition to this, the fact that the soak-away trenches crossed almost the complete close from east to west, meant that a representative proportion of the site was observed. The whole site was divided into an alpha-numeric grid and this is particularly useful in guiding the reader to the locale of particular discoveries. References such as J9 dotted throughout the text that follows should assist in rapidly spotting features referred to on the area plans (Illus 40–41).

THE NORTHERN CLOSE

Excavations to the north of the current cathedral building whilst investigating a much wider expanse of ground were restricted to the foundations for the new mason's huts, the stripping of former path surfaces and the excavation of soak-away trenches to improve drainage in the Close. Only the excavation of the soak-aways were deep enough to provide access to the pre-cemetery deposits (Illus 40, 41).

The soak-away trenches were not ideal environments for excavation. At only 0.6m wide, conditions were cramped and interpretation of features and deposits was difficult (Illus 42). The required excavation level within these trenches (c 1–1.2m below

Sufficient amounts of early pottery were present to indicate occupation and almost certainly industrial activity, similar to that reported on above from St John's Quad, continuing on the northern side of the cathedral.

Three sherds of Roman pottery were recovered from the area, one of which was found in a deposit also containing several sherds of a Saxon storage jar. Once again a tantalising hint of Roman activity

in the vicinity of the city but not enough to claim Roman occupation on the site.

Across the whole of this part of the site pottery from the 10th and 11th centuries was present. Although some sherds of pottery dating to this period were recovered from stratified deposits, the fact that early pottery commonly occurred in general graveyard deposits indicates that early stratified deposits must have been disturbed by subsequent grave digging. However, it is likely that deposits dating to the 11th century and earlier still remain in situ, below the excavation level required by the development.

Pottery dated to the 12th century recovered from the latest pre-cemetery stratified deposits indicates that the burial ground here must be contemporary with the present cathedral. All pottery later than this date was recovered from deposits post-dating the use of the site as a burial ground.

A number of patches of burning recorded here almost certainly indicated the proximity of smithing hearths. The burnt, sooty fill of a shallow, bowl-shaped feature (J6/J7) contained smithing slag and a high density of hammerscale. The area around it had been subjected to considerable heat making it almost certain that the feature was directly involved in the process, although due to the absence of other evidence it was not possible to identify its purpose (Illus 43).

Unfortunately, direct dating evidence was not present, but the feature was cut by a stone burial Cist suggesting a pre-13th century date.

A sequence of deposits identified in grid squares J6 and J7 gave the most undisturbed impression of pre-cemetery archaeology in the north of the Close (Illus 44). A mid-brown silty clay deposit was observed in the base of the soak-away trench. The top of the deposit was present at 55.27m OD and is believed to be the same as sterile silty clay observed in the base of the deep excavation in St John's Quad. A red burnt clay deposit, possibly a hearth, was cut into the silty clay and subsequently overlain by a charcoal rich layer containing 11th century pottery. This

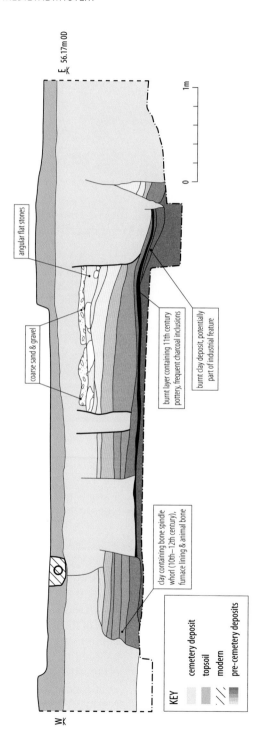

E 56.17m OD

angular flat stones

coarse sand & gravel

burnt layer containing 11th century pottery, frequent charcoal inclusions

burnt clay deposit, potentially part of industrial feature

clay containing bone spindle whorl (10th–12th century), furnace lining & animal bone

KEY
cemetery deposit
topsoil
modern
pre-cemetery deposits

W

0   1m

ILLUS 44
South facing section through pre-cemetery deposits (J6/J7)

ILLUS 45
Cattle radius polished flat on one side, 11th century (SF2244)

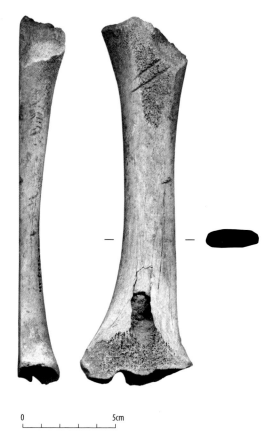

0   5cm

deposit was present over the full width of the trench for a length of 2.5m and appears to have been caused by a fire. A burnt deposit overlying this appeared to be domestic in origin, containing abundant charred cereal grain, charcoal and animal bone. A further four occupation layers were present in the sequence, containing a mixture of domestic and industrial material including lead slag, iron smithing slag, charred cereals and animal bone. A bone spindle whorl[37] dated to the 10th–12th century was also recovered (Illus 120) as well as another worked bone[38] (Illus 45). These occupational deposits were sealed by a surface of gravel and flat stones, the top of which lay at 56.03m OD.

The limited area of excavation and the truncation caused by later burials makes these deposits difficult to interpret but as mentioned above their presence does indicate intense activity on this part of the site prior to the 12th century. The nature of the material recovered derives from both industrial and domestic activity, a similar picture to that in St John's Quad. The survival of these deposits to such a high level and lack of their reoccurrence elsewhere in the soak-away trenches also illustrates how much archaeology has been destroyed by later burial activity. Although pre-cemetery deposits are present elsewhere to the

north of the cathedral, they rarely manifest themselves as much more than a shallow layer in the base of the trench.

During the excavation of a service trench to the west of the Old Deanery (H17), a wall was revealed on a north-south alignment (Illus 46). Whilst it didn't survive along its whole length the wall was observed intermittently for a distance of 25m, heading directly towards the south-east corner of the Cathedral Barn. It was 0.98m wide with a dressed face to the east and west and a rubble core surviving to a height of 0.4m. Although potentially a former boundary wall to the deanery, there is the possibility that it could be a return of the east-west wall revealed beneath the Cathedral Barn in 2009 (Illus 15).

37   SF1169
38   SF2244

ILLUS 46
Old deanery wall (H17)

ILLUS 47
West end of the Cathedral with remains of Building 7 in foregorund

THE WEST END

The excavations at the West End of the cathedral covered a larger area than the deep excavation in St John's Quad but were for the most part shallower (Illus 48). The renovation work here had been designed so that levels were built up adjacent to the Cathedral, with the intention of minimising the impact upon archaeological deposits. Deeper deposits were removed in the far west of the site adjacent to Palace Yard (the southern continuation of Broad Street), but even here the impact did not exceed a depth of 1m below existing ground level. Because the base of the excavation was not flat and rose up from west to east, strips of archaeology were revealed getting progressively later with increased distance from Broad Street. This meant that the earliest deposits were only encountered in the west of the area (G2, F2). Further to the east, excavation did not continue beneath the depth of burials.

The main focus of pre-cemetery activity exposed here appears to have occured

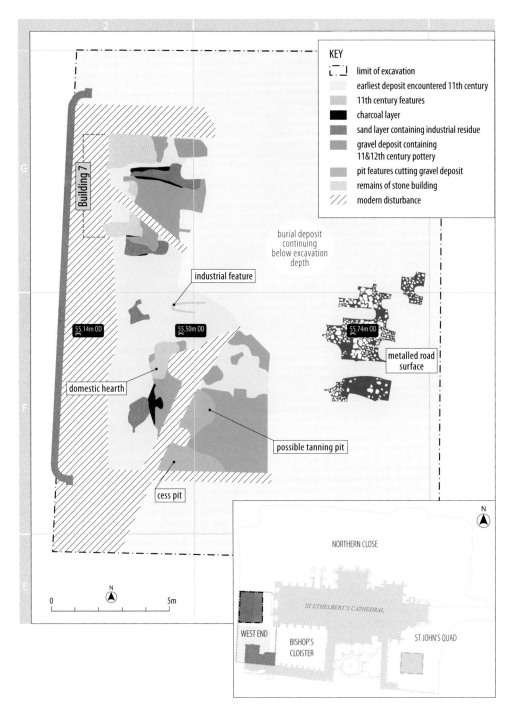

KEY

- limit of excavation
- earliest deposit encountered 11th century
- 11th century features
- charcoal layer
- sand layer containing industrial residue
- gravel deposit containing 11&12th century pottery
- pit features cutting gravel deposit
- remains of stone building
- modern disturbance

Building 7

burial deposit continuing below excavation depth

industrial feature

55.14m OD

55.50m OD

55.74m OD

metalled road surface

domestic hearth

possible tanning pit

cess pit

0   5m

NORTHERN CLOSE

ST ETHELBERT'S CATHEDRAL

WEST END   BISHOP'S CLOISTER   ST JOHN'S QUAD

ILLUS 48
Features at the West End

ILLUS 49
Remains of stone Building 7 (G2)

Immediately to its north were patches of heat affected white clay. A linear depression cut into a mounded deposit of this white clay may have had an industrial purpose. A sample taken from the clay was found to contain metalworking residues, fragments of glass, mortar and both burnt and unburnt animal and fish bone.

Overlying these earlier deposits was an intermittent layer of charcoal suggesting a widespread burning event. The deposit was up to 0.1m deep in places, and although heavily truncated by later activity it was identified across the full north-south extent of the excavated area. The charcoal layer was associated with an overlying deposit of fine yellow sand containing slag and other industrial residues. A deposit of orange gravel containing 11th and 12th century pottery sealed this evidence for early industrial activity extending across the whole of the area investigated. In places the deposit was up to 0.1m deep and appears to define a change in use. In the south of the site the gravel deposit was cut by two large pit features. The relatively clean, organic nature of the fill of the more southerly feature suggests that it may have been a cess pit. Pottery recovered from the feature was dated to the 11th century. The presence of a clay lining in the second pit suggested that its purpose may have been to contain liquids and may have been used for activities such as tanning. The feature contained pottery dated to the late 12th or early 13th centuries.

during the 10th and 11th centuries and in common with the other areas of the Close appears to include evidence for both domestic and industrial activity.

The earliest deposit excavated was a dark brown sandy silt containing 11th-century pottery. Environmental samples recovered from the deposit contained industrial residue and charred seed. The deposit continued below the required excavation depth so earlier deposits will still survive here. A small hearth cutting into this level appeared to be domestic in nature. Only the upper hearth deposits were available for excavation, but were found to contain fragments of burnt animal and fish bone and a sherd of pottery dated to the 10th or 11th centuries. Any related structure for the hearth could be below the level of excavation.

ILLUS 50
Potential road surface (F3)

The remains of a stone structure (Building 7) were revealed in the north-west of the excavated area (G2) (Illus 49). Preserved to a height of 0.65m, the irregular stones appeared to be part of a foundation course. The arrangement of the stones suggested that they represented the south-east corner to a building. Pottery recovered from between the stones dated to the late 13th century, although the wall was heavily disturbed and therefore the pottery cannot be considered as an entirely reliable means of obtaining a date for the structure.

What appeared to be a patchy road or yard surface comprising large flat stones, cobbles and gravel was present in the centre of the excavated area (F3) (Illus 50). Due to truncation by later burials it was not possible to establish its original extent or orientation.

The ground reduction requirements at the West End were not conducive to achieving a good understanding of the archaeological deposits. Some features of note, however, were observed.

The potential road surface in the centre of the site is of particular interest when considered alongside the pre-conquest road identified during the 1993 New Library Building excavation. The surface is broadly similar in appearance and in the correct location to be a continuation of the same road. A comparison of the level the two surfaces places the 1993 surface 0.16m lower than the surface revealed during the 2009–11 excavations. This slight difference in level could result from road sloping down towards the River Wye.

The remains identified as Building 7 relate to a structure that presumably continued to the west, outside the boundaries of the present Close. Historic maps of the Close do not show any structures in this position, and it is therefore assumed that it pre-dates the 17th century. It would appear to be positioned too far to the west to front onto Palace Yard, so may instead relate to the possible Saxon road identified to the east.

THE CONTRIBUTION OF POTTERY TO THE DATING OF THE SITE

There have been numerous references above to pottery dates but little consideration of exactly what types and dates of pottery were recovered from the site. The names and date ranges of different types of pottery have been set out in Table 1 below and are then discussed from the Saxon period onwards. Roman pottery aside, the earliest date at which pottery begins to be used in Hereford appears to be around the time of Alfred the Great at the end of the 9th Century. Pottery studies by Alan Vince in the 1980s[39] produced a pottery series for the city and the letters and numbers referred to as fabric codes relate to this sequence.

SAXON (10TH TO 11TH CENTURIES)

Saxon pottery was found in all excavated areas, though was concentrated in St Johns Quad. The pottery may date as early as the very end of the 9th and is certainly present from the 11th century onwards. It is apparent that considerable activity was taking place around the Saxon Cathedral and the types of ceramics present imply domestic occupation as well as industrial activity.

Early Cotswold ware cooking pots (fabric D1) date from as early as the late 9th century in Hereford and may have gone out of use in the city by the late 11th century. Hereford seems to have lain at the western limit of ceramic use during the late Saxon period and D1 was some of the earliest pottery to be used in the city[40]. This fabric was found in deposits predating the earliest medieval burials here. Six sherds contained 'kettlefur' type deposits indicating use in cooking. Further sherds were sufficient to indicate activity from this earliest period around the north and west sides of the cathedral.

Stafford-type ware (fabric G1) is thought to date in Hereford between the 10th and 11th centuries. In early 11th century deposits in Hereford it forms up to 70% of the material declining to about 12% of sherds by the late 11th century[41]. Excluding redeposited material found in the graves the total from St John's Quad area amounts to 60% indicating early 11th century activity.

SAXO NORMAN (11TH TO 12TH CENTURIES)

Several types of pottery indicate activity during this period and include Stafford-type ware (fabric G1) which may have continued to be used after the Conquest, Worcester-type unglazed ware (fabric C1) which is first found in Hereford during the latter part of the 11th century, Cotswold cooking pots and pitchers (fabric D2), occasional Stamford type spouted pitchers (fabric E1b) and Malvernian cooking pots (fabric B1) first used in Hereford in the early to mid 12th century. The latter was the most common medieval fabric found at the site, accounting for 39% of all medieval pottery in St Johns Quad. Eight of the thirteen rims found had cordon decoration placing them in the early to mid 12th century[42].

---

39   Vince 1985

40   Vince 2002, 54 & 66
41   Vince 1985, 62
42   Vince 1985, 46

LATER MEDIEVAL (13TH TO 15TH CENTURIES)

The majority of pottery from this period was of Herefordshire later wares including a chafing dish (fabric A7b) and jugs, a colander and a skillet[43] in Malvernian oxidised glazed ware (fabric B4). However, there was comparatively little pottery dating between the beginning of the 13th century and the advent of fabrics A7b and B4 in the later 13th and the 14th centuries respectively, although several sherds such as Worcester glazed ware jugs (fabric C2), Herefordshire siltstone tempered ware (fabric A4) jugs and jars, and sherds of Brill/Boarstall ware (fabric E3) may fill this gap.

FABRIC CODE	COMMON NAME	ST JOHNS QUAD	NORTHERN CLOSE (EAST)	NORTHERN CLOSE (WEST)	WEST END	OTHER	TOTAL	DATING
Roman								
A1/SVW	Severn Valley Ware	4	–	1	1	–	6	Roman
Saxon	10th to 11th century							
D1	Cotswold Wares – cooking pots	44	14	–	29	–	87	L9/11
G1	Stafford-type ware	70	18	14	15	–	117	10/11
A7a	Herefordshire Wares – early pitchers	–	1	–	–	–	1	11/12
Saxo-Norman	11th to 12th century							
C1	Worcester Wares – cooking pots	34	5	6	6	1	52	L11/13
D2	Cotswold Wares – cooking pots & pitchers	55	25	6	32	–	116	L11/12
E1b	Stamford Wares – spouted pitchers	13	3	–	–	–	16	11/12
B2	Malvernian Wares – tripod pitchers	3	–	–	–	–	3	12
B1	Malvernian Wares – cooking pots	108	18	6	36	–	168	12/14
Later medieval	13th to 15th century							
C2	Worcester Ware – jugs	1	5	–	2	–	8	13
B3	Malvernian Wares	3	1	–	–	–	4	13
A2	Herefordshire Wares	2	–	–	–	–	2	13
A3	Herefordshire Wares	–	2	–	–	–	2	13
E3	Brill/Boarstall Ware	3	3	–	–	–	6	13/14
A6	Herefordshire Wares	1	1	1	1	–	4	13/14

43   Vince 1985, fig 42.10

FABRIC CODE	COMMON NAME	ST JOHNS QUAD	NORTHERN CLOSE (EAST)	NORTHERN CLOSE (WEST)	WEST END	OTHER	TOTAL	DATING
A4	Herefordshire Siltstone-tempered Ware	2	4	1	1	–	8	13/14
A5	Herefordshire Wares	4	–	1	–	–	5	M13/E15
A7b	Herefordshire Later Wares	36	22	6	8	3	75	L13/15
B4	Malvernian Oxidised Glazed Wares	37	26	1	3	1	68	14/17
Post-medieval & Modern | 16th century onwards								
G6/TUDG	Tudor Green Wares	2	2	–	–	–	4	15/16
B4/B5	Malvernian Wares	–	–	–	2	–	2	16/17
G8/CSTN	Cistercian-type ware	27	4	2	7	–	40	16/17
F2	Rhenish Stoneware	12	3	2	–	–	17	16/18
MY	Midlands Yellow Ware	–	–	2	1	–	3	L16/17
BORDB	Border Ware – brown glazed	2	–	–	–	–	2	L.16/18
BORDY	Border Ware – yellow glazed	2	–	–	–	–	2	L.16/18
A7d/e	Herefordshire Wares	22	8	3	23	1	57	17/18
E6	Staffordshire Wares	17	8	4	6	1	36	17/18
G5	Tin-Glazed wares	3	2	–	1	2	8	18
Modern Wares	Creamware, Transfer Printed Modern Stoneware, Modern Whiteware	16	9	2	28	6	61	m.18+
U/I	Unidentified	24	9	3	4	–	40	–
Total		547	193	61	206	15	1,022	

TABLE 1
Stratified pottery distribution by sherd count and area

A BODY OF EVIDENCE

Widespread occupation and industry in the Close appears to have come to an end by the start of the 12th century. The archaeological evidence from both the 1993 New Library Building excavations and the current project suggest that once the construction of the Norman cathedral got underway little attention was paid to the Saxon layout of the area that became the cathedral precinct.

Although the deep quarrying and charnel pit excavated on the New Library Building site, and the quarry pits present in St John's Quad illustrate the destructive impact of the new cathedral on the Saxon town, the process was not immediate and occurred over a generation or more. Bishop Losinga (1079 – c 1095) was the first of the post-conquest Bishops to make a significant impact on the ecclesiastical precinct with the construction of his chapel. However, his greatest contribution to the development of the Close, was the transferral of the commercial centre of the town to the north of the defences following his arrangement with William FitzOsbern to establish a new market place[1]. Whether Robert or later

Bishops actually cleared the site of the Close in preparation for the new cathedral has not been clear to date. However, the previous chapter provides perhaps the most compelling evidence that the area surrounding the cathedral had served some other use and this must have been the case. The key to this evidence is the complete lack of burials (bar the one unusual example) that predate the construction of the 'new' Norman cathedral started when Bishop Reinhelm (1107–15) was incumbent[2].

Whilst a cathedral church is referred to in Hereford at the beginning of the 9th century and it might be assumed that regular burials were taking place from at least this date, this does not necessarily have to have been in the vicinity of the current cathedral. All the burials excavated as part of the current project post-date stratified occupational or industrial deposits of the early 11th century or later. The single exception to this was the 'foundation trench burial[3]' dated to the late 9th or early 10th century (Illus 20). The location of this burial, intentionally placed beneath the

---

1   Whitehead 1982, 17

2   Barrow 2000, 27
3   Sk5061

foundations of a building marks it out as exceptional and completely separate to the widespread burial within St John's Quad. Where the full sequence of deposits was observed, there was no evidence for burial beneath the stratified domestic and industrial deposits dating to the 10th and 11th centuries.

One of the earliest burials in St John's Quad relating to the use of the site as a burial ground[4] has been radiocarbon dated to 1025–1159[5]. Whilst the date allows the possibility that the burial is pre-conquest, the fact that the grave was dug into the fill of the 11th to 12th century quarry pits means it is considered to be post-conquest.

From this point on the archaeology of the Close is dominated by human burial. Although burial grounds and cathedral precincts in the medieval period were undoubtedly social places, used for games, animal grazing and trade, the archaeological evidence for these activities is limited to the occasional coin and trade token uncovered within the general soil deposits of the burial ground (Illus 51–52). A decorative book clasp[6] revealed within St John's Quad conjures up a vision of one of the Vicars Choral scurrying from his lodgings to work at the Cathedral and his battered religious text shedding its clasp (Illus 53).

We know that by the time St Guthlacs Priory moved off Castle Green in the 1140s,

0   2cm

ILLUS 51

Copper farthing trade token of Henry Jones, Hereford, cemetery deposits, St John's Quad, 1662 (SF0211)

0   2cm

ILLUS 52

Lead trade token, cemetery deposits, The Northern Close, 17th or 18th century (SF0965)

the recently consecrated cathedral was claiming exclusive burial rights over Hereford and some outlying parishes. From the late 13th century onwards there were instances of outlying parishes gaining some concessions from the cathedral with regard to burial rights, but the Close was still the final resting place for the people of the city until it was officially closed to burial in 1791. After this date burial within the Close was restricted to those who died within the precinct, but in practice it seems likely that occasional other burials were still permitted, particularly in existing vaults.

Although it is recorded that the Close was cleared of gravestones in 1796, stones recovered during the course of the excavation and within the Chapter House Yard revealed that burial was continuing on the Close until the mid 19th century. Research into the background of the individuals inscribed on the gravestones reveals them to be of the upper middle class and holders of positions of civic administration within the city. The latest of the dated stones belonged to William Symonds, a doctor who had served as both High Sheriff of Radnorshire and Mayor of Hereford before dying in 1844. It seems that during the first half of the 19th century burial was confined to notable local families, and by the time of the 1853 Burial Act which effectively outlawed inner city burial grounds, burial on the Close had ceased entirely.

---

4   Sk4993
5   WK34561, calibrated to 95%
6   SF0150A

the Cathedral itself, the middle classes and those below could expect a burial within the graveyard. A hierarchy of burial is generally acknowledged within Christian graveyards, with burial at the east end, close to the cathedral building considered the most desirable due to its proximity to the high altar. Increasing distance away from this focal point represents a reduction in desirability with the limits of the burial ground being the least popular. An often repeated belief is that the burial ground to the north side of a church is less popular than the south and was the burial place for thieves, outcasts and clandestine burials of un-baptised children.

Variations were observed in the burial density between different areas of the Close (Table 2). Density value was calculated by counting the number of partial and whole skeletons present within directly comparable areas. The area was fixed at 10m by 0.7m to enable the comparison of the soak-away trenches to the north of the cathedral (0.7m wide) with the open area excavations. The sample was always taken from east-west aligned trenches. The burial density of the medieval burial ground revealed during the 1993 excavation is included for comparison. Rather than being measured from a fixed area it is calculated from the total number of skeletons found within the excavated area.

ILLUS 53
Copper alloy book clasp, cemetery deposits, St John's Quad, 16th or 17th century (SF0150A)

DENSITY OF BURIAL

The 2009–11 Cathedral Close excavations revealed the articulated remains of 2,453 people. A glance at the impact plan (Illus 10) shows how little of the total Close area was actually excavated and thus what a small proportion this is of the numbers of burials present.

Observations on the density of burial can give an indication as to whether some areas of the Close were more favoured than others. Whilst those of sufficient status or wealth could aspire to burial beneath the floor of

AREA	GRID SQUARES	SAMPLE AREA (M²)	NUMBER OF BURIALS	DENSITY (BURIALS PER M²)
St Johns Quad	B13,B14	7	46	6.57
Northern Close (east)	J13,I13	7	68	9.71
Northern Close (west)	K3,K4	7	52	7.42
West End	F3	7	22	3.14
1993 New Library Building	C3, D3	200	1085	5.43

TABLE 2
Burial density

These can also be used to estimate the total number of burials within the Close which results in *c* 80,000 individuals being buried between 1100 and 1800, an average of 115 per year. This assumes that when the Close was reduced in level in the 19th century the Victorians simply removed mixed graveyard earth and stopped once they encountered actual articulated burials.

The results show a far greater density of burial in the north of the Close compared to the south and a comparatively low burial density at the west end of the Cathedral adjacent to the western entrance. It is possible that the higher burial density in the north of the Close reflects the social distinction alluded to above with the populous poor being buried here, and the secluded areas to the south, surrounded by cathedral buildings being reserved for the wealthier inhabitants of the city.

THE BURIAL GROUPS

Modern burial grounds appear well ordered, with neatly constructed rows of burials. The majority of graves bear a marker, more often than not giving the name and date of death of the deceased.

Undoubtedly a similar degree of order existed from the earliest days of burial in the Close. Unfortunately when grave markers are periodically cleared, burial plots are used and reused, landmarks used for grave orientation change along with preferences regarding burial depth. The result being that the relationship between individual burials can become confused.

An attempt was made to determine the sequence of burial by producing interconnected chains of burials. The level of disturbance caused to earlier burials by

later burials and absence of visible grave cuts made the task of identifying a precise order of burial difficult in many cases. However, what became evident was that a number of broad, easily identifiable characteristics of each burial seemed to fit a rough chronological model.

These trends had already been identified during excavation and assessment of the data confirmed that they represented a sensible basis for analysis. The trends are based on burial typology and whilst they cannot be considered rigidly chronological (ie providing an absolute date of burial) they consistently occur in the same sequence through time. There is certainly overlap between the groups and within a particular time period the status or wealth of an individual may have been the determining factor of burial type, rather than a certain time period rigidly employing a particular burial type. Nevertheless, as a means to begin analysis, division of the assemblage into five distinct burial groups was the most appropriate solution (Illus 54).

PRE-CIST BURIALS (*C* 12TH CENTURY)
Stone Cist burials were the earliest burials identified on a typological basis, but a number of simple earth burials had been physically cut when these were dug and therefore must be earlier. Because it was not possible to identify Pre-Cist burials when they were not physically related to a Cist burial, there is potential for burials of this group to have been grouped with the simple Bone Only burials.

CIST BURIALS (12TH TO 13TH CENTURIES)
The stone Cist burials could be identified by the presence of stone slabs placed vertically and lining the edges of the grave, sometimes also with capping stones (slabs placed horizontally over the burial and resting on the vertical stones) (Illus 55). There was no

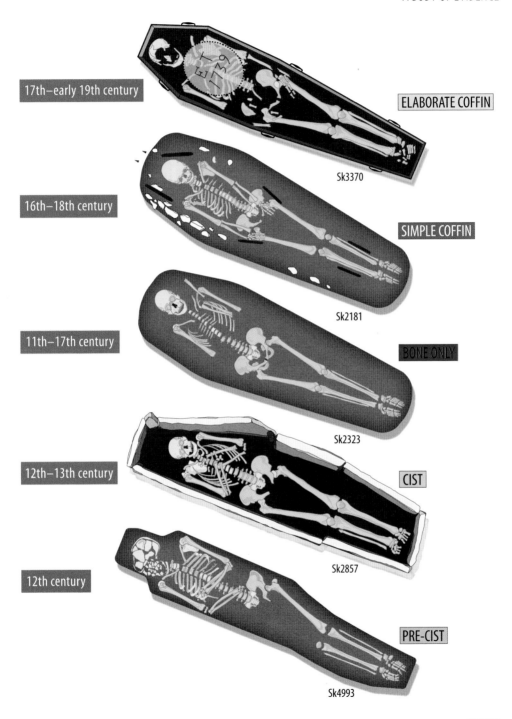

17th–early 19th century

ELABORATE COFFIN

Sk3370

16th–18th century

SIMPLE COFFIN

Sk2181

11th–17th century

BONE ONLY

Sk2323

12th–13th century

CIST

Sk2857

12th century

PRE-CIST

Sk4993

ILLUS 54
Burial typology

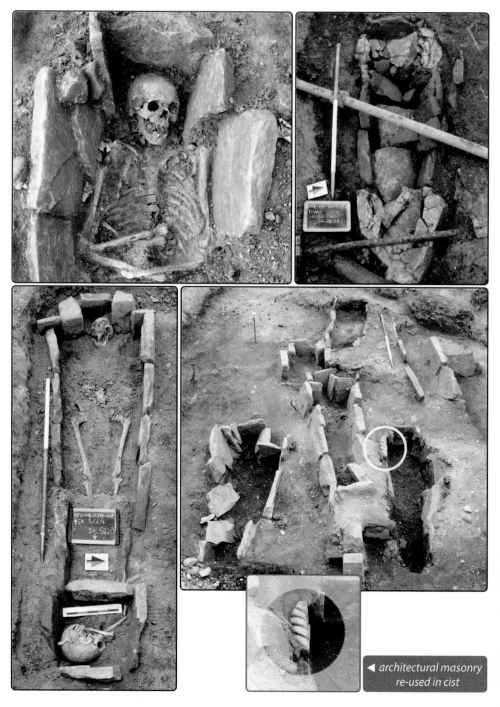

ILLUS 55
Cist burials

architectural masonry
re-used in cist

evidence to suggest that the stones were specifically cut or worked for use in the construction of the Cists, and they were not mortared or bonded in any way. The majority of stones used were un-worked; those that were had clearly been reused from elsewhere, were generally broken, and their decoration was typical of architectural stone.

The Cist burial tradition is relatively common in the early medieval period. At Bermondsey Abbey, two examples were cut by the foundations of the 12th century church and Cists were present at the pre 12th-century church of St Bride's, Fleet Street. They were the dominant form of burial in the 11th century cemetery on the south side of Holy Trinity at Aldgate. A continuing tradition of Cist burial is seen at St John's, Colchester where it is thought that the Cist burials were later than the 12th century. In Winchester's Paradise cemetery where Cist graves ranged in date from about 1200 to 1520 they formed about 39% of the burials excavated.

Five Cist burials including four children were revealed during the excavations on Castle Green, where they were considered to be amongst the final phase of burial before St Guthlac's Priory moved to the Bye Street site in 1143.

Of the 31 graves excavated at the later St Guthlac's site in Bye Street, four were Cists. Two of these cut earlier inhumations and were dated to the second phase of burial.

The radiocarbon dates obtained from two of the Bone Only burials predating the Cist burials during the 2009–11 excavations concur with the results of previous excavations and establish the Cist burial as a long-lived tradition, dating between the 11th and 13th centuries. This was supported during excavations for the New Toilet Block where Cist burials were also

ILLUS 56
Densely packed Bone Only burials

uncovered. The higher status of these was in some way confirmed through the presence of pattens and chalices, a rite reserved for priests and canons. On the basis of the style of chalice and a radiocarbon date from one of the burials these also appear to be 13th century.

The fact that the Cists form the earliest (sizable) burial group during the 2009–11 excavations adds weight to the argument that the Saxon burial ground was not present in the areas excavated.

BONE ONLY BURIALS (11TH TO 17TH CENTURIES)
In the case of Bone Only burials all that remains in the archaeological record is the bone itself (with the exception of 12 burials associated with pins that may have held the

shroud together) (Illus 56). There was no evidence for Cist stones and coffin fittings nor any evidence to suggest that the burial has been interred in anything other than a simple sewn, pinned or tied shroud.

Prior to the emergence of ready made shrouds in the 17th century it seems likely that shrouds were homemade or a suitable sheet acquired from the home to wrap the body in before burial. The use of shrouds continued well into the 20th century, but certainly from the 17th century onwards the shrouded body would be contained within a coffin.

Of the eight Bone Only burials sent for radiocarbon dating, six returned dates in the 13th century, the remaining two (which directly predate Simple Coffin burials, see Radiocarbon dating, below) dated to between the 15th and 17th centuries.

SIMPLE COFFIN BURIALS (16TH TO 18TH CENTURIES)

The Simple Coffin burials are those where evidence for simple coffin fittings were found with the skeleton. Iron nails and in some cases coffin handles confirm the former presence of a coffin. Although always occurring later than the Bone Only burials in their respective sequences, there could be a degree of overlap.

The use of the 'parish coffin' was common in the 16th and 17th centuries to transport the shrouded corpse to the grave, but rather than being buried with the individual was reused.

Until the mid 16th century the use of the private coffin was limited. Neither of the two prayer books of Edward VI, nor those of Elizabeth I and Charles II make any reference to coffins, and early coffins are generally

associated with intramural burial (burial within the church) and high status. Although excavations have revealed instances of pre-16th century coffined burial in churchyards, it was not the predominant form of burial for the common man, and occurrences are rare.

ELABORATE COFFINS (17TH TO EARLY 19TH CENTURIES)

The Elaborate Coffin burials are those with evidence for ornate coffins, using copper alloy studs and moulded brass plates for decoration (Illus 57). By the first quarter of the 18th century the funeral furnishing trade had become firmly established. Most coffins after 1750 were fabric covered with upholstery pins marking out details. Velvet coverings were the preserve of the wealthy, with black baize used to cover the coffins of the common man[7].

It is during this period that the brick-lined grave became a popular form of burial within the graveyard. Pressure from the upper and middle classes to be buried in family groups was alleviated by the construction of brick shafts within the cemetery capable of holding more than one coffin. This form of burial bridged the status gap between being buried within the cathedral itself, and being buried within a simple earth grave. The shafts created a re-usable space and had more in common with burial vaults than the common earth grave. The burials were vertically separated from one another by the use of iron or wooden bars fixed horizontally into the sides of the shaft. The shafts were then capped with stone slabs which could be removed to allow later interments.

THE COFFINS THEMSELVES

Most of the coffins do not survive leaving the grips, studs and nails to tell their own story.

---

7   Litten 1991, 99

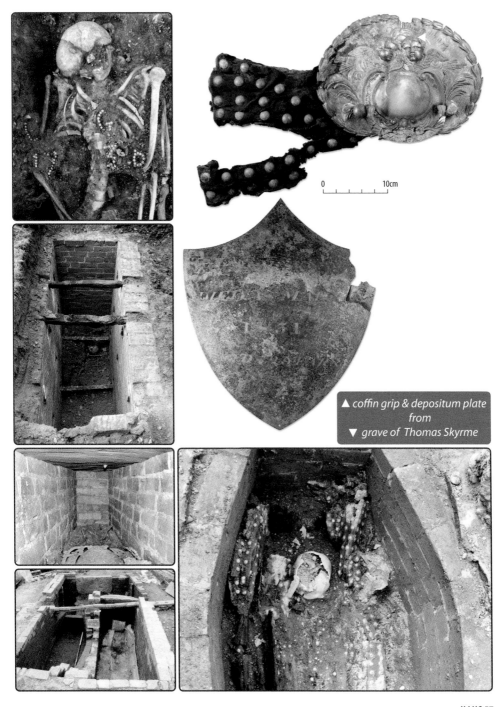

▲ coffin grip & depositum plate from
▼ grave of Thomas Skyrme

ILLUS 57
Elaborate Coffin burials

SF 0691A

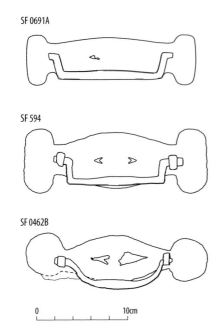

SF 594

SF 0462B

0   10cm

ILLUS 58
Iron grips and grip plates (SF0691A, SF0594, SF0462B)

Grips is the term generally given to coffin handles which were sometimes set within reinforcing and decorative grip plates. All but one of the grips at the site were made of iron, as were all but a handful of the grip plates in contrast to other 18th- and 19th-century graveyard assemblages, such as Spitalfields[8], which contain many more moulded brass and tin grip plates. Though the grips and plates are broadly similar in form, a lack of uniformity prevents the production of any clear typology and it is possible that rather than being mass produced by coffin furniture makers these were in fact produced by local blacksmiths. This would explain the conformity of convention, but the lack of exact patterns (Illus 58).

No. convincing differences were observed between grip and plate forms associated with

Simple Coffins and those with Elaborate Coffins. Only two were associated with direct dates, both in the 1730s and 40s. However, it seems likely that the earliest date back to around the mid 17th century when the use of coffins becomes near universal[9]. It is unclear whether the use of these simple iron fittings continue past the mid 18th century. There is no firm evidence for it, though similar simple plates have been found in 19th century coffins at other sites[10].

The lack of decoratively moulded plates in proportion to the high numbers of simple iron plates is perhaps more interesting, though this may in part be a matter of differential survival. The non-ferrous plates are very thin and delicate and some may have been completely destroyed. Fragmentary remains were found in a few graves. Dating may also be a factor, with a larger proportion of 17th- and early 18th-century coffins than found at comparative sites, as may be the relative status of the individuals interred. Alternatively it may represent a real regional difference in burial tradition, whether due to simpler or more sedate sensibilities or the strength of the local ironworking industry. Only one form of moulded non-ferrous coffin grip and plate were recovered, found in two graves, including that of Thomas Skyrme (d.1831), detailed below. The use of this form has been dated at Spitalfields to 1768–1847[11] but it seems likely that in this assemblage, its use is limited to the 19th century.

The studs (sometimes termed upholstery nails) were all of the same form, a domed head of various sizes with integral square sectioned shaft. They are the same form as others used commonly during the post-medieval period as upholstery studs for furniture. Evidence from other burial sites shows they were also used in a number of ways in coffin construction.

8   Reeve & Adams 1993

9   Litten 1991, 57
10   Boston 2008; Bashford & Sibun 2007
11   Reeve & Adams 1993, 144–7, fiche 1–2

Their basic function was to secure textile coverings to the exterior of the coffin, but their use went beyond the functional. They could be positioned in decorative patterns, sometimes highly elaborate[12], and could also be used to spell out biographical information on the coffin lid, usually in the simplified form of initials and date of death.

There were seven identifiable instances of coffins marked in this way (Table 3). The marked dates all fell between 1736 and 1746, with a late outlier in 1853. The last example[13], being over a century later would seem to be a conscious effort to return to an earlier tradition following the mid 19th century backlash against over-elaborate coffins[14]. There was little evidence for elaborate decorative designs in stud work, though a few of the coffins were well preserved enough for such detail to survive. Certainly the number of studs found associated with some burials implies there were some elaborate designs interred.

But for the studs, very little remained of objects which could be termed coffin decoration, and fewer still were found associated with their coffins. A small square copper alloy mount[15] was found in the grave fill of an Elaborate Coffin[16]. This was decorated with pressed rings of beading, however, it seems unlikely that it would have been used alone and as it was unaccompanied by any other decorative finds, it cannot be securely associated with this burial.

The one exception, in terms of the decorative use of plates and studs was the coffin of Thomas Skyrme[17], described in detail below.

BURIAL	INSCRIPTION	DATE OF COFFIN
Sk1090	C? G 1736?	1736?
Sk30378	B 173 (8?)7	1737?
Sk30284	T/F E 1?7?3?8?	1738?
Sk3370	ET 1739?	1739?
Sk4560	? ? ?743?	1743?
Sk1721	M 1746 +	1746
Sk2137	1816 1853 R W	1853

TABLE 3
Coffin stud inscriptions

THE COFFIN OF THOMAS SKYRME, 1831[18]

This was the best preserved of all the coffins, an Elaborate Coffin protected by a brick vault which had preserved large pieces of the coffin wood in sturdy enough condition to lift in tact (Illus 57, right). It was the only coffin from the site with brass grips. Six were found, spaced out along the sides[19] (Illus 57). On the lid over the chest, was a very sturdily made shield-shaped brass depositum plate[20] (Illus 57). Lastly there were two lid motifs: one, over the lower leg area was in the form of a large urn[21]; the other, was over the head area and was more fragmented but showed angels supporting a crown[22].

Putting the typological dating of all the coffin fittings together, the coffin has the date range 1827–47 and rather gratifyingly the clear engraved inscription on the depositum plate confirms just that. It reads 'Thomas Skyrme, died 18 March 1831, aged 72 years'.

---

12 Litten 1991, 99; Boston 2006, fig A2.41–8; Bashford & Sibun 2007
13 Sk2137
14 Reeve & Adams 1993, 77–8
15 SF0401
16 Sk1849
17 Sk11031

---

18 Sk11031
19 All of Spitalfields grip type 4, dated 1743–1847, and fixed to brass grip plates of Spitalfields grip plate type 3, dated at 1768–1847 (Reeve & Adams 1993)
20 St Martin's in the Bullring, Brimingham type 1, dated 1827–62 (Hancox 2006, 159)
21 Spitalfields lid motif type 2, dated 1795–1847
22 Spitalfields lid motif type 6, dated 1779–1847

There were also hundreds of brass studs used over the surface of the coffin meaning the overall effect of this coffin when new would have been very brassy, certainly compared to the more restrained iron fittings used on most other coffins. The weight of brass in the depositum plate and handles means these fittings would have been costly. It seems that Thomas Skyrme or his family at least were keen to publicly demonstrate their wealth.

Dating must be a large factor in why this coffin stands out so markedly from the rest found at the site. It is later than the majority, as it was interred after the ruling that burials in the cathedral grounds should cease. The gravestone that once capped this vault is still on display outside the toilet block[23]. It lists Isaac Skyrme (d.1799, aged 75), a city alderman, his wife Jane (d.1778) and son Thomas, the latter with biographical details matching the depositum plate. Oddly, the gravestone was recorded by Havergal[24] as originally lying in the Chapter House yard, close to where it now stands by the toilet block, but on the opposite side of the Cathedral to the location of the tomb itself (grid J8).

Thomas's death notice appeared in the Hereford Journal in 1831 mentioning a 'long and painful illness' (see Chapter 6). Otherwise few details are available of his life, work or family, though the manner of his burial suggests he was a man of some means and standing. It seems unlikely that he was the same Thomas Skyrme who in 1774 was listed as being in Hereford prison; he would have been 15 years old at the time. His late interment in the cathedral grounds is no doubt due to the presence of a pre-existing family vault.

FINDS ASSOCIATED WITH BURIALS

In keeping with the Christian tradition few grave goods were found. The level of intercutting between skeletons and the paucity of visible grave cuts meant that assigning finds to burials with any degree of confidence was rare. The majority of finds that were found within burial contexts were generally re-deposited, presumably dug up from the underlying stratified deposits and re-interred when the grave was back-filled.

EVIDENCE FOR CLOTHING

During the last quarter of the 17th century, the single piece long-sleeved gown replaced the winding sheet as the burial garment of choice. One problem with this garment was the positioning of limbs. Now that the corpse was more exposed, greater attention had to be paid to posture. One way of doing this was to tie the ankles together and pinion the arms against the side of the corpse with the waist band of the shroud[25]. Evidence from the excavation suggests that belts may also have been used to secure the body in position. Buckles were found associated with four skeletons, in various positions on the body. Only one was located on the pelvis suggesting a waist belt[26] (Illus 59). It was rare for corpses to be committed to the grave wearing day clothes[27], so the use of buckles to secure the shroud seems a likely alternative. The presence of single buttons in five graves is also likely to relate to shroud burials and is confined to burials in coffins. This was also the case for pins with a few exceptions.

GRAVE GOODS

Four burials were considered to have genuine grave goods. An Elaborate Coffin burial of an

---

23   Crookes 2001, last page; www.skyrme.info/places/index.htm, accessed 7th November 2014
24   Havergal 1881, reprinted in Crookes 2001, figs 10 and 11, no.3

25   Litten 1991, 81
26   SF1303, Sk31467
27   Litten 1991, 72

older male[28] was buried with a silver disc or coin in his mouth. The disc is featureless and may be a very worn silver coin, though given its otherwise very good condition, it seems more likely it was a purpose made blank disc to act as a token coin. It was bent at the edges and sat directly over the jaw bone as though it had been placed between cheek and jaw prior to burial. In addition to the silver coin, was a small crotal or rumbler bell located adjacent to his right knee (Illus 60, left).

0 ————————— 2.5cm

ILLUS 59
Copper alloy and iron buckle, right pelvis of Bone Only adult male burial, Sk31467, 1450–1550 (SF1303)

The tradition of placing a coin in the mouth of the deceased has been recognised in various cultures since at least the 5th century BC. The coin was placed with the deceased as a payment to the ferryman who conveyed souls across the river that separated the living from the dead. The tradition continued sporadically up until the early 20th century in Britain.

Crotal bells were used for a variety of purposes in medieval and post-medieval Britain. They were commonly attached to the harnesses of animals and were also used for decoration on clothing and as good luck charms on bracelets and necklaces. Devices involving bells were incorporated into coffins during the 19th century as a means to allay fears of being buried alive, although the small bell buried with this man is unlikely to have had any practical use, and appears to be more of a trinket. Taking into account the presence of the silver coin in the mouth of the deceased, the likelihood is that the bell relates to a further tradition or superstition.

In Christianity bells are rung to mark rites of passage such as births, marriages and deaths, and were believed by some to disturb the atmosphere and confuse evil spirits, possibly thwarting their designs on the escaping soul[29]. Although it is the more public church bells we usually associate with Christian worship, it may well be to this symbolism that the crotal bell alludes. The bell is not a unique or chance find as a further Elaborate Coffin burial[30] was found with a crotal bell adjacent to the upper left femur of the interred body (Illus 60, right). Whatever belief the bell alluded to it clearly extended beyond a single individual.

One further burial[31] was found to have a coin in the mouth, although there is some doubt as to whether it was intentionally placed there,

29 Richardson 1988, 27

ILLUS 60
Copper alloy crotal bells. Left, adjacent to right knee of Elaborate Coffin older male burial, Sk1306 (SF0173); Right, adjacent to upper left femur of Elaborate Coffin burial, Sk10085 (SF0667)

28 Sk1306

30 Sk10085
31 Sk40564

or whether it was deposited there through later disturbance of the grave. The silver half coin dated to the reign of Henry III (1216–72) but the coffin style (Simple Coffin) was clearly later and an 18th century button found within the grave appeared to confirm that this was not a 13th century burial. Potentially it was an early coin that had been placed within an 18th century grave, but evidence for disturbance around the skull suggested that the coin had been introduced to the grave at a later date.

Contained within the Elaborate Coffin of a young male[32] was a pair of compasses or dividers. (Illus 61) The measuring implement which was placed beneath the left lower leg of the body was initially believed to relate to the trade of the individual, with possibilities ranging from cartographer to stone mason.

0   5cm

ILLUS 61

Iron dividers, beneath left lower leg of Elaborate Coffin, young male burial, Sk2063 (SF0443)

However, another possibility is that the individual belonged to the order of Freemasons, first established in Hereford in 1729. The distinctive symbols of the fraternal society are the square and compasses, and although there is no evidence to suggest that freemasons were buried with identifying symbols, the brotherhood is known to conduct Masonic funerals for members.

A history of the Hereford Lodge was produced by Dr John Eisel in 2012 to mark its 250th anniversary. The document records that Brother Ross, a founder member of the lodge was buried in October 1763 with full Masonic honours. The place of burial is not recorded but in 1804, at the age of 44, Brother John Coren was buried in the Cathedral Close with full military honours. After the service a Masonic sermon was delivered at the graveside.

The identity of this young man as a Freemason is purely speculation, but the burial type is correct for the period when Masonic funeral rites were being carried out in Hereford and the society is renowned for its symbolism. The Hereford Journal records the funeral procession of John Cann in 1837, leaving from the lodge room at the Green Dragon Hotel on its journey to the place of burial (the location is not recorded). Preceded by a military band and members of the lodge, the coffin is recorded as having 'regalia on top of the pall'. Whether this regalia included a pair of compasses which were subsequently interred with the body is unknown, but it is not beyond the realms of possibility.

RADIOCARBON DATING

Thirteen burials were selected for radiocarbon dating. (Illus 62) The 'foundation trench burial'[33] was selected on the basis that it could provide dating evidence for the foundation of Building 1. The remaining burials were selected from 'chains' of intercutting burials in order to provide a temporal cross section of the burial ground, to test the viability of the burial groupings and to establish how quickly areas of the burial ground were being reused.

---

32   Sk2063

33   Sk5061

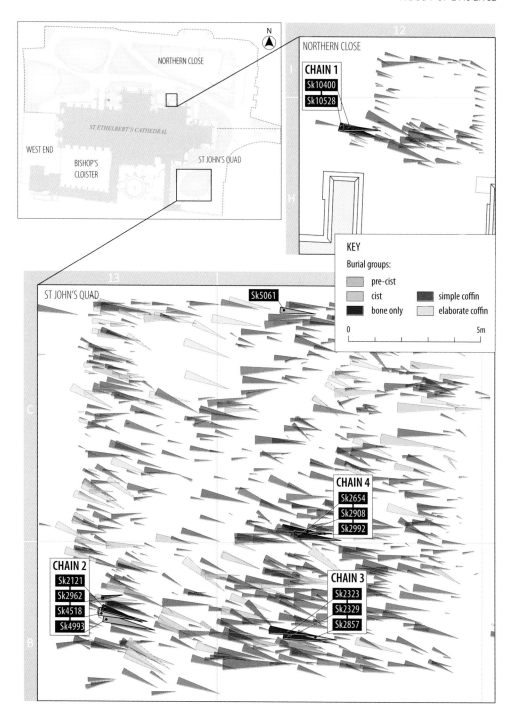

ILLUS 62
Skeletons selected for radiocarbon dating

SKELETON NUMBER	BURIAL GROUP	CHAIN	LABORATORY REFERENCE	UNCALIBRATED RADIOCARBON DATE (BP)	CALIBRATED DATE WITH A PROBABILITY OF		AGE/SEX
					68.2% (AD)	95.4% (AD)	
Sk5061	Pre-Cist	–	Wk-34563	1148±28	830–837 (3.1%) 868–903 (25.4%) 916–968 (39.7%)	780–792 (3.6%) 805–974 (91.8%)	Older Child/M
Sk10400	Bone Only	Chain 1	Wk-34564	372±29	1455–1516 (50.8%) 1597–1618 (17.4%)	1447–1526 (57%) 1556–1633 (38.4%)	Older Middle Adult/F
Sk10528	Bone Only	Chain 1	Wk-34565	757±34	1228–1232 (4.8%) 1241–1280 (63.4%)	1217–1288	Older Middle Adult/F
Sk2121	Bone Only	Chain 2	Wk-34553	711±27	1270–1292	1259–1303 (87.6%) 1366–1384 (7.8%)	Older Middle Adult/F
Sk2962	Bone Only	Chain 2	Wk-34559	759±28	1229–1232 (3.4%) 1241–1280 (64.8%)	1221–1283	Young Adult/F
Sk4518	Cist	Chain 2	Wk-34561	943±30	1032–1052 (15.2%) 1081–1128 (38.2%) 1133–1152 (14.8%)	1025–1159	Older Adult/M
Sk4993	Pre-Cist	Chain 2	Wk-34562	917±29	1044–1099 (42.1%) 1119–1142 (17.3%) 1147–1159 (8.8%)	1030–1185	Young Adult/F
Sk2323	Bone Only	Chain 3	Wk-34554	816±28	1212–1261	1171–1268	Older Adult/F
Sk2329	Bone Only	Chain 3	Wk-34555	791±26	1225–1261	1211–1278	Older Middle Adult/F
Sk2857	Cist	Chain 3	Wk-34557	844±25	1171–1221	1157–1259	Older Middle Adult/M
Sk2654	Bone Only	Chain 4	Wk-34556	302±29	1522–1575 (47%) 1584–1590 (4.1%) 1625–1645 (17%)	1490–1603 (70.4%) 1611–1652 (25%)	Sub Adult/M
Sk2908	Bone Only	Chain 4	Wk-34558	771±26	1226–1274	1219–1279	Younger Middle Adult/M
Sk2992	Bone Only	Chain 4	Wk-34560	807±26	1219–1258	1185–1271	Older Middle Adult/M

TABLE 4
Radiocarbon dated skeletons

Only skeletons selected for osteological analysis were considered for radiocarbon dating. There is therefore a bias towards skeletons from St Johns Quad (11 of 13) due to their increased levels of completeness and suitability for analysis.

To address the lack of information regarding the date range of the Bone Only burials, nine of the 13 dated burials belonged to this group. The Simple and Elaborate Coffined burials were assumed to be too late to be suitable for radiocarbon dating, although the last burial before a coffined burial was selected as the latest Bone Only in each chain.

The radiocarbon dating program produced some interesting results (Table 4). The dated skeletons from Cist and Pre-Cist burials were shown to be very similar in age. Sk4518 (Cist) which physically cut through Sk4993 (Pre-Cist) had an almost identical range of radiocarbon dates, suggesting that both burials occurred in the first half of the 12th century, during the building of the Norman cathedral. The possibility that two different burial practices were occurring in the same part of the graveyard at roughly the same time suggested that there had to be another factor determining which individuals received Cist burial and which received a simple earth burial. A further Cist burial returned a date range between the late 12th and early 13th century suggesting that the Cist burial tradition lasted for longer than a single generation, but matching the date range observed elsewhere in Hereford.

The date of Bone Only burials was an unknown quantity prior to radiocarbon dating. It was expected that the burials would span a period of up to four centuries. Analysis of the dated chains, however, gave this some definition. Of the nine dated

burials of this type, seven returned dates firmly in the 13th century implying a peak level of burial in St John's Quad during this period. The remaining two Bone Only burials, both being the final burials of this group in their respective chains were dated between the 15th and 17th centuries, confirming the long lasting tradition of non-coffined burial.

DISTRIBUTION OF THE BURIAL GROUPS
see Illus 63–66 and Table 5

PRE-CIST BURIALS
Burials could only be assigned to this group if there was physical evidence that they pre-dated a Cist burial. Therefore, the number of Pre-Cist burials identified is entirely dependent on the presence of Cist burials.

Those burials that could be proven to pre-date the Cist burials were limited in number and proportionally more came from the excavated assemblage in St Johns Quad than other areas. This could be due to the fact that greater excavation depths were reached in this area and the less confined excavation conditions enabled relationships to be identified more easily.

CIST BURIALS
Although present across all four areas of the site, the distribution of Cist burials is not even. It seems likely that the presence of Cist burials is dependent on the level of subsequent burial in the vicinity. It is apparent to the north of the cathedral, where clusters of Cist burials appear (J6, J8, J9) that overlying burials are less dense than in adjacent areas where no Cists are present (J7). The suggestion being that Cist burials were once more extensive in their distribution, but subsequent burial has removed evidence for this.

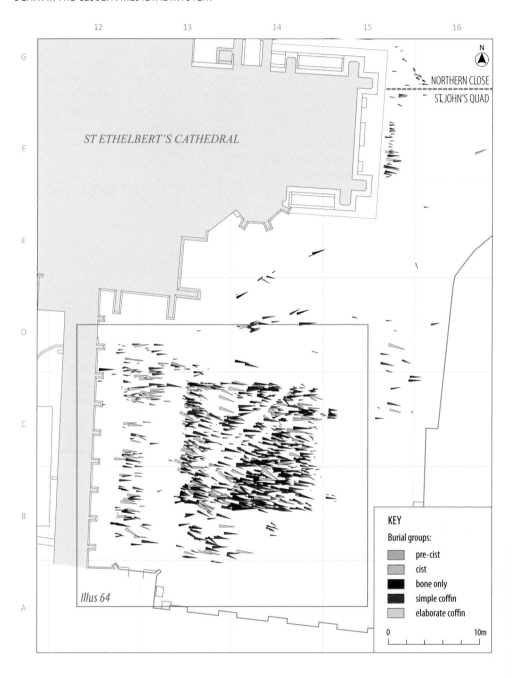

ILLUS 63
Distribution of St John's Quad skeletons coloured by burial group

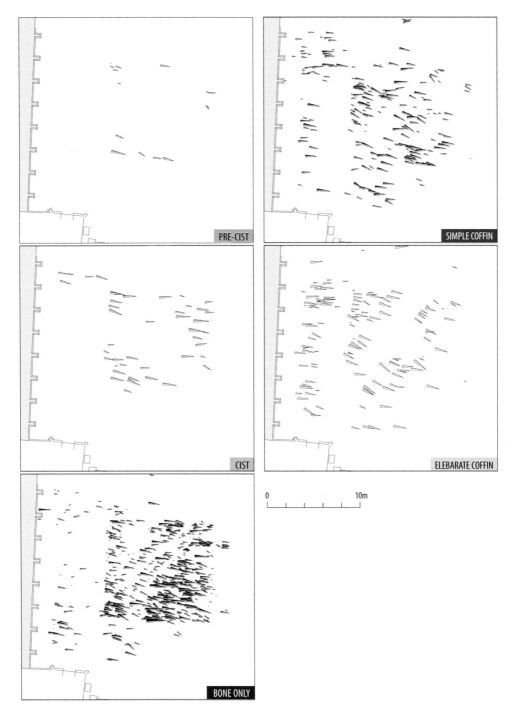

ILLUS 64
Distribution of St John's Quad skeletons isolated by burial group

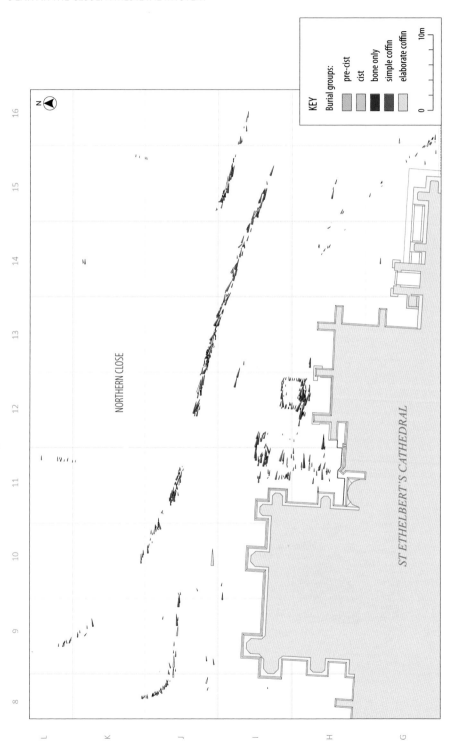

ILLUS 65

Distribution of Northern Close (east) skeletons coloured by burial group

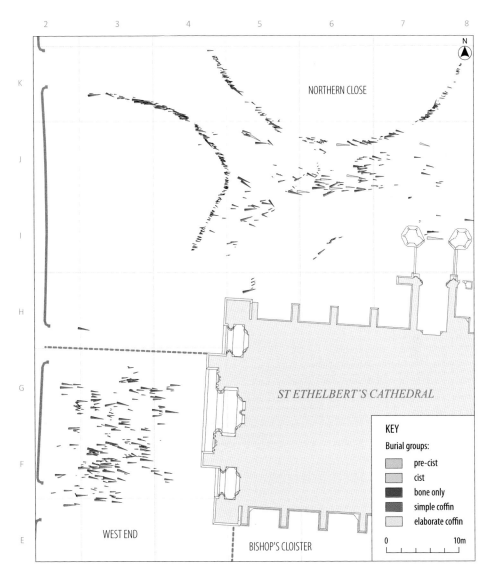

ILLUS 66
Distribution of Northern Close (west) and West End skeletons coloured by burial group

In St John's Quad, the level at which Cist burials are identified indicates a slope in the ground level from north-west to south-east, with burials in the north-west present at a level of *c* 55.90m and burials in the south-east present at *c* 55.30m.

The deep excavation area in St John's Quad was excavated to a consistent level and it would therefore be expected to have a relatively uniform distribution of Cist burials. This is not the case; burials appear to be concentrated around the edges of the trench with an area of *c* 40m^2 in the centre of the site entirely devoid

	PRE-CIST		CIST		BONE ONLY		SIMPLE COFFIN		ELABORATE COFFIN		TOTAL
St Johns Quad	16	0.7%	50	2%	671	27%	235	9.6%	142	5.8%	1114
North east	2	0.1%	18	0.7%	513	20.9%	86	12.3%	30	1.2%	649
North west	2	0.1%	14	0.6%	364	14.8%	57	2.3%	14	0.6%	451
West end	0	0%	2	0.1%	210	8.6%	27	1.1%	0	0%	239
Total	20	0.8%	84	3.4%	1758	71.7%	405	16.5%	186	7.6%	2453

TABLE 5
Distribution of the burial groups

of both Cist and Pre-Cist burials. Potentially this is the result of truncation and removal by later burials, but alternatively the burials could be respecting a since lost topographic feature in the centre of the site.

BONE ONLY BURIALS

This was the dominant burial type accounting for 71.7% of the total assemblage. Unfortunately no variables were observable amongst these burials to provide further sub-divisions.

These types of burial demonstrate consistently high burial density across the site. In the St Johns Quad deep excavation the density increases towards the south-east of the area. This may relate to the slope of the land previously discussed, with a preference to bury the dead on the flatter ground to the south-east. Within the area of greatest density (B14) up to nine generations of intercutting Bone Only burials were identified.

SIMPLE COFFIN

When considered as a percentage of total burials excavated, burials in Simple Coffins remain consistent across the north and west sides of the Cathedral. In St John's Quad, however, the proportion of burials is significantly higher. This may indicate a preference for burial at the south-east of the Close during the 16th to 18th centuries or the greater proportion of coffined individuals here could be a function of status and wealth. If, as suspected, coffin burial was the preserve of the wealthier individuals in society, then the high numbers identified to the south-east of the Cathedral may suggest that it was a preferred area of burial and reserved for those who could afford to be buried there.

ELABORATE COFFINS

The distribution of burials in Elaborate Coffins identifies a clear preference for burial at the east end of the Close where they form nearly 6% of the burials as opposed to less than 2% in the remaining areas. The complete lack of these burials at the West End may indicate that burial had stopped in this area by the 18th century. Indeed, the conclusion reached by the excavators of the New Library Building site to the south was that the area had ceased to be used as a burial ground by the beginning of the 17th century.

CONCENTRATIONS OF BURIAL TYPES

An analysis of the distribution of burials by sex did not produce any distinctive patterns. It appears that there were no distinct areas of the burial ground exclusively reserved for the burials of males or females. Analysis of the distribution of juveniles and adolescents also showed them to be evenly distributed within the burial ground, with the exception of a cluster of Cist burials which were all juveniles or adolescents. In this case seven burials were identified within an area measuring approximately 1.5m² (Illus 67). The stature of the individuals suggested that they were all children, and of the three burials that were osteologically analysed, one was classed as an infant and two were younger children. No. adult burials were present and the disordered arrangement of burials and intercutting of earlier burials by later ones, suggested that the practice of child burial within this particular area of the Close had taken place over a considerable period of time. Of the nine sub-adult Cist burials, six were excavated from grid square J6. The remaining three sub-adult burials were excavated in grid squares J15, C14 and H12. Although excavations were limited and conclusions tentative, there would appear to be evidence for burial segregation of the young during the period covered by Cist burial (12th to 13th centuries).

THE BOUNDARIES OF THE BURIAL GROUND

NORTH

The most northerly burial was encountered in the north of the trench present in grid square L11. This Simple Coffin burial was revealed at a depth of 1.2m below ground level and further burials were excavated immediately to the south. Due to the increased burial overburden and limited excavation in the north of the Close, little can be said with confidence about the extent of burials in this area.

The most northerly excavations, in grid square M8 revealed evidence for 11th century occupation buried at a depth of 1.5m below the present ground surface. Overlying this was a homogenous brown loam deposit similar to the general graveyard deposit, however no human remains were revealed.

Based on the evidence available it is reasonable to assume that the northern boundaries of the Close have not changed dramatically since the Norman period.

EAST

The most easterly burial (Bone Only) was excavated in grid square F16. Excavations to a depth of 1.5m were carried out for the creation of parking bays in grid squares G18 and G19 and excavations to a depth of 1.8m took place in grid square F18 for the installation of a petrol interceptor tank. No. human remains or archaeologically significant deposits were found during either excavation. The deposits were disturbed and appeared to comprise imported material. A number of masonry blocks and a spread of mortar were identified that are likely to relate to buildings that are shown on this part of the site on Taylor's map of 1757.

The potential boundary wall revealed in grid square H17, would appear to fit both the archaeological and cartographic evidence. If the line of the wall is extended southwards, then it does divide the region to the west where burials were found and to the east where no burials were found. Speed's 1606 draft map of Hereford appears to show a wall enclosing the Cathedral precinct passing through this location. The same square area is fossilised in today's layout of the buildings around the green.

SOUTH

John Speed's draft map of 1606 appears to illustrate a clearly defined southern edge

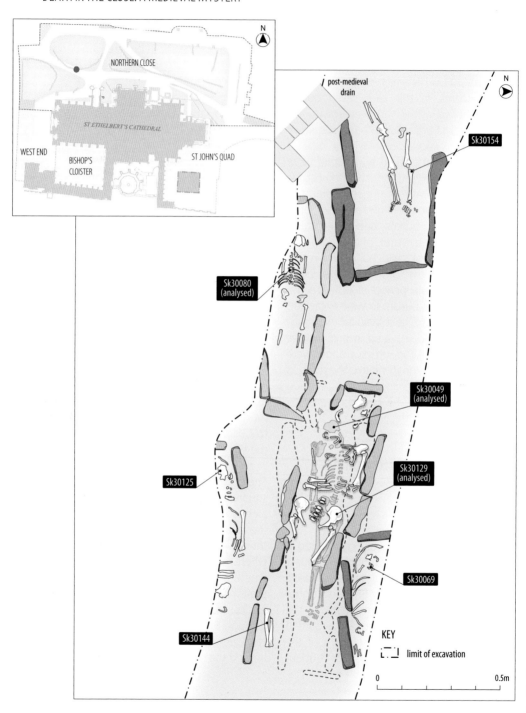

ILLUS 67
Cluster of child Cist burials, Northern Close, J6

to the Close. It is however, difficult to place too much faith in Speede's map, as the proportions are askew and key features, such as the south cloister are missing. Given the evidence for potential walls enclosing the north and east of the Close, revealed during the current excavation and the Cathedral Barn excavation of 2009, there is clearly the potential for the southern boundary of the Close to have been marked by a wall.

Analysis of burial distribution in the south of the Close has failed to establish a historic boundary. Both Bone Only and coffined burials continued up to the southern edge of grid square B13. Ground works to the south of this were low impact and not to sufficient a depth to encounter further burials. The fact that Cist and Pre-Cist burials were not encountered to the south of the deep excavation is probably simply due to the limited depth of excavation.

The construction of the College of the Vicars Choral and the south cloister in the 15th century would have formed a natural boundary to the Close, but the extent of burial to the south, prior to the appearance of these buildings is unknown. No. southern boundary to the burial ground was identified during the New Library Building excavations, with burials continuing to the edge of the excavated area. There is therefore potential for the burial ground to have continued beyond the line of buildings currently forming the southern boundary to the Close.

WEST
In grid square K3, a deposit of loose stone was identified in the trench section. The stone was not coursed in any way, but it was apparent that burials were not present to the west of this feature. The stone deposit may have been the remains of a robbed out boundary wall,

mirroring the wall revealed in grid square H17. There is however, the possibility that it relates to the buildings that are known to have occupied this part of the Close until the 1930s. What is clear, is that burials continued beneath the Broad Street buildings as shown on Taylors map of 1757. All the burials present within the footprint of the houses were Bone Only. Simple Coffin burials were present immediately to the east of the former properties and suggest a boundary for the Close equating to that shown on Taylors map during the early post-medieval period.

Although at a greatly reduced density, Cist burials are present in the west of the Close. Two Cist burials occurred within grid square F3. The lack of Cist burials to the west of this may suggest that the boundary to the Close was slightly further to the east during the 12th and 13th centuries, but it is difficult to draw such a conclusion based on the evidence of two burials. Later Bone Only and Simple Coffin burials continue up to the area of modern disturbance at the western extent of the excavated area.

ARM POSITION
During excavation it was noted that the arms of the skeletons were in different positions and that these demonstrated a degree of consistency that suggests deliberate action on the part of those carrying out the burial rite.

Six major variations in position were noted during excavation (Illus 68). The 1993 New Library Building excavations had also revealed variations in arm position and attributed them to changes in burial practice over time. A preference for the arms crossed and resting on the pelvis in the earliest burials was followed by a preference for the arms to be folded across the stomach in the 13th century. Later arms were crossed over the chest, whilst the

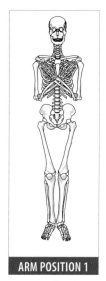

ARM POSITION 1

arms crossed on chest

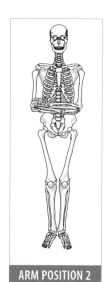

ARM POSITION 2

arms crossed
on waist (folded)

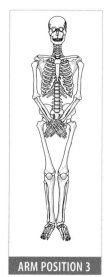

ARM POSITION 3

arms on pelvis
(hands on abdomen)

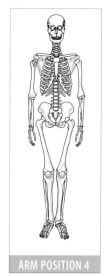

ARM POSITION 4

arms on sides

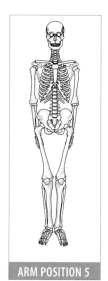

ARM POSITION 5

arms on sides
(forearms under pelvis)

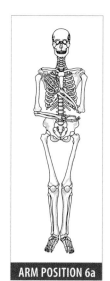

ARM POSITION 6a

left hand on chest
right one on pelvis

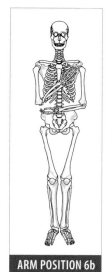

ARM POSITION 6b

right hand on chest
left one on pelvis

ILLUS 68
Different arm positions

latest burials had the arms crossed over the chest with the hands placed on the shoulders.

Of the 2,453 skeletons excavated during the current project, it was possible to determine the arm positions of 666 (27.1%). The remaining burials were either too badly truncated to determine arm position or the upper part of the skeleton lay outside the excavated area and was therefore not observed.

An analysis of arm position in relation to burial type does appear to show changes in arm position over time, although the changes in preference are not clear cut and instead appear as broad trends (Table 6, Illus 69). Rather than attaching a symbolic meaning to these changes it is probably more helpful to look for an explanation in the ways the bodies were deposited in the ground.

In instances where the shroud or winding sheet was containing and providing support to the body (Pre-Cist, Cist and Bone Only burials) the folding of the lower arms over the torso (arm positions 1, 2 and 3; plus variations 6a and 6b where the body may have been disturbed) is the most popular method of placement. It might be supposed that the arms are placed over the torso and secured by the winding sheet or shroud to prevent limbs falling out of position whilst the body is manoeuvred into the grave.

The emergence of coffin burial meant that the position of the arms at burial was no longer such an important consideration and arm positions 4 and 5 become popular. The data clearly shows the correlation between arm positions 4 and 5 and coffin burials.

The relatively equal dominance of arm positions 2 and 3 within Cist and Bone Only burials raised the question as to whether the difference was one of male and female arm position. However, the osteological data

ARM POSITION	PRE-CIST	CIST	BONE ONLY	SIMPLE COFFIN	ELABORATE COFFIN
1	3	7	25	5	–
2	3	16	126	26	1
3	2	10	140	30	10
4	–	2	19	36	42
5	–		17	29	34
6a	1	2	11	6	–
6b	1	3	19	–	–
Other	1	2	30	6	1
No. Data	9	42	1,371	267	98

TABLE 6
Distribution of arm positions by burial group

suggested a fairly even number of males and females exhibiting both arm positions. No correlation was evident when arm position was compared to age or sex.

Variations in arm position would appear to relate to the practicalities of burial rather than having any particular symbolic importance. The placing of the arms on top of the body prior to wrapping in a winding sheet would make a corpse easier to handle and prevent arms falling away from the body at inopportune moments. Burial within a coffin reduced the importance of folding the arms like this and there appears to be a trend towards placing the arms at the side of the body, a position more in keeping with the shape of the coffin itself.

ORIENTATION OF BURIALS
The majority of burials were interred in the Christian tradition, supine and orientated on an approximate east-west alignment with the head to the west. Variations were observed

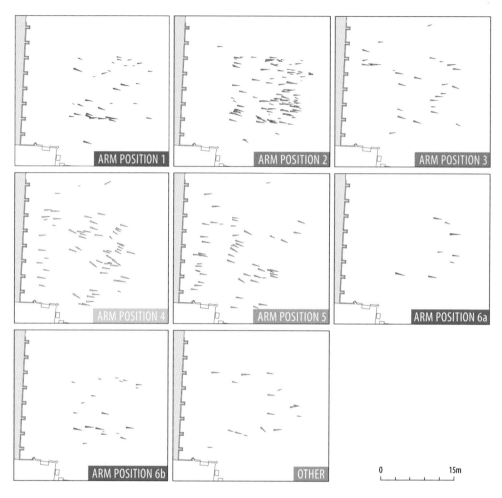

ILLUS 69
Distribution of St John's Quad skeletons by arm positions

within the orientation of burials, but the reasons appear to be terrestrial rather than spiritual.

Using the deep excavation in St John's Quad as the most complete dataset, there are a number of observations that can be made regarding burial orientation.

The general orientation of burial is slightly north-west/south-east of true east-west. This mirrors the orientation of the Cathedral which is 2.8° off true east-west.

Earlier burials are orientated on a truer east-west alignment than later burials

The maximum variance from east-west within Pre-Cist, Cist and Bone Only burials is 24° which is less than 6% variance from the orientation of the Cathedral.

The orientation of Simple Coffin and Elaborate Coffin burials towards the centre of the excavated area display a greater displacement towards a north-west/south-

ILLUS 70
Tree-lined path in St John's Quad from the decorative border of Taylor's Map of Hereford (1757)

east alignment. The maximum observed variation is 50° from true east-west (14% variance).

Discounting minor variations in orientation which are likely to relate to the varying skills of individual grave diggers, the overall picture is of two major variations in orientation. The first of these, east-west with a slight bias to north-west/south-east, clearly uses the Cathedral buildings as its guide. The second variation, confined to the coffin burials and showing a far larger bias towards north-west/south-east appears to be referencing a landscape feature not present at the time of excavation.

Taylor's 1757 map shows the feature that is likely to have been responsible for this change in burial orientation. A footpath sweeps around the south-east corner of the Lady Chapel and

traverses St John's Quad before stopping outside the entrance to the college of the Vicars Choral. The path is depicted as tree-lined on both the map and on a drawing of the Quad included within the decorative border of Taylor's map where the trees appear to be mature and of long-standing (Illus 70). In September 1726, reference is made (in the Cathedral act books) to the repair and enlargement of the gravel walk leading from the north end of the college cloister to Castle Street[34].

In drawings of the Lady Chapel dated 1827 and 1842 the path can be seen but the trees are no longer present.

Considering that repair and enlargement of the path were called for in 1726, we might assume that it existed for a period of time

---

34 Morgan 1976, 16

91

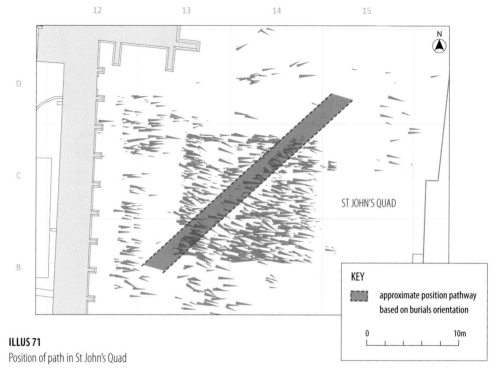

ILLUS 71
Position of path in St John's Quad

before this date. Although the remains of the path were not identified during excavation, its former position can be traced using the burials as a guide (Illus 71). The postulated path is approximately 2.5m wide and passes through the centre of the deep excavation area at an angle of 50°. The burials beneath the path and therefore earlier, conform to the orientation of the Cathedral. Those burials immediately to either side of the path and of Simple and Elaborate Coffin types are generally orientated at 90° to the path. As the distance from the path increases, the coffin burials appear to revert back to the orientation of the Cathedral.

At what point the trees were removed and a different path arrangement was configured is not so clear. The trees were apparently cleared by 1827, but burials may have been orientated to the path until the closure of the burial ground around 1850.

A further example of orientation to pathways can be seen to the north of the deep excavation area, where burials on a north-east/south-west orientation appear to be buried adjacent to the edges of a path running alongside the southern edge of the Lady Chapel. This path is visible on Taylor's map, but considering that Cist burials are also aligned to it, a path is likely to have existed in this position since at least the 13th century when the Lady Chapel was constructed.

ATYPICAL BURIALS

Five burials were found to be buried with their heads at the east end of the grave, the reverse of the standard Christian practice of burying the dead with their heads to the west, in preparation for resurrection on the day of judgement when they would sit up and face east. Although it has always been believed that this burial method is indicative

ILLUS 72
Leper burial, St John's Quad, Sk2971

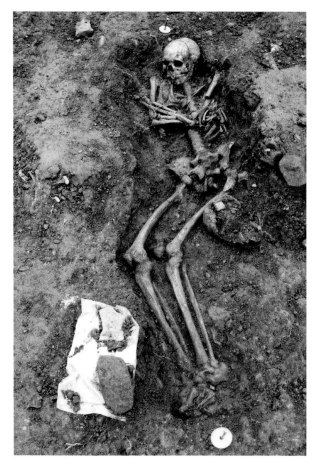

of a priest burial (rising up to face his flock), the medieval priestly burials from the New Toilet Block excavations were all facing the same way as their congregation. The practice of burying priests with their heads to the east is likely to be a post-medieval custom[35].

Four of the five corpses buried in this reverse manner belonged to Simple Coffins and one belonged to an Elaborate Coffin. Other than orientation, there was nothing else within the graves to mark them out as any different from other burials. The five burials amount to 0.2% of the excavated assemblage and the possibility exists that corpses entirely covered by a winding sheet, or contained within a simple wooden coffin, that may have been little more than a rectangular box, would occasionally be buried backwards purely by accident or lack of attention.

A further interment worthy of mention is the burial of a *leprosy* victim in a slightly flexed position[36] (Illus 72). The only leper burial also being the only crouched burial excavated is presumably not a coincidence, although the reason for burial of a leper in this manner is not entirely clear.

Attached to the eastern end of a Cist in St John's Quad was an additional stone

box containing the disarticulated remains of a further individual. The most likely explanation is that when the digger of the grave encountered the remains of a previous burial, rather than simply removing them and reburying them within the backfill of the grave, the additional stone-lined space was created and the bones laid out in a respectful manner.

The respect shown to the disinterred remains in this instance is not repeated during later use of the burial ground. Excavations carried out at Kellington Church in Yorkshire, identified a major shift in the care of burial that took place in the 12th century; before that date, bodies were

---

35   Daniell 1997, 149
36   Sk2971

carefully laid out and any bones which were discovered were treated with reverence. After that date less care was taken about cutting through existing graves and disturbed bones were simply thrown back into the grave with the backfill[37]. It has been argued that this change in attitude reflected a change in belief from the Day of Judgement (when the deceased would physically rise up) to Purgatory (a more spiritual reckoning of the character of the individual).

---

37   Daniell 1997, 146

SUSPECTS OR VICTIMS?

'Insensibly one begins to twist facts to suit theories, instead of theories to suit facts'
Sherlock Holmes

It is difficult to know exactly how many people have been buried within the Cathedral Close. However, it has become evident over the past three decades that any attempt to estimate the quantity that might be disturbed by groundworks on any given occasion can be guaranteed to be less than the number finally affected. Another fact is that there is no such thing as an unlimited budget either in finance or time. Archaeologists, architects and builders alike were faced with the difficult question as to how to tackle such a great unknown? It is perhaps ironic that most of the sensitivities of this scheme with respect to buried human remains were brought about by the previous major re-landscaping of the close in *c* 1850. As a result of these works, burials were encountered within 100mm of the ground surface and could be guaranteed to be densely-packed for a further three-quarters of a metre. The result was the excavation in 2009–11 of 2,453 inhumations in various states of completeness and preservation.

The aim of this chapter is to outline what tales these individuals have to tell. Through the study of their skeletal material (osteological analysis) small clues about the lives of people who once occupied the city of Hereford might be extracted and measured alongside roughly contemporary historical accounts. However, the reader needs to be forewarned that as always a number of factors contrive to confound the inquisitor in this respect. What questions can be asked of this silent cohort? Certainly it is possible to quiz the assemblage about what it might tell us regarding the make-up of the population at different points in the past (demography). It is also possible to compare it against other excavated populations and seven comparative skeletal assemblages were chosen containing relatively large numbers of individuals, from both rural and urban sites of similar dates within England for this purpose (Table 7). The significant treatise by Roberts and Cox[1] is also widely referred to for comparison.

Due to the dense and intermixed nature of the burials across the majority of the site any attempt at more than a very broad chronology was thwarted. As mentioned in previous chapters

---

1   Roberts & Cox 2003

SITE	DATE (CENTURY)	TYPE	NO. SKELETONS	REFERENCE
St Andrew's, Fishergate, York	11th – 16th	Urban lay & canons, wealthy	402	Stround and Kemp 1993
St Helen on the Walls, York	10th – 16th	Poor urban parish	1,068 1,014	Dawes & Magilton 1980 Grauer 1993
St Peter's, Barton-on-Humber	8th – 19th	Rural, Anglo-Saxon to post- medieval	2,750	Waldron 2007
Wharram Percy	–	Rural medieval, late Anglo-Saxon to post-medieval	687	Mays 2007a
Blackfriars, Gloucester	13th – 16th	Urban medieval	129	Wiggins et al. 1993
Fishergate House, York	Medieval	Urban medieval, low socio-economic status	244	Holst 2005
Blackfriars, Ipswich	13th – 16th	Lay benefactors of the priory, middle class traders and craftsmen	250	Mays 1991a

TABLE 7

Main comparative assemblages referred to in the text

it has been necessary to rely on the physical manifestation of each burial (forming a typology) to develop this. Therefore whilst these groups are roughly chronological they present a risk that contemporary burials may be considered as parts of different groups on the basis of their burial rite.

Whilst there are many analyses that can be undertaken on human skeletal remains it is rare that these would all be used, and certainly it is not always expedient to do so. As the excavation unfolded it became apparent that there was a notable variation in levels of preservation and completeness across the site. In comparison with the well preserved remains in St John's Quad, more than half of those at the West End exhibited poor preservation as they lay directly beneath constructed surfaces. It was also notable that the Bone Only burials had the worst preservation of all the burial groups, perhaps indicating that coffins and cists may have afforded individuals some protection from the burial environment.

The majority of skeletons uncovered during excavation were less than 25% complete. St John's Quad exhibited the most complete individuals, followed by the West End, probably as a result of the open-area excavation strategy employed in these cases. In other locations burials were excavated from within narrow drains and soakaways contributing to lower levels of completeness. Sub-adults were relatively less complete with poorer surface preservation compared to the adult assemblage, which conforms to the general trend seen in excavated human remains at other sites (Illus 73).

At an early stage during the excavation 100 skeletons were selected at random from the St John's Quad area. These were assessed and the results used to dictate future approaches to obtaining information from the assemblage, and the extent to which burials needed to be processed. Factors considered were how much of the skeleton survived, its level of preservation, and whether there was a correlation between these two factors (which is also noted in many of the comparative assemblages eg Blackfriars, Ipswich[2]), as well as the reliability and amount

2   Mays 1991a

of data that could be obtained from skeletons of varying degrees of completeness.

Archaeologists become accustomed to having to make 'professional judgements' in the face of results that only go part of the way to answering their queries. Therefore it was somewhat surprising to see how categorical the results of this first osteological exercise were. Before briefly considering this further it is worth familiarising ourselves with the main objectives for undertaking the study (ie the types of information the project aimed to extract from the data set). In a rough order of priority:

• Preservation levels of the skeletal remains
• Age at death
• The biological sex of adults
• Estimation of adult height (stature)
• The nature, presence and frequency of skeletal and dental pathology (signs of illness/injury)
• Recordable differences between skeletons (metric and non-metric variation)
• The minimum number of individuals present

The data quite clearly illustrated four significant points regarding this assemblage. Firstly, there appears to be a direct relationship between how well the bone was preserved and how much of the skeleton survived. The reasons for this are clear; the main reason that less of a skeleton survives is because it has continuously been dug through over the centuries to bury more bodies. Secondly, once less than 50% of the skeleton survived it was considerably less likely that its sex could be ascertained. Thirdly, as with sex, a refined age for individuals was much more likely to be obtained in those skeletons where more than 50% of the skeleton survived. For sub-adults, often only 25% of the skeleton was needed, due to the relative ease with which an age can be obtained for the pre-pubertal skeleton.

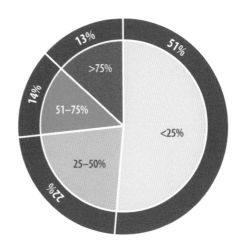

ILLUS 73
Completeness of excavated skeletons

CATEGORY	ABBREVIATIONS	AGE
Sub-adult	Sub-AD	<18 years
Foetus	F	3rd foetal month- 40 weeks in utero
Neonate	N	Birth +/- 2 months
Infant	I	Birth–1 year
Younger child	YC	1–6 years
Older child	OC	7–12 years
Adolescent	AO	13–17 years
Adult	AD	18+ years
Younger adults	Y AD	18–25 years
Younger-middle adults	Y–M AD	25–35 years
Older-middle adults	O–M AD	35–45 years
Older adults	O AD	45+ years

TABLE 8
Age categories and abbreviations

BURIAL GROUP	TOTAL NO.	% OF TOTAL BURIALS	NO. ANALYSED
Pre–Cist	20	0.8	8
Cist	84	3.4	44
Bone Only	1,758	71.7	409
Simple Coffin	405	16.5	153
Elaborate Coffin	186	7.6	96
Total	2,453	100	710

TABLE 9
Burials selected for analysis

However, the conclusion of the exercise was quite a surprise. The presence or absence of any pathology was logged against each individual and this was plotted against percentage completeness of the skeleton. Naturally it was anticipated that the more of the skeleton that survived the more likely it would be that one form of pathology or another would be observed. But what transpired was that where the individuals were very complete they always exhibited some pathology, and that the ability to observe this rapidly decreased with a reduction in the amount of the skeleton surviving.

The above clearly underlines the conclusions of the assessment that adult individuals over 50% complete and sub-adult individuals over 25% complete provided the highest quality dataset for analysis. Furthermore, those below the cut-off percentages had very limited potential for demographic and pathological information and would have had little impact on the quality of data obtained. As a result 710 of the more complete skeletons, 29% of the total individuals recovered from the site, were the only ones selected for analysis (Table 9).

Given the above assessment then quite clearly even less would be gained from collecting and studying the disarticulated human bone. It is widely acknowledged when recovered from 'cemetery soil' (rather than discrete contexts) that this is of limited scientific value[3]. A 'rapid scan' of the bone was undertaken for interesting or rare pathology, and a count of the bones to obtain a minimum number of individuals buried within the excavated areas. The results of this latter exercise emphasise the shortcomings of such fragmentary remains as the minimum number of individuals (MNI) within the excavated area estimated on this basis was 2,103 which is 350 less than the number of individuals lifted during the excavation[4].

Regardless as to their likely selection for further processing and analysis all individuals were excavated according to professional guidelines[5]. This included producing a measured plan with a photograph prior to disturbing the remains, and sieving to recover small bones such as wrist, feet and hands, as well as the small bones of infants and young children.

Does the method of selecting skeletons for further study mentioned above affect the results of the analysis? The strategy applied

---

3   English Heritage 2004
4   At least some of the disarticulated bone would have originated from the articulated burials which were incomplete and therefore the MNI is calculated by counting and siding all articulated and disarticulated bone elements and the most common element present represents the MNI. The most common bone part in the adult population was the right proximal epiphysis of the femur and for the sub-adults it was right proximal femoral metaphysis. The MNI for adults is 1763 individuals and for non-adults is 340, giving a total of 2103 individuals. The MNI represents the absolute minimum number of individuals that can be proven to be present and in reality will be lower than the actual number of skeletons present.
5   McKinley & Roberts 1993

here is referred to as a stratified sample and is commonly used to ensure that only relevant information is collected, so within the assemblage there is unlikely to be a negative effect. However, there is also a need to compare the findings from this site with other assemblages and it is here that potential problems could arise. The occurrence (or prevalence) of various observations are reported as the true prevalence rate (TPR) as this is not affected by the completeness of the skeleton and therefore can be compared with results from other sites.

Another issue facing interpretations of an osteoarchaeological nature, is that the people buried in the burial ground might not be representative of the living population. This is an area that can be tested using a small range of statistical analyses, but in doing so there needs to be a statistical norm, and should the living population not conform to this there is always a chance that differences will be interpreted as being due to variations in burial practice or the use of different areas of the burial ground for different segments of the population rather than an actual variation in the living population itself.

WHO WERE THEY?

We assume that the individuals unearthed here were citizens of Hereford City and documentary evidence seems to support this. It appears that by at least 1108 the Cathedral was claiming exclusive burial rights within the city. By 1143 people buried there came from all the five city parishes as well as several outlying ones. However, this rather lucrative monopoly, which carried with it mortuary fees, offerings and legacies left for anniversaries, obits and trentals (types of church service), was frequently contested by other churches in the area, and with some success. In 1298 as a consequence

of a protest by the Rector of Hampton Bishop, any parishioner whose goods at the time of death exceeded 6s in value (enough to meet the fees) was to be taken to the Cathedral for burial, while women and children and the poorer folk might be buried nearer home though had to pay 1s a year for this privilege[6]. In the early 14th century Allensmore made a bid for autonomy leading the Cathedral to permit local burial of children and paupers[7] and St Guthlac's managed to secure parochial burial rights for c 150 years around 1300. In 1348 due to the 'inadvertent' burial of some of the wealthier individuals within local parish churchyards, the Cathedral gave such churches general burial rights in exchange for any funeral profits. Furthermore, Reverend Side, the vicar of St Peter's started carrying out funerals (the burial ground was at St Guthlac's monastery in the Bye Street suburb) and retaining the profits and although the chapter took him to court, the courts found for Side in 1376 with a papal decree acknowledging funerary autonomy for St Peter's.

This is an interesting insight into the workings of medieval burial practices. What it means for the inquisitive archaeologist is that people were being selected from the population and that the nature of this selection changed over time. The records above imply that it might be expected for the Cathedral Close to contain less women than men after 1298 as well as less children. It might also be expected that in the later medieval period at least the wealthier end of the spectrum of the population were buried here, paupers being buried within their local parish. Thus the excavated burials do not represent a random cross-section of the population of the city. Some degree of error

6   Shoesmith 2000, 305
7   Swanson & Lepine 2000, 79

99

AGE CATEGORY	MALE		FEMALE		UNKNOWN		TOTAL	
	No.	%	No.	%	No.	%	No.	%
Y AD	21	7.7	14	7.0	1	25.0	36	7.6
Y-M AD	57	21.0	51	25.6	0	0.0	108	22.8
O-M AD	116	42.8	81	40.7	2	50.0	200	47.2
O AD	57	21.0	47	23.6	1	25.0	104	21.9
AD	20	7.4	6	3.0	0	0.0	26	5.5
Total	271	100	199	100	4	100	474	100

TABLE 10
Adult age & sex distribution

BURIAL GROUP	MALES	FEMALES	RATIO (M:F)
Pre-Cist	1	5	0.20
Cist	27	8	3.38
Bone Only	132	98	1.35
Simple Coffin	59	56	1.05
Elaborate Coffin	52	32	1.63
Total	271	199	1.36

TABLE 11
Male-to-female ratio by burial groups

is also introduced by the very fact the sample is skeletal and therefore does not represent the normal, healthy, population from which it is drawn[8].

The sex of an individual is commonly determined using differences in morphology or shape of the skull and pelvis, as well as consideration of the overall size of bones[9]. However because secondary sexual characteristics do not develop until late puberty and early adulthood the sex of sub-adult individuals cannot be ascertained. The age and sex distribution of the analysed adults shows no statistical difference in the age structure of males and females[10]. Both men and women show a peak in adult mortality occurring between the ages of 35 and 45 years (Table 10).

The male-to-female ratio of 1.36:1 in the adult assemblage is slightly in excess of the 1.06:1 expected within any population[11]. It has been noted that there is often a bias towards identifying males in a skeletal assemblage,

however, the excess is particularly great in some burial groups. Cist burials have, by far, the greatest male majority, however, the small sample size may have biased the results (Table 11). Of the Cist burials previously uncovered in Hereford five had sex established and include one female and four males[12]. There was no evidence for spatial segregation of burials in the Cathedral burial ground in regard to sex and therefore selected excavation of differing areas of the burial ground is unlikely to play a part in this bias. As mentioned above the preference to let some individuals be buried in local parishes including women may be a possible contributing factor to the lower numbers of females uncovered at the Cathedral.

The presence and preservation of the pelvis is also important for the estimation of adult age[13] although as many criteria as possible were used[14]. The dentition was not used as a sole criterion for estimating the age of an individual due to its unreliability, especially in post-medieval assemblages probably as a result of changes in the diet compared to

8   Johnston 1962
9   Mays & Cox 2000
10   $x^2 = 1.52$, p = 0.68
11   Rousham & Humphrey 2002, 128

12   Shoesmith 1984; Shoesmith 1980
13   Allowing different stages of bone morphology and degeneration to be identified at the pubic symphysis (Suchey & Brooks 1990) and/or the auricular surface (Lovejoy et al 1985)
14   Sternal rib morphology (Iscan et al 1984; 1985) and dental attrition were also considered (Brothwell 1981)

earlier periods[15], and it exhibited a tendency to underage within this assemblage. It should be remembered that adult skeletal age-at-death represents physiological age rather than actual chronological age. Several studies[16] have shown that age-at-death estimations from the skeleton frequently underestimated age for older adults.

In simple terms of the 2,453 articulated individuals excavated, 2,020 were adults and 433 sub-adults. In recent societies lacking modern medical care and sanitation, about 20–56% of deaths may occur under 16 years of age[17]. Percentage-wise the 17.7% found at Hereford Cathedral is much lower than that at Burton-on-Humber (37.6%) Wharram Percy (44.6%), and the St-Helens-on-the-Walls 27.3%. In fact the low percentage is more akin to the numbers of sub-adults found on monastic sites such as St Andrew's Fishergate (22.4%) and not far off the 20.5% recorded for the New Library excavation in Hereford (excluding the plague pit which had a greater bias towards sub-adult burial of 39.3%). In sub-adults consideration of primary and secondary *ossification* centres[18], dental formation and eruption timings[19] as well as long bone length[20] were used to calculate age. The low numbers of sub-adults from Hereford cover all periods of the use of the burial ground. So what factors might contribute to this low percentage?

Whilst it might be that burial practice skewed the relationship between the buried and living populations resulting from the interment of children in areas segregated from the main burial ground, the fact that such low figures have been obtained from

such a range of excavation areas weighs against this. There was no distinction between the distribution of adults and sub-adults across the close and given this latter point we may be safe in assuming that the proportions of the ages of the individuals is representative of the living population. The only evidence to contradict this was recovered from the excavation of a group of seven sub-adults in Cists outside the west door of the Cathedral. However, it has also been established that poorer women and children may have been buried in their local parishes, and this could have an impact on how representative the assemblage is.

Despite the above it may be possible to use the ages for the individuals excavated to compare life expectancy curves for both the medieval (Pre-Cist, Cist and Bone Only burials) and late-medieval/post-medieval (Simple and Elaborate Coffined burials) populations (Table 74). These indicate greater life expectancy in sub-adults in the later of these two groups. There are a couple of interesting differences between the assemblage excavated across the Close and that from the 1993 New Library excavation. The latter burials more closely match those of the later medieval and post-medieval groups from the current excavations. In the case of the medieval population excavated, life expectancy is a lot lower in the medieval period than later for under 12s, with the 5 year and unders having a life expectancy in line with the plague pit burial assemblage. The other discrepancy between the two assemblages occurs in the 35–45 year age band where the life expectancy across the Close is about 5 years lower than that observed in the 1993 excavations. This seems to be the case for both the earlier and later periods of burials and men and women equally. The resulting conclusion is that a large proportion of the population

---

15   Walker et al 1991, Brickley et al. 2006

16   eg Molleson & Cox, 1993, Miles et al. 2008

17   Hewlett 1991

18   Scheuer & Black 2000 & 2004, Schaefer et al. 2009

19   Ubelaker, 1989

20   Fazekas & Kosa 1978, Maresh 1970

PRE-CIST, CIST & BONE ONLY

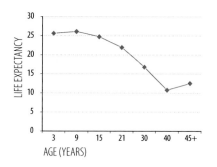

SIMPLE COFFIN & ELABORATE COFFIN

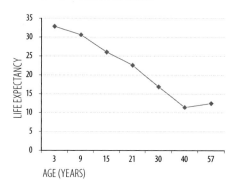

ALL

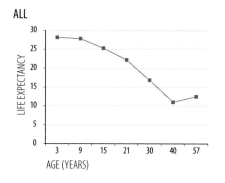

ILLUS 74
Life expectancy curves

was dying between the ages of 35 and 45 years. Even so this is higher than observed in other medieval populations where documentary sources for the period suggest a life expectancy for males at the age of 20 years of between 24 and 36 years increasing gradually from the mid 13th to the end of the 15th century[21]. It is perhaps more in line with the post-medieval London Bills of Mortality where it was recorded that the highest percentage of adult deaths occurred within the 30s and 40s from 1728 to 1810[22].

It does not appear that there is a significant enough bias in the assemblage to suggest that unbaptised infants were buried elsewhere[23] and the argument in Hereford for the use of the abandoned site of St Guthlac's Priory for the interment of 24 infants[24] has been subsequently overturned by the realisation that this was in fact a parish burial ground too. In fact in medieval times children could be baptised by a lay-person if the priest was not present and was usually undertaken one week after birth[25] but if the life of the newborn appeared in danger it would be baptised immediately or if it appeared the child might be stillborn any limb that emerged could be baptised by the midwife[26]. As children (along with women and the poorer members of society) were allowed to be buried nearer home in parish burial grounds around Hereford the assemblage could be biased in this respect. Thus the further consideration, that children were healthier than the national average in Hereford perhaps could simply be caused by greater numbers of children being buried in other burial grounds.

21 Dyer 1989, 182
22 Roberts & Cox 2003, 304
23 Ulrich-Bochsler 1997
24 Shoesmith 1980, 51
25 Shahar 1990, 46
26 Ibid

All 236 sub-adults analysed could be placed within an age category (Illus 75). The five foetuses and 17 neonates were either stillborn, or died following birth. Four of the foetuses were between 28 and 38 weeks old and had been born prematurely, all were within Bone Only burials with the exception of one Elaborate Coffin. One foetus, aged 24–28 weeks old was found within the pelvic cavity of an adult female[27] (Illus 76). The peak in those who died occurred in the 1–6 year age group, accounting for 40% of sub-adult deaths. The causes of death in these very young children are likely to have been similar to those in modern developing countries[28]. Breastfeeding protects the infant against diarrhoeal diseases but the child becomes susceptible after it is weaned at approximately 1–2 years old[29]. The majority of possible causes do not show skeletal changes including gastro-intestinal and other infections caused by poor nutrition, inadequate sanitation and the absence of a clean water supply[30], in utero infections, prematurity, very low birth weight, and respiratory distress in newborn children.

It is generally considered that once over the age of 5 years, average life expectancy of an individual would be greatly increased, a fact that is borne out

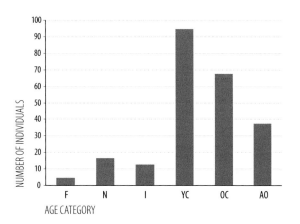

ILLUS 75
Sub-adult age distribution

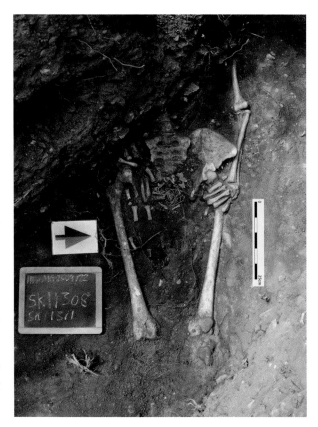

ILLUS 76
Foetus Sk11311 found within pelvic cavity of adult female Sk11308

---

27   Sk11311, Sk11308, respectively
28   Walsh 1989; Assefa et al. 2001
29   Mays 2007a, 93
30   Black et al. 2003

BURIAL GROUP	MALE			FEMALE		
	Mean	No.	SD	Mean	No.	SD
Pre-Cist	–	0	–	162.06	4	3.09
Cist	172.25	26	5.27	161.19	6	4.05
Bone Only	169.76	105	5.44	159.45	73	5.83
Simple Coffin	170.51	52	5.32	158.67	44	4.46
Elaborate Coffin	170.65	40	5.47	159.13	27	6.39
Total pop.	170.38	223	5.44	159.30	154	5.51

SD = standard deviation

TABLE 12
Adult stature (cm)

by both demographic and archaeological data[31] and this appears to have been the case in both the medieval and later burial groups.

WHAT WERE THEY LIKE?

There are a number of ways in which further information can be obtained about a buried population. Some of these involve the measurement of particular bones and the use of a comparison of these, either against known data to provide conclusions such as the height of individuals, or against each other to produce an index that can be used to identify racial traits. This is commonly referred to as metric data. Further observations can also be made on a wide range of bones throughout the skeleton. These are commonly referred to as non-metric traits and are seen as defining racial properties within an assemblage[32].

STATURE AND GROWTH

The stature was estimated using complete and fully fused leg bones (femur/tibia). Stature has been used as a rough yardstick to indicate the overall health of individuals and of populations. Provided the genetic component of the populations does not change (as would happen, for example, with an influx of people of differing average stature). Everybody has a maximum genetic potential to reach a certain adult stature, however, physical and emotional[33] problems during childhood and adolescence, such as malnutrition, infection or chronic illness, may prevent individuals achieving this potential. The growing body can 'catch-up' growth after such an event; however, where the factors affecting the individual are too severe or prolonged they will become permanently stunted.

Stature could be estimated for 377 adult individuals including 223 males and 154 females (80% of the adults analysed) (Table 12).

The mean height within the five different burial groups indicates that females are taller in Cist and Pre-Cist burials and show a general decline in height through time, but the difference is not statistically significant[34]. For the males, there is distinctly less variation in mean stature, however, the mean height is also highest in the Cist burials; again no statistically significant difference is present between the groups[35]. Females had a range of 145–177cm and males 155–190cm; this reflects the height differences of a normal population and is consistent with stature distributions from other medieval and post-medieval cemetery populations.

---

31 Kausmally 2004; Roberts and Cox 2003
32 Stature has been calculated using Trotter's regression formulae (1970). Standard metrical data was recorded, where preservation allowed, following the guidelines of Buikstra & Ubelaker (1994) for infants and Brothwell & Zakrzewski (2004) for adults. The cranial, meric and cnemic indices were calculated for adults (Bass 2005) and non-metrical traits recorded (Brothwell & Zakrzewski 2004;

Finnegan 1978).
33 Pine et al 1996
34 one-way ANOVA $F=0.58$, $p=0.68$
35 $F=1.52$, $p=0.21$

Comparisons between mean statures of populations from different periods has traditionally shown a marked increase of height during the Anglo-Saxon period, with a reduction in height during the later medieval period[36]. This reduction in stature has been attributed to increasing urbanization during the medieval period, with its associated problems, including pollution, increased spread of disease and less access to fresh produce[37]. The mean female stature calculated for a number of sites in the later medieval period was 159cm and for post-medieval sites was 160cm[38] and the male mean was 171cm for both periods. The mean stature of the Hereford population is most similar to the urban poor at Fishergate

House, York (Table 13). However, it is notable that in comparing different sites, there is no distinct separation in stature between urban and rural sites.

SITE	CONTEXT	MALE		FEMALE	
		Mean	No.	Mean	No.
St Andrew's Period 6	Urban	171.0	205	159.0	73
Hereford Cathedral	Rural/urban?	170.4	223	159.3	154
Fishergate House	Urban	170.1	48	159.1	42
St Peter's	Rural	170	216	158	156
Blackfriars	Urban	169.7	25	155.4	19
St Helens-on-the-Walls	Urban	169.3	not stated	157.4	not stated
Wharram Percy	Rural	168.8	169	157.8	119

TABLE 13

Stature comparison of urban and rural archaeological assemblages (cm)

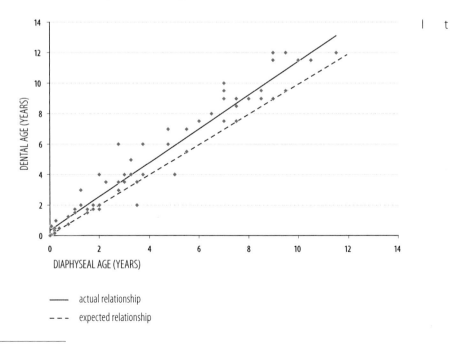

actual relationship

- - - expected relationship

36   Caffell 1997, 48
37   Ibid
38   Roberts and Cox 2003

ILLUS 77

Sub-adult growth by dental age and long bone growth

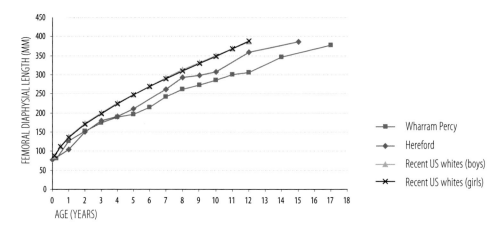

ILLUS 78
Comparison of sub-adult long bone growth

is possible to compare long bone growth in sub-adults against dental development, which is not so severely affected by environmental conditions. Because the final range of statures is a result of growth in childhood, such comparison can be used to compare the growth achieved with what would be expected under optimum conditions. Such measurements were achieved in 74 sub-adult individuals. When plotted it is clear that bone growth was almost always equal to or lower than dental age (Illus 77).

Sub-adult growth in the Hereford assemblage reflects characteristic human growth showing a steep increase during infancy, followed by a slower steady increase until another sharper incline at puberty. The Hereford sub-adults are shorter than modern (American) children of a similar age. Studies of long bone growth in archaeological populations are sparse as large populations with an adequate representation of sub-adults are uncommon. However, comparing the Hereford sub-adults to those at Wharram Percy indicates that they are relatively tall compared to contemporary children living in a rural environment (Illus 78).

RACIAL TRAITS

The shape of the skull (cranial or cephalic index) is believed to be primarily determined by genetics but climate and diet may also have some effect[39]. Research has shown apparent changes in the mean cephalic index from the Neolithic period onwards and early physical anthropologists used it to attempt to define race, and to trace the migration of different peoples[40]. There is a growing body of data indicating a tendency for medieval populations in western Europe to become increasingly broad-headed (brachycephalic: index >80), in contrast with earlier periods, when the greater proportion were long-headed (dolichocephalic, index <75) or mid-way between (mesocephalic 75–80).

At Hereford, only 45 adult skulls were sufficiently intact for measurements to be taken, and once the data had been grouped by sex and by burial group the number of individuals involved was very low. Both males and females followed a similar pattern with a fairly even spread across the indices and a need

---

39   Mays 2000, Sparks and Jantz 2002
40   Brothwell 1981, 87

to create an extra broad-headed group to accommodate the range of results (Table 14). Despite some very broad-headed individuals in the medieval population there are hints of a trend towards lower indexes (ie longer heads) in the chronologically later coffined burials. This does not conform to the pattern observed across the rest of the country and could well indicate a racial distinctiveness to the local population here, or some racial mixing in the later medieval period onwards Table 15).

It is also believed that non-metric traits might be used in an attempt to measure genetic differences between populations[41]. However, it remains uncertain whether the presence or absence of these traits is purely genetic or effected by environmental factors such as stress or repetitive movement. Eighteen cranial and 13 post-cranial traits were recorded for adult individuals during the study. A few selected examples that might contribute to understanding or comparing the population are discussed below.

Sutures are the name given to the joints between sections of the skull. A number of non-metric traits relate to these junctions such as when they don't fuse (**metopism**) or when other bones form between them (wormian or inca bones). *Metopism* is likely to be genetically determined and it shows considerable geographical variation[42]. With the exception of Fishergate House, York the 14.9% seen at Hereford Cathedral is higher than that of the

INDEX	MALE		FEMALE	
	No.	%	No.	%
Dolichocephalic (<75)	11	37	6	40
Mesocephalic (75–80)	7	23	5	33
Brachycephalic (80–85)	6	20	2	13
Hyperbrachycephalic (85+)	6	20	2	13
Total	30	100	15	100

TABLE 14
Cranial index

BURIAL GROUP	MALE				FEMALE			
	Mean	No.	SD	Range	Mean	No.	SD	Range
Pre-Cist	–	–	–	–	–	–	–	–
Cist	79.06	6	10.49	73.73–90.36	–	–	–	–
Bone Only	79.41	11	6.86	73.58–93.91	82.57	7	7.43	74.71–95.09
Simple Coffin	72.31	4	7.90	63.92–81.49	70.17	6	8.61	60.21–83.5
Elaborate Coffin	77.82	9	4.54	72.48–87.2	73.82	2	2.00	71.82–72.82
Total pop.	77.91	30	7.68	63.92–93.91	76.44	15	9.49	60.21–95.09

TABLE 15
Mean cranial index by burial group

adult population of most comparative sites[43]. Amongst the most frequently occurring traits was the palatal torus a bony prominence along the mid-line of the palate. Both genetic and environmental factors are thought to be involved in producing them[44] and tori may be associated with high levels of masticatory stress[45]. A higher prevalence occurs in males

---

41   Berry and Berry 1967; Berry 1974; Hanihara et al. 2003
42   Hanihara and Ishida 2001b

43   St-Helens-on-the-Walls at 11%; St Andrews period 6 at 7.4%; Barton 3.6%. Fishergate House recorded 21.7% but from relatively small numbers of observable frontal bones (13/60)
44   Seah 1995
45   Roberts and Manchester 1995, 54

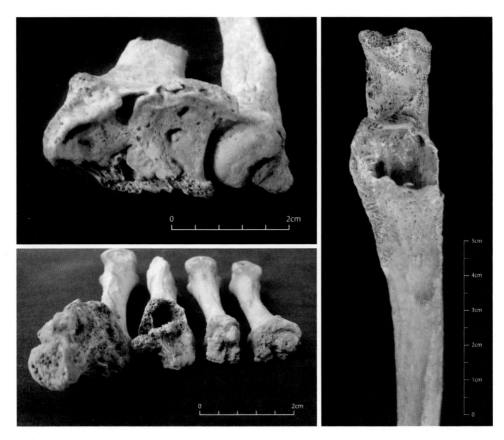

ILLUS 79
Lesions caused by psoriatic arthritis or Reiter's syndrome, Sk1809

in the assemblage[46], so was the meat tougher in Hereford than elsewhere or does this mean men were using their teeth as tools?

In the Cist burials some non-metrical traits[47] exhibited a relatively high frequency in comparison to the other burial groupings possibly indicating racial variation in this group.

It is possible for bone growth to extend to surrounding softer tissues. Something similar to this occurs in the spine with calcification of cartilage, which occurred in three individuals in

the assemblage. In these instances whilst there are a variety of potential causes the most likely explanation was thought to be an inherited condition called **ochondrosis**. Symptoms usually appear in midlife as a chronic backache.

Other conditions that might be genetic include a group of joint diseases called sero-negative arthropathies. Two individuals in the assemblage showed fusion of joints in the lower spine and part of the pelvis (sacro-iliac) a condition called **ankylosing spondylitis**. These were both older adults and probably suffered from aching pain in the lower buttocks radiating to the upper thighs.

---

46   13 out of 54 males (24%), 6 out of 34 females (18%)

47   *Metopism*, lambdoid wormian bones, mastoid foramen extra-sutural and multiple infra-orbital foramen

LEVEL OF LESION	MALE	FEMALE	SUB-ADULT
C5	0	1	0
L3	1	0	0
L4	3	2	0
L5	4	6	1
Total	8	9	1

TABLE 16
Individuals with vertebrae affected by spondylolysis

Two other conditions were quite difficult to segregate in the assemblage, these being **psoriatic arthritis** and **Reiter's syndrome** (Illus 79). The spines of these individuals were unfortunately poorly preserved and therefore are only possible cases. There were five possible cases in the assemblage, probably too few to form any definitive conclusions, but it is worth drawing attention to the plight of the most severely afflicted of these, an older adult female within an Elaborate Coffin[48]. She no doubt experienced so much pain in her left arm that it resulted in a disability the evidence being the more gracile appearance of bones here compared to the right arm probably as a result of the inflammation and destruction of the cartilage and bone in the joints the pain severely restricting its use.

Eighteen individuals from the site were affected by **spondylolysis**, a condition believed to be genetic, where parts of one vertebral body separate (Table 16, Illus 80). As alarming as it sounds there are usually no symptoms. This condition has been observed in 3–7% of modern Caucasian populations[49], at Barton it was 4% and at Wharram Percy 10%. In the Hereford assemblage, using only adults for comparison purposes it was 4%. Given the

ILLUS 80
Spondylolysis

probable genetic nature of this condition it is interesting that three affected individuals[50] were buried directly over one another in St John's Quad and may represent a family group.

WHAT DO WE KNOW ABOUT THEIR LIVES?

ACTIVITY
Observations across a wide chronological range suggest that the shafts of leg bones have tended to become more rounded, perhaps reflecting a general trend towards a more sedentary lifestyle[51]. The measurement is called the femoral or tibial index (measuring upper and lower leg bones respectively) and a lower index value reflects a flatter shaft cross-section and generally tends to indicate a more

---

48   Sk1809
49   Resnick and Niwayama 1988

50   Sk5080, Sk2550 and Sk3231
51   eg Buxton 1938; Brothwell 1981

active lifestyle[52]. However, as this is more greatly influenced during childhood and adolescence then an active adult lifestyle is less likely to be represented by the index[53]. At the Cathedral 645 femurs were measured (364 males and 281 females). The overall mean index for both sexes was broad and flat in shape. There appears to be a statistically significant difference[54] between male femora which tend to be rounder (higher index) than that of females (Table 17). The mean index does increase over time from the medieval (Pre-Cist, Cist and Bone Only burials), through the later-medieval/early post-medieval (Simple Coffin burials) to the later post-medieval period (Elaborate Coffins) which is in line with general observations of other populations. There was no real difference in the tibial index between the sexes but this again followed the normal chronological trend with males showing an increase in roundness from the medieval to later post-medieval period. Considering the femoral index and how it is predominantly determined during the developmental years of an individual then this appears to suggest that girls and young women were more active and undertaking more physical tasks than their male peers.

WEAR AND TEAR

There are a number of skeletal manifestations that can indicate the extent of and groups affected by manual labour.

A type of fracture (**osteochondritis dissecans**) that is most common in young adults and affects joint surfaces can be the result of repeated activities such as can be seen from modern day sports men and women and was particularly prevalent in burials in Simple Coffins (Illus 81). It is thought that the most likely origin of the lesion is some kind of

INDEX	MALE		FEMALE	
	No.	%	No.	%
60-	17	4.7	31	11.0
70-	121	33.2	121	43.1
80-	162	44.5	92	32.7
90+	64	17.6	37	13.2
Total	364	100	281	100

TABLE 17
Femoral index

micro fracture that results from repeated low intensity activity. In the Hereford assemblage 63 individuals were noted with the lesion, including 20 females, 36 males and seven sub-adults (Table 18). Slightly more males are affected than females, which is the case in modern populations[55]. The results imply activities that caused repeated impact at either the shoulder, elbow or ankle joint and therefore is not inconsistent with areas of the body that might be affected by manual activities such as using axes to cut wood, digging in hard ground, and maybe even impacts on the ankles from simply walking whilst carrying heavy loads.

Other more serious effects of repetitive activity can occur through **rotator cuff disease**, which is a frequent cause of shoulder pain and is linked to degenerative causes as it becomes more common with age. Studies also report an association with repetitive heavy use of the shoulder complex[56]. Sixteen individuals[57] showed skeletal changes consistent with *rotator cuff disease*, the majority (11) being male, and in eight of these cases

52   Larsen 1997, 222
53   Jurmain et al. 2011
54   t=-4.18, p=<0.001

55   Aufderheide and Rodriguez-Martin 1998, 82
56   Hagberg and Wegman, 1987; Park et al. 1994
57   The prevalence of *rotator cuff disease* was 4.05% increasing with age as expected (16/395 individuals with rotator cuff inserts observable)

TABLE 18
Prevalence of osteochondritis dissecans

BURIAL GROUP	MALE		FEMALE		SUB-ADULT		TOTAL	
	No.	%	No.	%	No.	%	No.	%
Pre-Cist	0/1	0.0	1/5	20.0	0/2	0.0	1/8	12.5
Cist	3/27	11.1	0/8	0.0	1/9	11.1	4/44	9.1
Bone Only	14/132	10.6	8/98	8.2	5/176	2.8	27/406	6.7
Simple Coffin	12/58	20.7	9/56	16.1	1/37	2.7	22/151	14.6
Elaborate Coffin	7/53	13.2	2/32	6.3	0/12	0.0	9/97	9.3
Total	36/271	13.3	20/199	10.1	7/236	3.0	63/710*	8.9

*includes four unsexed individuals

both shoulders were affected. All except one male younger adult were aged over 35 years.

Three male individuals in Bone Only burials suffered from **clay-shoveller's fractures** (Illus 82). Here, each exhibited a fracture to the spinous process of a thoracic vertebrae. In two of the individuals[58] the fractures were well-healed, however, in one[59] the bones were un-united at the time of death. This fracture is caused by an overload on the spinous process due to forceful muscular action which has been widely associated with work involving shovelling especially in heavy soils[60]. Amongst the drift geology of Herefordshire are a large proportion of heavy bolder clay deposits[61].

In the past, as now, heavy lifting can also affect the back. Repetitive or acute excessive spinal compression from such activities potentially causes a rupture of the discs between vertebrae creating a dent in the vertebral body. This is technically referred to as a **Schmorl's node** (Illus 83). In

the adults, 230 were affected by a *Schmorl's node*, including 151 males and 79 females, giving a prevalence of 50% of adults with one or more vertebra present (Table 19). Furthermore, nine adolescent individuals exhibited nodes on a combined total of 43 vertebral bodies. The mid part of the spine (thoracic vertebrae) was most commonly affected and the upper part (cervical vertebrae) were not affected at all. Adult males were affected to a greater extent than adult females, although this difference was not statistically significant[62]. There does

62   $x^2=3.94$, p=0.05

58   Sk10440, Sk30278
59   Sk30220
60   Knusel et al. 1996
61   Bloodworth et al. 1999

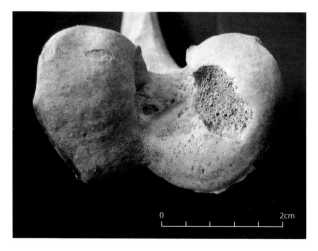

ILLUS 81
Osteochondritis dissecans

	CERVICAL VERTEBRA		THORACIC VERTEBRAE		LUMBAR VERTEBRAE		TOTAL	
	No.	%	No.	%	No.	%	No.	%
Male	0/858	0.0	505/2196	23.0	181/968	18.7	687/4022	17.1
Female	0/615	0.0	183/1671	11.0	66/741	8.9	250/3027	8.3
Total adults*	0/1480	0.0	688/3883	17.7	247/1715	14.4	937/7078	13.2
Adolescents	0/102	0.0	29/266	10.9	8/119	6.7	37/518	7.1

*figures include data from four unsexed adults

TABLE 19
Prevalence of Schmorl's nodes, by vertebrae

not appear to be any great difference in the prevalence of this condition over the time span of the burial ground. For the less anatomically literate reader it may be helpful to understand that the spine is divided into four groups of vertebrae. From the top down these are called cervical vertebra (which include two vertebrae below the skull called the atlas and axis), thoracic vertebrae (the most numerous central section of the spine), lumbar vertebrae (in the lower part of the spine), and the sacrum (the group of fused vertebrae to which the pelvis is attached) at the bottom.

Another comparable condition is **intervertebral osteochondrosis**, probably caused by stress resulting in herniation of the disc. It has been found in populations with more physically

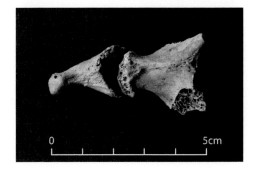

ILLUS 82
Clay-shoveller's fracture

arduous lifestyles. In the Hereford assemblage 31 adults exhibited this condition[63], a prevalence of 6.8% of adult individuals.

In the bottom half of the spinal column (lower thoracic and lumbar vertebrae) five individuals exhibited **anterior vertebral erosions** which are not consistent with *intervertebral osteochondrosis* (Illus 84). Individuals affected included two younger-middle adult males[64], one younger-middle adult female[65] and a younger adult female[66] all from Bone Only burials, as well as one younger-middle adult female[67] within a Simple Coffin. In these five individuals the erosions were varied in size and quite large[68]. Erosions of the vertebral body such as seen here have been used to diagnose brucellosis in skeletal material, a disease passed to humans from animals, commonly through milk[69]. However, the erosions could also be caused by *trauma*[70]. As four of the five individuals exhibited other

63   37 thoracic vertebrae, 12 lumbar vertebrae
64   Sk31470, Sk40198
65   Sk40300
66   Sk2883
67   Sk31003
68   Like those seen in traumatic anterior disc herniation (Mays 2007b)
69   Capasso 1999; Anderson 2003
70   Mays 2007b, 115

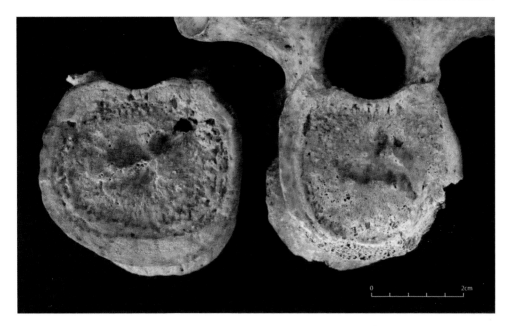

0   2cm

ILLUS 83
Schmorl's nodes

spinal *trauma* including *Schmorl's nodes* and/ or compression fractures of the vertebral bodies this increases the likelihood that *trauma* was the cause.

A common trait observed within the assemblage relates to indentations at the end of the leg bone where it meets the ankle (the distal end of the tibia). These are more technically referred to as squatting facets and as their name suggests are believed to be in part due to repetitive and prolonged hyper-extension of the ankle joint when individuals regularly undertake tasks near the ground and are forced to squat for periods of time. From the 246 individuals where the observation could be made, 36% exhibited a squatting facet[71] (Table 20). Females had a significantly higher prevalence than males[72] which was similarly the case at Barton (5.8%

and 2.2% respectively), although, there, from a much smaller group. The sex difference may suggest that females attended to tasks lower to the ground such as tending a fire; in the medieval community women were more involved in tasks centered around the dwelling such as caring for infants, cleaning, preparing of food etc. A higher prevalence of squatting facets was found at Fishergate House, again, more commonly in women, with 61– 62.5% of females and 31.5–38.5% of males displaying this trait and at Wharram Percy where 55% (107/193) of adults had facets. The latter high prevalence was considered in part due to the rarity of chairs in medieval peasant life. This compares markedly to the post-medieval middle classes of Spitalfields[73] who had a 2% prevalence (9/455).

Another trait that also could be stress related is associated with the acromion, the most

---

71 Either medial or lateral
72 x^2=13.3, p=0.00027

---

73 Molleson and Cox 1993

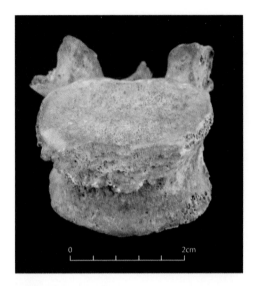

ILLUS 84
Anterior vertebral erosions

CONDITION	MALE				FEMALE			
	R		L		R		L	
	No.	%	No.	%	No.	%	No.	%
Squatting facets	28/108	25.9	29/105	27.6	38/92	41.3	39/96	40.6
Os acromiale	6/147	4.1	6/151	4.0	0/110	0.0	2/109	1.8

TABLE 20
Prevalence of squatting facets and os acromiale by sex

prominent bone on the top of the shoulder which is made up of sections of bone that usually fuse together between the ages of 22 and 25 years. One of the traits observed within the Hereford assemblage and others elsewhere is termed **os acromiale** and relates to the non-union of the acromion process. There is considerable evidence that it may be the result of *trauma* or be caused by occupational factors with chronic stress preventing fusion. Therefore certain habitual activities involving the shoulder may increase the frequency of this condition. On the Tudor Warship, the *Mary Rose*, for example, it was linked to the regular

use of bow and arrows from a young age. This trait has a relatively low prevalence within the Hereford population, but interestingly there is a higher prevalence in males and it only occurred in females on the left side (Table 20). Males were also affected to a greater extent than females at Barton (4.7% and 0.6%) and St Andrews[74] (8.4%–10.3% and 0%–5.6%). At the latter site it affected the individual's right side more frequently than the left (9.5% and 7.1%).

Degenerative joint disease is one of the most common pathological conditions identified in skeletal material and the Hereford assemblage is no exception. Degenerative changes to the joints include *osteoarthritis* and *degenerative disc disease* in the spine. These are strongly age related, but there are many contributing factors including genetic predisposition and *trauma*, although it seems that mechanical strain on the joints also plays an important role[75].

Degeneration of the discs held between the vertebral bodies (**degenerative disc disease**) results in the discs losing their 'cushioning' and individuals can suffer from neck and back pain as well as possible pain in the corresponding ligaments. The latter symptoms arise as a result of strains or tears of spinal ligaments[76] (Illus 85). Overall, 40%[77] of individuals at Hereford Cathedral, with one or more vertebrae, exhibited *degenerative disc disease* (Table 21). This is a little higher than the 35%[78] found at Wharram Percy and 29%[79] at Ipswich Blackfriars.

---

74 Period 6
75 Simon et al. 1972; Radin et al. 1980; Croft et al. 1992; Videman and Battie 1999; Lawrence 1969
76 Lawrence 1969
77 183/461
78 125/360
79 51/173

SEX	CERVICAL VERTEBRA		THORACIC VERTEBRAE		LUMBAR VERTEBRAE		FIRST SACRAL VERTEBRAE		TOTAL	
	No.	%	No.	%	No.	%	No.	%	No.	%
Male	134/858	15.6	175/2196	8.0	84/968	8.7	15/200	7.5	408/4022	10.1
Female	102/615	16.6	131/1671	7.8	42/741	5.6	9/162	5.6	284/3027	9.4
Total adults*	236/1480	15.9	307/3883	7.9	128/1715	7.5	26/364	7.1	697/7078	9.8

*figures for total adults includes data from four unsexed adults

TABLE 21
Prevalence of degenerative disc disease in differing regions of the spine, by vertebrae

At Hereford, as expected the occurrence of *degenerative disc disease* increased with increasing age although there does not appear to be a significant difference between males and females affected[80]. Overall the disease is most prevalent within the upper part of the spine (cervical vertebrae) for both sexes although men seem to be affected in the lower spine (lumbar and sacral vertebrae) more than women.

The spine is also a frequent site of changes related to **osteoarthritis** and 31% (147/468) of individuals, with one or more vertebral facet, at Hereford Cathedral were affected (Illus 86). Changes caused by this were present in all areas of the spine. There does not appear to be a significant difference between the sexes in any of the age bands but the disease was much more prominent in individuals of 35 years and over with only 11 people younger than this affected (Table 22).

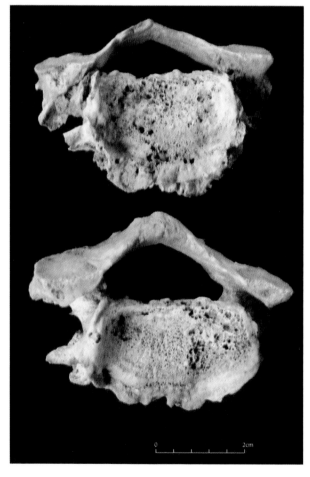

ILLUS 85
Degenerative disc disease

80　Male 109/264 (41.3%), female 71/193
　　(36.8%); p=0.33

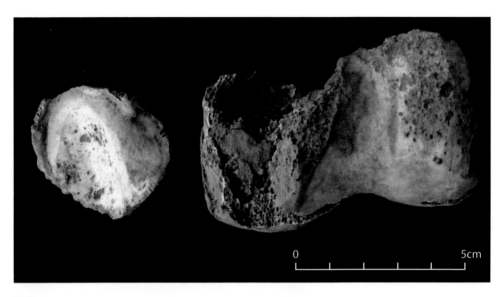

ILLUS 86
Osteoarthritis

	CERVICAL VERTEBRA		THORACIC VERTEBRAE		LUMBAR VERTEBRAE		FIRST SACRAL VERTEBRAE		TOTAL	
	No.	%	No.	%	No.	%	No.	%	No.	%
Male	146/3413	4.3	204/7200	2.8	89/3772	2.4	10/378	2.6	449/14763	3.0
Female	85/2494	3.4	173/5541	3.1	108/2906	3.7	18/288	6.3	384/11229	3.4
Total adults*	231/5936	3.9	380/12792	3.0	200/6729	3.0	28/616	4.5	839/26100	3.2

*figures for total adults includes data from four unsexed adults

TABLE 22
Osteoarthritis in differing regions of the spine, prevalence by vertebral facets

A difference in prevalence between the sexes of *degenerative disc disease* and *osteoarthritis* has been considered to reflect functional differences between the vertebral bodies and neural arch facet joints. The function of the vertebral bodies is primarily support whereas the facets allow varying degrees of movement therefore weight bearing might be expected to have less of an effect on the distribution of facet joint degeneration[81]. An examination of the prevalence of *degenerative disc disease* in occupational groups[82] concluded that 'sex distribution probably depends more on occupational differences between the sexes than on any hormonal or other influence'[83]. In the case of the lumbar spine, it was found that more strenuous occupations, such as

81 Bridges 1994; Knusel et al. 1997
82 Lawrence 1969
83 Ibid, 133

coal-mining, outdoor work such as farming, road-making and unskilled labouring are associated with the highest prevalence. The results here indicate that male and female lumbar spines are not undergoing significantly different amounts of weight bearing stress and movement. It would therefore appear that heavy tasks were fairly equally distributed between the men and women of Hereford in the past.

A total of 164 adults (35%) exhibited *osteoarthritis* in parts of the body other than the spine, and 93 of these also had the spinal condition. Whilst overall there is not a significant difference in the occurrence of *osteoarthritis* between the sexes, males have a higher prevalence of the condition around the shoulder joint, whereas females have a higher prevalence in the hip and knee. In individuals less than 35 years at death only females exhibited *osteoarthritis* in the hip and knee (6/35, 17%) and as oestrogen loss, one possible cause for the onset of the condition, occurs at the time of menopause (c 40–61 years of age) then the above observation is more likely to be due to occupational or environmental factors (Table 23).

Jobs requiring kneeling or squatting along with heavy lifting are associated with especially high rates of both

JOINT	MALE		FEMALE		UNSEXED		TOTAL	R+L TOTAL
	No.	%	No.	%	No.	%	%	%
R Jaw	5/138	3.6	2/114	1.8	–	0.0	2.8	3.0
L Jaw	4/140	2.9	4/102	3.9	–	0.0	3.3	
R Upper Shoulder	12/188	6.4	6/36	4.4	0/1	0.0	8.0	7.0
L Upper Shoulder	15/183	8.2	5/134	3.7	0/3	0.0	6.3	
R Chest	5/172	2.9	2/128	1.6	0/1	0.0	2.3	2.3
L Chest	5/171	2.9	2/126	1.6	0/2	0.0	2.3	
R Shoulder	6/206	2.9	1/158	0.6	0/2	0.0	1.9	1.8
L Shoulder	4/202	2.0	2/151	1.3	0/3	0.0	1.7	
R Elbow	14/223	6.3	9/165	5.5	1/3	33.3	6.1	5.1
L Elbow	10/221	4.5	6/168	3.6	0/3	0.0	4.1	
R Wrist	24/246	9.8	17/184	9.2	1/4	25.0	9.7	9.8
L Wrist	25/242	10.3	16/175	9.1	1/4	25.0	10.0	
R Hand	10/237	4.2	9/176	5.1	1/4	25.0	4.8	4.7
L Hand	10/229	4.4	8/175	4.6	1/4	25.0	4.7	
R Hip	15/235	6.4	18/182	9.9	0/3	0.0	7.9	8.7
L Hip	18/243	7.4	23/182	12.6	0/4	0.0	9.6	
R Knee	8/201	4.0	8/158	5.1	0/4	0.0	4.4	4.0
L Knee	4/194	2.1	9/163	5.5	0/4	0.0	3.6	
R Ankle	0/153	0.0	0/129	0.0	0/3	0.0	0.0	0.3
L Ankle	1/153	0.7	0/132	0.0	0/3	0.0	0.3	
R Foot	9/141	6.4	7/121	5.8	0/3	0.0	6.0	5.9
L Foot	8/145	5.5	8/126	6.3	0/3	0.0	5.8	

Jaw = temporomandibular joint; Upper shoulder = acromioclavicular joint between clavicle and scapula; Chest = sternoclavicular joint, between clavicle and sternum; Wrist = distal radius, distal ulna, carpals & proximal metacarpels; Hand = distal metacarpels & phalanges; Ankle = distal tibia, distal fibula and corresponding surfaces of talus.

TABLE 23
Prevalence of osteoarthritis in all extra-spinal joints

JOINT	MALE		FEMALE		% DIFFERENCE BETWEEN THE SEXES
	No.	%	No.	%	
Upper Shoulder	23/222	10.4	7/161	4.3	6.0
Hip	26/260	10.0	28/197	14.2	4.2
Shoulder	10/241	4.1	3/184	1.6	2.4
Knee	9/219	4.1	11/174	6.3	2.2
Hand	16/257	6.2	15/192	7.8	1.6
Chest	8/206	3.9	4/154	2.6	1.3
Jaw	8/154	5.2	5/127	3.9	1.3
Spine	85/268	31.7	60/196	30.6	1.1
Wrist	35/261	13.4	23/185	12.4	1.0
Foot	14/156	9.0	11/133	8.3	0.7
Ankle	1/169	0.6	0/143	0.0	0.6
Elbow	18/260	6.9	13/190	6.8	0.1

Spine = individuals with one or more vertebral facet affected of those individuals with one or more facet

TABLE 24
Osteoarthritis in male & female individuals ranked by difference in prevalence

knee and hip *osteoarthritis*[84]. Significantly more females[85] than males[86] exhibited squatting facets in the assemblage, and of the females affected by *osteoarthritis* of the knee or hip 25% also had squatting facets, the case in only 6% of males.

Affliction of the upper shoulder joint was significantly more common in males and had a significantly different distribution by age between the sexes. Only older adult females were affected, whereas in males nearly half[87] were aged 35–45 years at death with three

younger than that. *Osteoarthritis* of this joint can be found in association with *rotator cuff disease* and four males in the assemblage exhibited both. Amongst the causes for this are injury to the joint (today a high prevalence is found in collision sports) or lifting weighty objects (Table 24).

The main shoulder joint seems to have been affected to a lesser extent than the upper shoulder joint and does not seem to affect individuals under the age of 35 years. In patients younger than 40 years, instability of this joint generally follows a history of either full or partial dislocation[88], although certain occupations, such as heavy construction or overhead sports, are also contributory factors[89].

Overall, 46%[90] of the Hereford population exhibited *osteoarthritis* which is similar to Ipswich Blackfriars 38%[91] and almost identical to the prevalence at Wharram Percy 47%[92]. These are all higher than the mean for a range of later-medieval sites at 28%[93].

Assuming that mechanical factors are the main cause of *osteoarthritis* and *degenerative disc disease* then it seems that Herefordians had more in common, in terms of lifestyle, with the low status rural people of Wharram Percy than with other populations considered. Within the Hereford population *degenerative disc*

---

84 Felson et al 1991; Coggon et al 1998
85 52/114 (45.6%)
86 34/130 (26.2%)
87 11/23 (48%)

88 Ibid
89 Millett et al. 2008
90 218/474
91 80/211
92 170/360
93 Roberts and Cox 2003, 282

disease was at its most prevalent in Bone Only and Simple Coffin burials. *Osteoarthritis* had a more consistent prevalence, but again, individuals buried in Simple Coffins showed the highest frequency (Table 25).

One slightly different aspect of life is reflected in the presence of **bunions** (hallux valgus), which causes the big toe to point inwards towards the second digit. This is commonly associated with individuals wearing ill-fitting or pointed footwear (Mays 2005). Of those individuals with a big toe (first metatarsal bone) surviving, 16.8%[94] suffered from this. Females had a slightly higher prevalence (18.2%[95]) than males (15.8%[96]) indicating women may have worn more restrictive shoes. The condition affected both feet in 26 cases and the prevalence increases in the later burial groups[97].

BURIAL GROUP	DEGENERATIVE DISC DISEASE		OSTEOARTHRITIS	
	No.	%	No.	%
Pre-Cist	2/6	33.3	2/6	33.3
Cist	10/34	29.4	17/35	48.6
Bone Only	105/230	45.7	104/234	44.4
Simple Coffin	43/108	39.8	56/114	49.1
Elaborate Coffin	23/83	27.7	39/85	45.9
Total	183/461	39.7	218/474	46.0

(for inclusion individuals had one or more vertebral bodies)

TABLE 25
Prevalence of adults with degenerative disc disease and spinal osteoarthritis by burial groups

SUMMARY

So overall what does the above analysis tell us about the population? There appear to be slightly more male burials than female, something that might be explained by allowances to bury women and children in other burial grounds outside of Hereford. A proportionately lower number of children in the assemblage possibly also underlines this. An alternative explanation might be one of status based on an assumption that the south-east part of the graveyard is commonly reserved for higher status citizens. With the exception of the Cist burials

where within the small number excavated there was a predominance of males (a wider volume of data within the city supporting this selectivity), there was no apparent distinction between the sexes across the burial ground.

Regarding life expectancy, does this match what might be normally expected? Certainly in the sub-adults, and in particular the under 12s, there does appear to be an increase in life expectancy in the post-medieval period. The under 5s in the medieval population have a life expectancy much in line with that of the plague pit burials excavated in 1993. Despite the life expectancy being five years less in the 35–45 age band in both medieval and post-medieval populations from the 2009–11 excavations by comparison to the 1993 excavation, overall life expectancy appears to be higher than that observed elsewhere in medieval populations.

The Hereford population clearly has similarities with other contemporary groups and this is very much underlined by the estimated stature (height) of individuals with men being taller

---

94   37/220
95   18/99
96   19/120
97   Pre-Cist 0/0; Cist 1/18; Bone Only 13/95; Simple Coffin 10/58; Elaborate Coffin 13/46

than women and a slight reduction in the height of both from the medieval period through to the post-medieval. Factors that have been blamed for this (increased urbanisation, poor health and pollution) could be prevalent within Hereford City and in particular in the medieval period which would have seen population growth. Following the Welsh sacking just prior to the Conquest, which decimated the population, it increased to an all-time medieval high in the 13th century. Considered alongside this data the population appears to most closely match assemblages such as the urban poor at Fishergate. Also, perhaps underlining this Hereford children appeared to be slightly taller than rural communities like the one at Wharram Percy.

There is some evidence to suggest some degree of racial distinctiveness in Hereford. The cranial shape is possibly slightly narrower than elsewhere in the country, and also there seems to be a higher prevalence of non-metric skeletal traits in Cist burials than others, again suggesting this group (or elements of it) may be racially distinct. It was also interesting to note that despite there being very few cases of one type of condition (*spondylolysis*), which is considered to be hereditary, a group of three individuals buried in the same part of the cemetery all exhibited this.

It is probably safe to assume that the population of Hereford were not idle and that medieval and later lifestyles required considerable numbers of manual tasks.

There is evidence to suggest that these were shared fairly equally between the sexes although some distinction in the nature of these tasks is evident in the skeletal record. Women show some indication that they spent more time undertaking tasks nearer the ground than men which is to an extent supported by a much greater coincidence of squatting facets and *osteoarthritis* of the knee joint in women than men. It also appears that young women were more active than young men in respect to tasks that involved using their legs. Men on the other hand demonstrated greater evidence for lifting as well as manual jobs that involved repetitive stress on the shoulder joint and spine. One condition associated with archers seems to have affected more men than women and the few cases of *bunions* seem to imply either ill-fitting shoes, or continued use of shoes from adolescence into adulthood.

A holistic view of people living in medieval and later Hereford would not place them significantly apart from other contemporary populations although there are some indications that in the early Norman period there were possibly some distinctive racial differences. Hard work seems to have been relatively evenly distributed between the sexes although younger women perhaps did more fetching and carrying than their male counterparts and older men undertook slightly heavier tasks and jobs involving more repetitive strain to the upper body whilst women did more jobs nearer the ground.

6

INTERROGATING THE WITNESSES

The previous chapter outlined the make-up of the population alongside the difficulties in determining the breakdown of society from burial remains alone. Here we are going to try to tackle the day to day lives of these early Herefordians, how they might have lived, perceived others around them and the effects of external influences on the population as a whole. Human remains are very good at providing thought provoking snapshots of the influence of things such as environment, diet and disease on the population.

What indications might there be within the skeletal record of what people's lives were like? Individuals' daily diets can affect their growth and development and different individuals show evidence for too little or too much food. Evidence can also be seen of disability and disfigurement. Severe injuries often leave traces in the skeleton as do some infectious diseases.

POLLUTION

We now tend to take for granted the effect of pollution on our health. Though often seen as a modern evil, the use of solid fuels in the past for heating and cooking resulted in noticeable effects from smoke inhalation. It is possible that this was a contributing factor to infection in the sinuses which shows up as something called **maxillary sinusitis** (Illus 87).

Forty-two individuals from Hereford Cathedral showed evidence for chronic infection in this area, though it must be noted that the condition could not be seen in complete or semi-complete skulls (without breaking them) so the final number could be much higher (Table 26). As a result the observation could only be made in 223 individuals. Adults made up 180 of these 20% being affected, considerably more than the 14% of cases observed in sub-adults. Whilst it might be expected that more women should be infected if they spent more time working in smoky, poorly ventilated homes than men apparently the difference is not statistically significantly[1] suggesting it was not necessary to spend too long in smoky environments before the condition manifested itself. The infection can also be caused through a dental condition but as this only occurred in seven cases, an environmental cause for the infection seems most likely in the rest of the population. As

---

1    $x^2 = 4.54, p = 0.04$

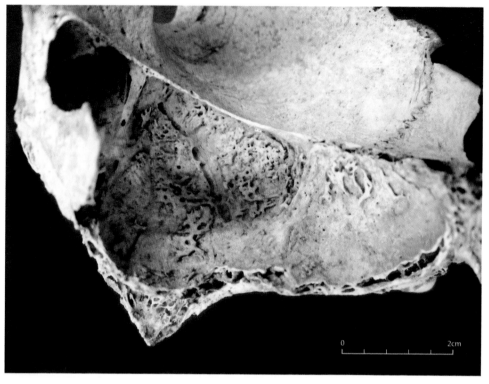

ILLUS 87
Maxillary sinusitis

BURIAL GROUP	NO.	%
Pre-Cist	0/3	0.0
Cist	4/15	26.7
Bone Only	26/134	19.4
Simple Coffin	9/48	18.8
Elaborate Coffin	3/23	13.0
Total	42/223	18.8

TABLE 26
Prevalence of maxillary sinusitis (of individuals with at least one sinus present to observe)

Hereford was not heavily industrialised in the post-medieval period then a reduction in the prevalence of the condition might be expected with improvements in household ventilation. This appears to have been the case as there is an observable decrease in sinusitis over time.

The total prevalence of 19% of individuals affected[2] is relatively low compared to 72%[3] at St-Helens-on-the-Walls and 51% at Wharram Percy[4]. The latter suggests that even rural environments were not free of predisposing factors. The low levels at Hereford imply it may have had a healthier environment.

2   42/224 individuals with 1+ sinus
3   82/114
4   Roberts et al 1998

SKELETON	BURIAL GROUP	AGE	SEX	DESCRIPTION OF SKELETAL MANIFESTATIONS	STATUS*
Sk1998	Bone Only	1.5–6 mths (I)	–	Lateral bowing of the right radius and left ulna; porous flared rib ends; porotic lesions on ectocranial surface of cranial vault fragments and on the squama of the temporals.	Active
Sk5215	Bone Only	6 mths–1yrs (I)	–	Marked lateral bowing of the radii and ulnae; medial tilting of tibal distal growth plates; porosis of cranial fragments (	Active;
Sk12455	Bone Only	6 mths (I)	–	Bowing of humeri laterally, posterior radii and ulnae and tibiae anterior-medially, flaring of metaphyseal distal ends of radii and femurs, porosity of the metaphyseal ends of long bones, flared sternal rib ends with highly porotic ends, medial tilting of the distal tibiae and radii epiphyseal surfaces, marked roughening of the bone underlying growth plate in humeri, radii, femurs, tibiae and fibulae, porosis of ectocranial surface of cranial frags (parietal?).	Active
Sk40187	Bone Only	1.5–2 yrs (YC)	–	Medial bowing tibiae and fibulae and anterior bowing femora, medial tilting of distal tibial growth plate	Active
Sk10431	Bone Only	1.5–2 yrs (YC)	–	Right femur anterior bowing with a thickened	Healed?
Sk10290	Bone Only	3–4 yrs (YC)	–	Medial bowing of right tibia and lateral bowing of right fibula (L NP), active woven bone on concavity of bending of shafts, short limb bone length for age.	Healed
Sk30016	Bone Only	15–17 yrs (AO)	–	Severe anterior bowing and thickening as well as medial-lateral flattening of the proximal left femur.	Healed
Sk1514	Elaborate Coffin	35–39 yrs (O–M)	F	Lateral bowing of the femurs, anterior bowing of tibiae and fibulae.	–
Sk5611	Elaborate Coffin	45–49 yrs (O AD)	M	Left femur anterior bending, lateral bending right fibula and tibia	–
Sk11548	Elaborate Coffin	30–34 yrs (Y–M)	M	Posterio-m	–

*Active and healed *rickets* was diagnosed on the basis of criteria presented by Mays et al 2006.

TABLE 27
Individuals exhibiting skeletal manifestations of rickets

DIET

Delving into the skeletal record of the past occupants of Hereford certainly begins to put metaphorical flesh on the term 'you are what you eat'. Of the metabolic diseases that relate to diet and other dietary deficiencies and that leave identifiable traces on the bone, the following are perhaps the most commonly seen. Lack of vitamin D (although not entirely dietary) results in *rickets* and *osteomalacia* and can be quite clearly visible in the skeletal record. *Gout*, caused by an excess of uric acid can also be clearly seen.

More subtle traces of vitamin C deficiency, which presents itself in *scurvy*, can also be recorded. Calcium deficiency is probably the most obvious dietary effect that will manifest itself within the skeleton causing conditions such as age-related bone loss (or *osteoporosis*) alongside other general stress indicators that are not related to calcium deficiency (ie *cribra orbitalia, porotic hyperostosis and dental enamel hypoplasia*).

Rickets is infrequently observed in medieval cemeteries in comparison to post-medieval

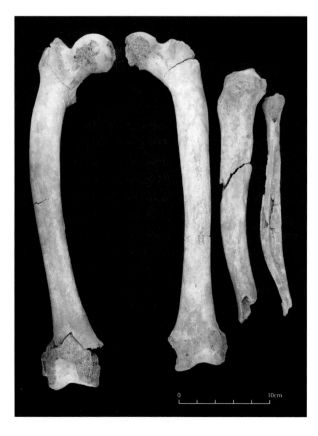

ILLUS 88
Rickets bending deformities

this category. Poor transport links meant that the price of coal was a lot higher than elsewhere in the country, and thus any industrial development on a major scale was stalled[6]. Certainly at St Martin's in Birmingham the prevalence of *rickets* was a lot higher at 7.5%[7].

The seven sub-adults that appeared to have had *rickets* were all from Bone Only burials. In three infants and one younger child the disease was active at the time of death and in one adolescent and two younger children it was healed. By contrast the three adults who exhibited possible bending deformities associated with residual *rickets* were all from the later Elaborate Coffin group.

ones (Table 27, Illus 88); there was a great rise in *rickets* in the 19th century and this is mainly due to the high amounts of urban atmospheric pollution blocking sunlight. It may also be the result of swaddling of infants or seen in sick children who are kept indoors to recover from another disease. The 3.0% prevalence within the Hereford assemblage fits with that found at other sites[5]; at Wharram Percy eight individuals (1.2%) exhibited active *rickets* all between the ages of 3 and 18 months, ten at Barton-on-Humber (0.4%), Fishergate House had six possible cases (5.3%) and St-Helens-on-the-Walls two cases (0.2%). The disease is more likely to occur in major urban and industrial centres where pollution was, on the whole, greater. Post-medieval Hereford does not really fall into

The above seems to confirm the interpretation as to why the disease occurs in medieval populations with the deaths of the youngest sufferers possibly implying other underlying illnesses that prevented them from going outside and were eventually fatal. Given the small number of adults with the condition, and the greater mobility of the post-medieval population it could be that these individuals were brought up in urban centres such as Birmingham and London where the effects of pollution were much greater or alternatively survived long periods of childhood illness.

Two adult females from Bone Only burials were diagnosed with the adult form of vitamin D

5   Roberts & Cox 2003, 247–8

6   Roberts 2001, 91
7   Brickley et al 2006, 132

ILLUS 89
Osteomalacia-related pseudofracture of scapula

deficiency, **osteomalacia**, resulting in the weakening of the bone and characterised by the appearance of small fractures (Illus 89). Along with the high risk of fracture, symptoms include muscle and bone weakness and/or pain[8]. As well as pollution and low levels of nutrition, a loss of calcium and phosphorus due to closely spaced pregnancies and prolonged lactation in the past would have made females especially vulnerable to a vitamin D deficiency[9]. It is tempting to suggest this was the cause here as both affected individuals were women old enough for child-bearing[10].

Vitamin C whilst present in numerous vegetables in varying amounts, is highest in citrus fruits. It is destroyed at high temperatures (boiling destroys 50% of effective vitamin C) and by exposure to air[11]. As such, populations in colder climates where fruit is less abundant and that consume mainly cooked foods are prone to develop a deficiency. **Scurvy** is also associated with hardship, famine, and war, as well as the better known case of prolonged trips at sea (from the 15th to 18th centuries). Infantile *scurvy* (or Moller-Barlow disease) is seen primarily in infants with low birth weight, such as premature babies, or twin births, as well as infants who are fed prepared food or condensed milk[12].

In the Hereford assemblage four cases of possible *scurvy* were recorded and include individuals aged between 6 months and 2 years; one infant had *scurvy* concurrent with *rickets*. Two of these were from Bone Only burials the other two in later Simple Coffin and Elaborate Coffin burials. Clinical manifestations of *scurvy* can appear following as little as 2–4 months of inadequate intake of vitamin C[13]. The most rapid proportionate growth occurs in infancy and early childhood, and therefore the probability of forming defective blood vessels in this age group is the greatest[14]. Clinical manifestations include ulceration, swollen and bleeding gums, fracturing and re-fracturing and death[15].

Some evidence for iron or vitamin B12 deficiency occurs in the form of a porous or finely pitted area in the eye socket, **cribra orbitalia** (Illus 90). Lesions are generally present in both orbits when they occur and therefore individuals with one or more orbits observable were scored for *cribra orbitalia* (Table 28).

The overall prevalence of 38.4% at Hereford is relatively high. Of 34 comparable assemblages, the prevalence at Doonbought Fort, Co. Antrum

8   Holick 2005
9   Prentice 2003
10 Sk31232 25–29 years; Sk31657 18+years
11 Wyatt 1976
12 Stuart-Macadam 1989, 202

13 Tamura et al 2000
14 Ortner et al 2001
15 Stuart-Macadam 1989, 202

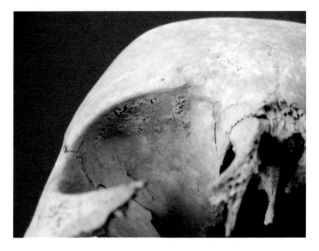

ILLUS 90
Cribra orbitalia

at 33.3% [16] and Wharram Percy at 33.2% were closest. The higher prevalence of *cribra orbitalia* in females in Hereford was not statistically significant[17], though women are generally more susceptible to developing iron-deficiency anaemia (particularly during pregnancy) and higher frequencies in females occurred in seven of nine sites listed by Stuart-Macadam[18].

Cribra orbitalia is more frequent in sub-adults than adults: it was found in 57.8% of sub-adults and 31.3% of adults. The highest prevalence was present in the younger child cohort; the pattern here fits with the findings of a number of previous studies in which it is noted that the condition was most common in individuals under 12 and decreases with advancing age[19]. The greater frequency in sub-adults may be the result of those individuals suffering from anaemia being more likely to die prematurely, however, progressive obliteration of lesions by bone remodelling in adult life could mask earlier signs and produce a similar pattern.

Iron deficiency anaemia does not normally occur prior to six months of age unless iron stores at birth are inadequate[20] but prematurity

AGE GROUP	CRIBRA ORBITALIA			POROTIC HYPEROSTOSIS		
	No.	%	Remodelled	No.	%	Remodelled
F	0/2	0.0	–	0/4	0.0	–
N	0/7	0.0	–	0/12	0.0	–
I	2/7	28.6	0	0/11	0.0	0
YC	28/40	70.0	0	7/62	11.3	0
OC	12/18	66.7	0	10/29	34.5	1
AO	10/16	62.5	0	9/22	40.9	0
Y AD	7/16	43.8	0	10/19	52.6	5
Y–MAD	16/59	27.1	2	31/77	40.3	8
O–MAD	33/101	32.7	11	54/132	40.9	17
O AD	16/52	30.8	3	15/72	20.1	8
AD	4/52	26.7	3	8/23	34.8	6
Total	128/333	38.4	19	144/463	31.1	45

TABLE 28
Prevalence of cribra orbitalia and porotic hyperostosis by age

16	Roberts & Cox 2003, 234
17	= 0.01, p= 0.914
18	Stuart-Macadam 1985
19	Roberts & Manchester 1995, 169
20	Mensforth et al. 1978

and low birth weight can cause a deficiency. At Hereford Cathedral, no individual under nine months of age exhibited either *cribra orbitalia* or *porotic hyperostosis* (where a similar pitting can be seen on other bones in the cranial vault). The lack of both in early infancy may indicate that at birth, iron stores were generally adequate and therefore low birth-weight was not a regular problem. It should be considered, however, that individuals could have died before developing lesions.

The majority of younger children with *cribra orbitalia* were aged between 1 and 3 years old. A potential cause of anaemia at this age is 'weanling diarrh'oea' as weaning onto adult food exposes the child to a range of gastro-intestinal pathogens[21]. It may be that this was a significant contributor to morbidity in young children in this population.

Porotic hyperostosis was present in 31.1% of individuals with either a parietal or occipital present (Table 28). Although recording methods are different between sites, it can be seen that the Hereford assemblage sits closer to, although still significantly higher than the prevalence at rural Wharram Percy (Table 29). Of those affected, at Hereford in the adults there is a decrease with age and 57.9%[22] of lesions were remodelled at the time of death, however, in sub-adults it increased in frequency from younger child age to adolescence.

In 331 individuals where both the orbit/s and parietal/occipital were observable 63 individuals (19.0%) exhibited a co-occurrence of *cribra orbitalia* and *porotic hyperostosis*. It has been suggested that *porotic hyperostosis* requires more a prolonged and severe disease to develop[23].

Calcium deficiency is a little harder to diagnose. Whilst **osteoporosis** can relate to this it is also

SITE	PRESENT	%	REMODELLED	ACTIVE
Hereford Cathedral	144/463	31.1	45 (31.25)	99 (68.8%)
Wharram Percy	125/502	24.9	52	73 (58.4%)
St-Helen-on-the-Walls	267/460	58.0	203	64 (24.0%)

*differing recording methods used – Wharram Percy prevalence by parietal; St-Helens-on-the-Walls by frontal and/or parietal; Hereford Cathedral by parietal and/or occipital.

TABLE 29
Porotic hyperostosis comparison with other sites

symptomatic of aging. Five males and six females exhibited broken wrists (*Colles' fractures*) eight being present in individuals between the ages of 35 and 44 years at death and two in older males. It is unknown if any of these represent osteoporotic fractures, with the exception of one female older-middle adult[24] who had a *Colles' fracture* combined with other evidence[25].

Vertebral compression fractures were observed on a total of 83 individuals in the assemblage and older adults again had the highest prevalence[26]. Biconcave vertebral fractures or 'cod-fish vertebrae' that are more likely to be associated with *osteoporosis* were present in eight of these individuals, seven were older adults, six of which were females. However, a possible case of bone cancer (malignant *neoplastic lesions* in the spine) in one of the female individuals[27] may have exacerbated bone loss and fracture. Just taking the eight individuals with cod fish fractures, as cases of confirmed *osteoporosis*, the prevalence of the condition within the assemblage is 1.7%.

An important indicator of general health in a population is the presence of defects in tooth enamel. A growth disruption in the

---

21   Mittler & van Gerven 1994
22   44/76
23   Hengen 1971

24   Sk5186
25   Two biconcave vertebral fractures, plus a thinned trabecular network observed on broken vertebrae
26   26/100
27   Sk4486

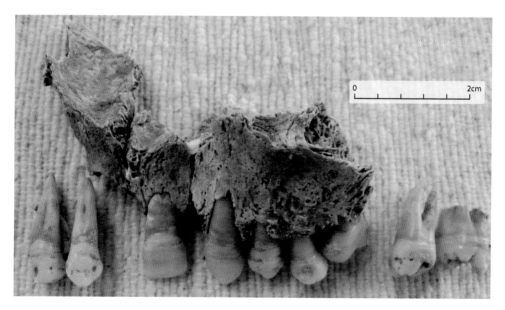

ILLUS 91
Dental enamel hypoplasia

BURIAL GROUP	NO.	%
Pre-Cist	4/6	66.7
Cist	13/33	39.4
Bone Only	136/248	54.8
Simple Coffin	57/108	52.8
Elaborate Coffin	14/53	26.4
Total	224/448	50.0

TABLE 30
Prevalence of dental enamel hypoplasia by burial group

enamel, **dental enamel hypoplasia**, can be a result of stress such as malnutrition, disease or low birth weight (Illus 91). Defects are only accumulated during enamel formation, up to around the age of approximately 12 years and defects are observable as lines, grooves or pits on the surface of the crown[28].

In total, 50% of the population was affected by one or more episodes of this condition[29]. These numbers are reasonably low. Individuals from Bone Only (including Pre-Cist) and Simple Coffin burials were the most frequently affected with the post-medieval Elaborate Coffin and Cist burials exhibiting a notably lower prevalence compared to these. Whilst it is difficult to be statistically certain, there is a possibility that these figures hint that burials in Cists and Elaborate Coffins may on average have enjoyed healthier early lifestyles to the rest of the population. Consideration of the breakdown of the occurrence of this condition by age lends some weight to this argument.

The total number of *dental enamel hypoplasia* shows males were much more significantly[30] affected than females in Hereford (Table 31). So at what age was this happening? Some sources suggest that most of the impacts occurred in

---

28   Hillson 1996

29   224/448 total; 135/142 sub-adults, 239/306 adults
30    $x^2 = 12.44$, p= 0.0004

childhood as the most commonly affected teeth were canines which develop between four months before birth up to seven years[31]. However, the prevalence in the adult teeth points to a later period of stress. Comparing the sub-adult and adult prevalence using the commonly acknowledged order of eruption of adult teeth[32] then the most elevated prevalence is in the earlier teeth, peaking with the canines and tailing off in the later teeth. The results suggest that the sub-adult population was most at risk of infection and disease from birth through to the point when adult canines erupt (around about early puberty).

Levels of dental disease[33] are affected by the general health of the population and diet. In total 275 individuals with dentition exhibited *caries* with the molars being the most frequently affected tooth type and of these the second molar the most common (Table 32–33).

Bacteria within dental plaque can cause destruction of the tooth leading to the formation of a cavity in the crown or root surface[34]. Carious lesions can cause severe pain, infection, and tooth loss. Whilst there are many things that can cause *caries*, sugar is the main culprit and is found occurring

NO. OF DEH	1	2	3	4	5	TOTAL LESIONS
Males	330	191	46	17	–	584
Females	213	92	12	3	–	320
All adults	543	283	58	20	–	904
Sub-adults	374	118	43	2	2	539
Total	917	401	101	22	2	1,443

TABLE 31
Frequency of dental enamel hypoplasia lesions (DEH) by teeth

	INDIVIDUALS		TEETH	
	No.	%	No.	%
Male	121/172	70.3	418/3,102*	13.5
Female	97/134	72.4	357/1,958	18.2
All adults	218/306	71.2	775/5,060	15.3
All sub-adults	57/141	40.4	134/1,836	7.3
Total population	275/447	61.5	909	13.2

*including two adult deciduous teeth which have been retained in two male individuals

TABLE 32
Prevalence of dental caries

naturally in foods such as fruits, vegetables and honey as well as in carbohydrates such as cereals. Small amounts of sugar began to be imported into England in the 12th century, but it was a scarce luxury in the medieval period. It was not until around 1700 that sugar imports increased dramatically due to imperialist policies[35]. This may account for the fact that individuals in the latest Elaborate Coffin burial group, exhibited the highest frequency of *caries* (Table 34). In fact there appears to be a steady increase in the condition from the earliest to latest burial groups.

31 Scheuer & Black 2004
32 incisor, 1st molar, canine, 2nd and 3rd molar
33 The dentition survives the rigours of the burial environment relatively well, being less prone to demineralisation and weathering than bone, so the dental health of a population can be studied with a greater degree of confidence. *Caries* and *calculus* were scored as absent or present for each erupted tooth. Ante-mortem tooth loss and periapical *abscesses* were recorded as absent/present for each erupted tooth position and *periodontal disease* by erupted teeth present within a socket. The severity of *calculus* and *periodontal disease* were recorded following Brothwell (1981). The tooth surfaces affected were also noted for both *calculus* and *caries* and this information can be found in the site archive.

34 Hillson, 1996

35 Moore & Corbett 1978

SIDE	Right								Left							
TOOTH	M3	M2	M1	PM2	PM1	C	I2	I1	I1	I2	C	PM1	PM2	M1	M2	M3
	Maxilla															
Total teeth	109	114	120	156	168	171	125	121	133	121	174	154	149	114	118	109
Carious teeth	23	32	31	28	28	24	10	14	16	11	27	35	30	32	30	22
%	21.1	28.1	25.8	17.9	16.7	11.7	8.0	11.5	12.0	9.1	15.5	22.7	20.1	28.1	25.4	20.2
	Mandible															
Total teeth	150	161	112	191	208	219	193	158	165	190	235	218	192	138	162	140
Carious teeth	22	38	27	31	27	13	14	9	4	8	22	29	27	26	49	22
%	14.6	23.6	24.1	16.2	13.0	5.9	7.3	5.7	2.4	4.2	9.4	13.3	14.1	18.8	30.2	15.7

TABLE 33
Distribution of dental caries by tooth position in the adult permanent dentition

BURIAL GROUP	INDIVIDUALS		TEETH	
	No.	%	No.	%
Pre–Cist	3/6	50.0	5/87	5.7
Cist	18/33	54.6	50/618	8.1
Bone Only	143/248	57.7	441/4,020*	11.0
Simple Coffin	74/10	68.5	254/1,475*	17.4
Elaborate Coffin	37/52	71.2	159/696	22.8

*includes an adult deciduous tooth which has been retained

TABLE 34
Prevalence of dental caries in total population by burial group

	INDIVIDUALS		TEETH	
	No.	%	No.	%
Male	44/189	23.3	85/4,182*	2.0
Female	35/145	24.1	49/3,011	1.6
Total	79/334	23.7	134/7,193	1.9

TABLE 35
Prevalence of abscesses in the adult permanent dentition

Caries can also develop into **dental abscesses** where bacteria enters the pulp cavity, other causes include high levels of wear, *trauma* to the teeth or *periodontal disease*. The bacteria cause inflammation and pus accumulates; once pressure builds up the pus is drained out by the formation of a hole in the surrounding bone[36]. Men and women appear to be equally affected with molars and teeth in the upper part of the jaw most predisposed to the condition (Table 35–36).

Consideration of *abscesses* amongst burial groups shows a slightly lower occurrence in the more prestigious Elaborate Coffin group which is notable against the higher level of *caries* in this burial population Table 37). It would perhaps imply that a richness of diet may be associated

36   Roberts & Manchester 1995; Hillson 1996

SIDE	Right								Left							
TOOTH	M3	M2	M1	PM2	PM1	C	I2	I1	I1	I2	C	PM1	PM2	M1	M2	M3
Maxilla																
Total	111	150	164	189	215	218	211	204	201	211	206	202	185	166	139	105
Abscesses	0	3	10	3	12	4	6	7	3	7	7	8	6	5	9	2
%	0.0	2.0	6.1	1.6	5.6	1.8	2.8	3.4	1.5	3.3	3.4	4.0	3.2	3.0	6.5	1.9
Mandible																
Total	234	286	287	284	280	278	265	256	259	265	271	282	274	284	284	225
Abscesses	0	0	6	4	2	4	3	2	3	4	2	3	3	4	2	0
%	0.0	0.0	2.1	1.4	0.7	1.4	1.1	0.8	1.2	1.5	0.7	1.1	1.1	1.1	1.4	0.0

TABLE 36
Distribution of abscesses by tooth position in the adult permanent dentition

BURIAL GROUP	INDIVIDUALS		TEETH	
	No.	%	No.	%
Pre-Cist	2/4	50.0	2/91	2.2
Cist	6/25	24.0	11/622	1.8
Bone Only	40/157	25.5	67/3,472*	1.9
Simple Coffin	22/95	23.2	36/1,892*	1.9
Elaborate Coffin	9/53	17.0	18/1,114	1.6

TABLE 37
Prevalence of abscesses in adults by burial group

BURIAL GROUP	INDIVIDUALS		TEETH	
	No.	%	No.	%
Pre-Cist	4/6	66.7	35/87	40.2
Cist	28/33	84.8	307/618	49.7
Bone Only	194/248	78.3	1,977/4,020*	49.2
Simple Coffin	74/109	67.9	724/1,487*	48.7
Elaborate Coffin	36/52	69.2	363/684	53.1

TABLE 38
Prevalence of dental calculus in total population by burial group

with tooth infection but might equally assist, through a healthier diet, in fighting off more serious infection causing *abscesses*.

The build-up of tartar or **calculus**, is associated with carbohydrate consumption and a lack of oral hygiene[37] (Illus 92). Dental hygiene is believed to have been little practised at this time although toothpicks are known to have been used[38]. The teeth closest to the salivary glands (anterior teeth of the mandible) tend to have the greater *calculus* deposits as saliva is a source of minerals[39]. No. significant difference was observed either between the sexes or different burial groups (Table 38).

37 Hillson 1996

38 Ring 1985
39 Hillson 1996, 255

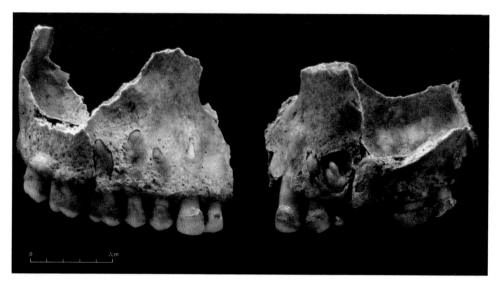

ILLUS 92
Calculus

	GRADE 1		GRADE 2		GRADE 3		TOTAL TEETH	
	No.	%	No.	%	No.	%	No.	%
Male	223/2,612	8.5	211/2,612	8.1	83/2,612	3.2	516/2,612	19.8
Female	135/1,657	8.2	130/1,657	7.8	71/1,657	4.3	337/1,658	20.3
All adults	358/4,269	8.4	341/4,269	8.0	154/4,269	3.6	853/4,270	20.0
Sub-adults	23/28	82.1	5/28	17.9	–	0.0	28/1,158	2.4
Total	381/4,297	8.9	346/4,297	8.1	154/4269	3.6	881/5,428	16.2

TABLE 39
Frequency and grade of periodontal disease by teeth

If this is truly an indication of a lack of dental hygiene then further consideration of the prevalence of *caries* and *abscesses* is required because these latter conditions show trends over time whilst *calculus* remains fairly uniform. Interestingly the presence of *abscesses* seems to show an opposite trend to the presence of *caries* with a reduction in prevalence from earlier to later burial groups. It is difficult to see how this could relate to better treatment,

or how it can be explained by diet (as in the latter case the trends in tooth decay should match one another) and there is little evidence in the dentition for better treatment over time. Evidence for the use of teeth as tools (see Chapter 5) was particularly noted during the earlier medieval period and it could simply be that in earlier times teeth suffered greater wear and tear.

Other bacterial effects resulting from poor oral hygiene include **periodontal disease** whose symptoms can range from bad breath through to tooth loss. Of the sub-adults, with one or more erupted teeth within a socket, seven (6.4%) exhibited *periodontal disease* (Table 39–40). This included two younger children (six deciduous teeth), one older child (three permanent teeth) and four adolescents (19 permanent teeth). The vast majority of these showed only slight

BURIAL GROUP	INDIVIDUALS		TEETH	
	No.	%	No.	%
Pre-Cist	1/4	25.0	5/63	7.9
Cist	13/30	43.3	87/503	17.3
Bone Only	80/221	36.2	483/3,074	15.7
Simple Coffin	34/98	34.7	185/1,184	15.6
Elaborate Coffin	17/47	36.2	121/603	20.1

TABLE 40
Prevalence of periodontal disease in total population by burial group

	INDIVIDUALS		TEETH	
	No.	%	No.	%
Male	152/189	80.4	965/4,182*	23.1
Female	117/145	80.7	892/3,011	29.6
Total	**269/334**	**80.5**	**1,857/7,193**	**25.8**

*includes an adult deciduous tooth which has been retained

TABLE 41
Prevalence of ante-mortem tooth loss in the adult permanent dentition

SIDE	Right							Left								
TOOTH	M3	M2	M1	PM2	PM1	C	I2	I1	I1	I2	C	PM1	PM2	M1	M2	M3
	Maxilla															
Total teeth	111	150	164	189	215	218	211	204	201	211	206	202	185	166	139	105
Carious teeth	25	50	61	44	47	29	32	32	29	38	31	50	48	67	41	29
%	22.5	33.3	37.2	23.3	21.9	13.3	15.2	15.7	14.4	18.0	15.1	24.8	20.3	40.4	29.5	27.6
	Mandible															
Total teeth	234	286	287	284	280	278	265	256	259	265	271	282	274	284	284	225
Carious teeth	102	130	170	76	53	30	40	41	35	30	22	39	71	146	119	101
%	43.6	45.5	59.2	26.8	18.9	10.8	15.1	16.0	13.5	11.3	8.2	13.8	25.9	51.4	51.4	44.9

TABLE 42
Distribution of ante-mortem tooth loss by tooth position in the adult permanent dentition

periodontal disease. In the adults *c* 48% of both males and females were affected although female teeth exhibited a higher prevalence of severe *periodontal disease*.

Tooth loss[40] itself predominantly occurred in adults, with only two instances recorded from 127 sub-adults. It can be a result of dental

disease, *trauma*, or tooth extraction. In the adult population 80.5% of individuals experienced this with 25.8% of teeth being lost (Table 41–42). Whilst males and females were equally affected, women tended to lose more teeth than men. In the mid 15th century the Royal Commonality of Barber Surgeons was created and by 1551 the first specified 'tooth-drawer' was mentioned, suggesting the beginnings of dentistry as a

40 This is recorded as ante-mortem tooth loss, ie tooth loss that occurred before the individual died rather than within the burial environment.

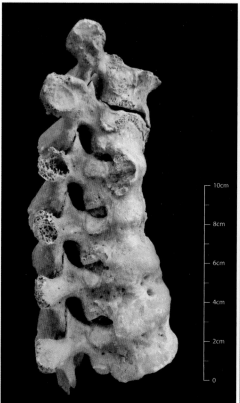
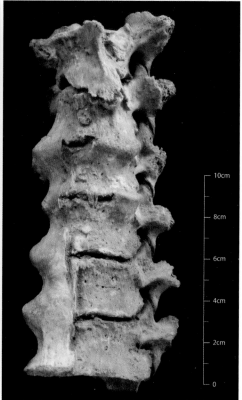

ILLUS 93
DISH

specialisation[41]. Tooth loss was significantly higher in the Elaborate Coffined burials[42] (Table 43).

Increased sugar and possibly richness of diet played a role in the onset of diffuse idiopathic skeletal hyperostosis or **DISH**, a fusing together of bones in the body (Illus 93). Whilst there are many factors affecting its onset, it is commonly believed to in part be associated with rich diet and obesity. It is therefore likely to have affected the later or more prestigious elements of society represented within the burial ground.

41   Ring 1985
42   Verses Pre-Cist, Cist and Bone Only groups (x^2= 13.63, p=0.0002) and Simple Coffins (x^2= 8.85, p=0.0003)

BURIAL GROUP	INDIVIDUALS		TEETH	
	No.	%	No.	%
Pre-Cist	3/4	75.0	14/91	15.4
Cist	17/25	68.0	83/622	13.3
Bone Only	120/157	76.4	704/3,472*	20.3
Simple Coffin	77/95	81.1	643/1,892*	34.0
Elaborate Coffin	52/53	98.1	414/1,114	37.2

TABLE 43
Prevalence of ante-mortem tooth loss in adults by burial group

Altogether 21 individuals showed indications of bone growth in the spine consistent with *DISH* (Table 44). Only nine of these individuals meet the criteria for *DISH* giving a prevalence of 1.8% (of individuals with three or more vertebral bodies). The other 12 skeletons showed an early stage of the disease where *ossification* was insufficiently advanced to meet the diagnostic criteria. Of these 12, two skeletons had only two vertebral bodies fused and the other individuals exhibited characteristic bone growth but without fusion of the bones.

It is interesting that of the nine individuals mentioned above the prevalence of *caries* (*c* 67%) does not differ dramatically from the rest of the population. Also the number of *caries* per individual across all 21 affected is below the average of the whole assemblage at 2.8 rather than 3.3 per individual. There are other indications that the diets of these individuals were good, as none of them suffered from signs of iron or vitamin B12 deficiency as described above, or signs of stress in childhood through the presence of *dental enamel hypoplasia*.

DISH is more common in males than females and rarely occurs under the age of 40 years. The male dominance is present within the Hereford assemblage and affected individuals were aged above 35 years at death. The highest frequency of *DISH* was present within Elaborate Coffin burials (Table 45). A survey by Roberts and Cox[43] found that there was a rise in the prevalence of *DISH* through time. Those most affected in the medieval period were found on monastic sites[44], while in the post-medieval period they were from the middle classes[45].

	EARLY-STAGE DISH*		DISH+	
	No.	%	No.	%
O–M Male	4/106	3.8	5/102	4.9
O AD Male	5/51	9.8	1/46	2.2
All male	9/244	3.7	7^/231	3.0
O–M female	2/71	2.8	2/66	3.0
O AD female	1/41	2.4	0/39	0.0
All female	3/176	1.7	2/168	1.2

*Prevalence by individuals with one or more thoracic vertebrae; +prevalence by individuals with three or more thoracic vertebrae; ^includes one adult of unknown age.

TABLE 44
Prevalence of 'early-stage DISH' and DISH by age and sex

BURIAL GROUP	EARLY-STAGE DISH		DISH	
	No.	%	No.	%
Pre-Cist	0/5	0.0	0/5	0.0
Cist	1/32	3.1	0/29	0.0
Bone Only	5/209	2.4	1/197	0.5
Simple Coffin	4/99	4.0	3/97	3.1
Elaborate Coffin	2/77	2.6	5/73	6.8

TABLE 45
Prevalence of 'early-stage DISH' and DISH by burial group

Another condition connected to obesity is **gout**[46] (Illus 94). It is also associated with alcohol consumption as well as a genetic predisposition, or impaired efficiency of the kidneys. Acute *gout* is characterized by severe joint pain, after which, if chronic *gout* develops, the collection of urate crystals and inflammatory tissue cause erosion of the areas in and around the joints. Life

43   Roberts & Cox 2003
44   Rogers & Waldron 2001
45   eg Spitalfields; Molleson & Cox 1993

46   Chen & Schumacher 2008

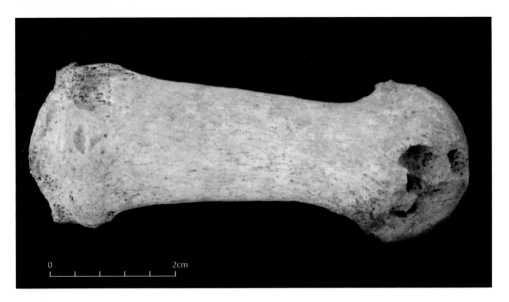

0   2cm

ILLUS 94
Gout

expectancy is not materially reduced in patients with *gout*[47], however, deposition of urate crystals in the kidneys of individuals with chronic *gout* can lead to kidney disease, and if untreated, renal failure and death[48].

Only one individual[49] in the Hereford assemblage exhibited signs of *gout* out of 474 adults. This was an older-middle adult male buried within a Cist. The evidence was noted in the big toe, this being the most common site of gouty changes in the skeleton. *Gout* is fairly rare in archaeological skeletal assemblages, however, ten cases were reported at Burton-on-Humber.

SOCIAL ATTITUDES

It is difficult to know how people behaved towards one another and what was acceptable, in effect the social mores of the past. Whilst the following cannot really answer such questions they help raise

consideration of the issues and indicate levels of tolerance towards habits and appearance.

Evidence for **smoking** is prevalent in the artefact record but some indications can also be seen in the skeleton. Eight individuals had evidence of pipe facets in their dentition including six males and two females (Illus 95). One of these individuals was found in a Bone Only burial, the others in Simple Coffins and Elaborate Coffin. In Britain, pipe-making began soon after the introduction of tobacco from North America in the mid 16th century. Smoking, or 'tobacco drinking' as it was known, was believed to bring medicinal benefits. Writing his *Great Chronologie* in 1573, William Harrison noted that: 'In these daies the taking-in of the Indian herbe called 'Tobaco' by an instrument formed like a little ladell, whereby it passeth from the mouth into the hed and stomach, is gretlie taken up and used in England, against Rewmes and some other diseases engenderd in the longes and inward partes and not without effect.'[50]

---

47 Talbott and Lilienfeld 1959
48 Talbott & Terplan, 1960
49 Sk11805

---

50 Harrison 1573

ILLUS 95
Pipe facets

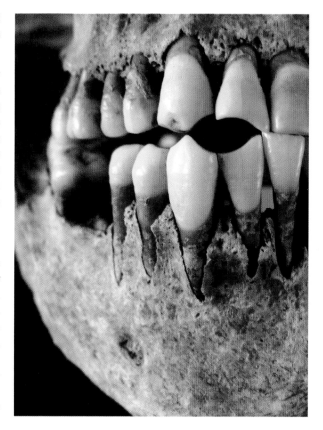

The above evidence does show that Bone Only burials must have extended at least into the late 16th century. It is perhaps also interesting (although the sample size is not large enough to comment on significance here) that the two females exhibiting pipe facets were found in Simple Coffin burials.

Hereditory symptoms, medical conditions and general wear and tear can result in a variety of effects on the skeletal structure that in some cases can become quite visible. This must certainly have been the case for a male older adult[51] in a Bone Only burial who had badly affected upper (thoracic) and middle (lumbar) parts of the spinal column[52] consistent with a diagnosis of **Scheuermann's disease** (Illus 96). This would have given him a markedly stooped profile.

Some conditions can be traced back to pregnancy and birth. One individual, an older adult male from a Bone Only burial[53] showed signs of a defect relating to injury during birth known as **Erb's palsy** (Illus 97). This manifested itself as wasting away of the left upper arm, forearm, shoulder and half of the collar bone. The left wrist and hand were unaffected. The injury also appears to have affected development of the upper two vertebrae

(with asymmetry in the atlas and axis, both of which slope downwards laterally to the right side and skull), and the right occipital of the skull appearing more flattened than the left. These features may indicate that this individual suffered from a twisted neck in which the head is tipped to one side, while the chin is turned to the other (called torticollis).

The skeletal manifestations are most consistent with a diagnosis of *Erb's palsy*. The combination of the stunted growth of the arm and the deformities of the epiphyses suggests that *trauma* occurred at an early age, and most probably at birth[54]. Brachial plexus injuries at

---

51 Sk2098
52 *Invertebral osteochondrosis* with destruction of annular rings on the superior bodies of vertebrae T7 to L5 accompanied by anterior wedging and *kyphosis*
53 Sk2874

---

54 Obstetrical injury affects 0.19% of live births, Evans-Jones et al 2003

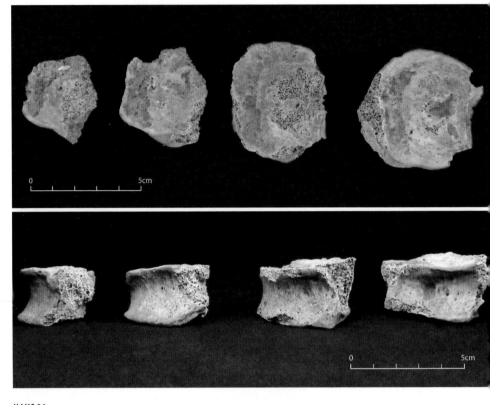

ILLUS 96
Scheuermann's disease

birth most commonly occur when the baby's shoulder becomes stuck against its mother's pubic bone (shoulder dystocia) and in the process of trying to manoeuvre the child out excessive force is applied to the baby's neck and head resulting in stretching and/or tearing of the brachial plexus nerves causing paralysis of the upper limb and torticollis[55].

It is interesting to note that this presumably medieval individual survived to become an older adult despite a considerable disability for the period.

The above example probably falls outside of the group of congenital diseases which are conditions that an individual is born with and can either be caused by an inherent genetic defect or by factors affecting the foetus during development such as infection or malnutrition. It is estimated that around 40% of congenital conditions affect the skeleton[5] and range from very slight skeletal changes that do not have any recognisable external symptoms (asymptomatic) to serious defects that are incompatible with life.

The most prevalent congenital developmental defects in individuals from Hereford Cathedral related to the vertebral column and rib cage (Table 46).

---

55   Becker et al 2002

56   Aufderheide & Rodriguez-Martin 1998, 51

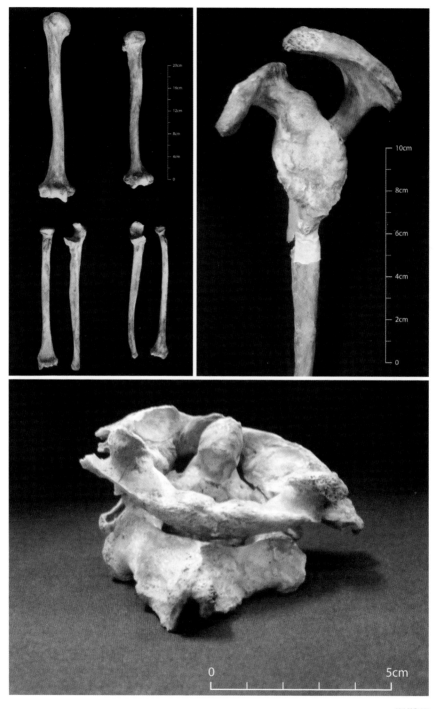

ILLUS 97
Erb's palsy

CONDITION	NO. OF CASES	PREVALENCE CALCULATED FROM	PREVALENCE
Congenital scoliosis	2	461 individuals with 1 + vertebrae	0.4%
Klippel-Fiel syndrome	4	394 individuals with 2+ cervical vertebrae	1.0%
Cleft cervical arch	2 cervical 2 C1	401 cervical arches (older child +) 194 individuals with C1	0.5 1.0%
Cleft sacral arch	69	250 individuals with sacral arches (adult)	27.6%
C8	3	427 C7 present	0.7%
L6	20	568 L5 present	3.5%
T13	11	526 T12 present	2.1%
Cranial border shift at the thoracic-lumbar junction	3	427 C7 present	0.7%
Caudal border shift at the thoracic-lumbar junction	1	563 L1 present	0.2%
Sacralisation of L5	26	364 individuals with S1 present	7.1%
7th cervical rib	4	427 C7 present	0.9%
Rib segmentation error	1	661 individuals with 1+ ribs	0.2%
Pigeon chest	1	305 individuals with a sternum	0.3%

TABLE 46

Congenital defects of the spine and rib cage

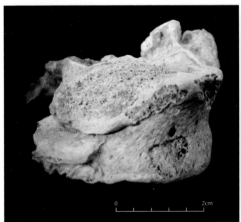
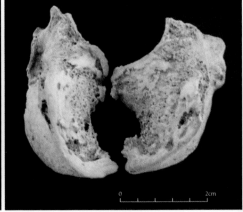

ILLUS 98
Scoliosis — cuneiform shaped vertebra and butterfly vertebra

CONDITION (EXTRA-SPINAL)	NO. OF CASES	PREVALENCE CALCULATED FROM	PREVALENCE
Mendosa suture retained	1	316 individuals with an occipital (adults)	0.32%
Craniosynostoses (brachycephaly)	2	45 individuals with intact cranial vaults	4.45%
Agenesis of hamate hook	6 individuals	133 individuals with a hamate (adults)	4.50%
	9 hamates	482 total adult hamates	1.87%
Bipartite medial cuneiform	3 individuals	258 individuals with a medial cuneiform	1.16%
	3 m. cuneiforms	409 total medial cuneiforms	0.73%
Non fusion of navicular epiphysis	1 individual	224 individuals with a navicular (adults)	0.45%
	2 naviculars	356 total naviculars	0.28%
Tarsal coalition – Calaneo-navicular	1	346 individuals with 2 plus tarsal bones	0.29%
	1	355 individuals with a calcareous or navicular	0.28%

TABLE 47
Defects of the skull and appendicular skeleton

Like the individual noted above with *Scheuermann's disease*, two further individuals are likely to have exhibited stooping, in this case as a result of **scoliosis**, a condition that results in a curvature of the spine (Illus 98). The first is an older Bone Only male[57], the second younger Simple Coffin male[58], clearly both surviving into adulthood.

A younger middle male Cist burial[59], had a wide and short sternum with a pronounced outward (anterior) curve consistent with **pigeon chest** which can be associated with a number of major health complaints and affect breathing (Illus 99). It is also likely to have had a pronounced visual appearance marking him out from his peers.

Congenital defects of the skull and appendicular skeleton were also observed during analysis (Table 47).

It is worth considering a few of the cases and considering these alongside other conditions that had an impact on people's lives within the city.

Two individuals in the assemblage had a condition which forces the skull to grow wide relative to its length (**craniosynostoses**), although it should be remembered that in the Hereford assemblage there were relatively few skulls which were sufficiently intact to observe cranial deformities.

An older female from an Elaborate Coffin[60] is likely to have suffered from restrictive ankle movement (due to *tarsal coalition* in her left foot), pain and potentially a form of painful flat foot called peroneal spastic flatfoot[61]. It is likely that the individual would at least have walked with a pronounced limp, and potentially needed to use some form of support such as a stick. Again this is another individual that seems to have suffered into older age. Given that her condition was potentially quite painful it is interesting to ponder on the types of treatments she might have been given over her lifetime.

57 Sk31487
58 Sk2308
59 Sk30194

60 Sk11886
61 Leonard 1974

There are other examples where individuals may have had a limp such as five adults exhibiting skeletal changes consistent with a diagnosis of **Legg-Calvé-Perthes disease**. In total, three females, including two younger-middle and one older-middle adult[62], as well as two older-middle males[63] were affected, giving a prevalence rate of 1%[64]. In addition to this, three individuals also showed a **slipped femoral capital epiphysis**, another condition affecting the head of the femur (Illus 100). This condition did not appear to be specific to any particular period affecting Cist, Bone Only and Elaborate Coffin burials.

Benign tumours are growths where the cells are not likely to invade surrounding tissue, but nevertheless may have some health effects. A total of 27 adults were affected by these[65] comprising 15 males and 11 females (Table 48).

The most common type of tumour was a small button-like growth of bone called an **osteoma**.

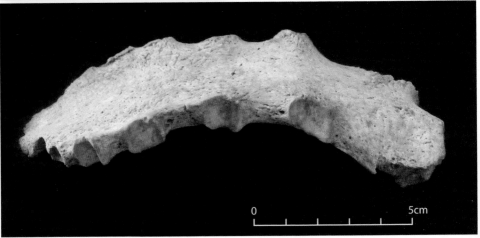

ILLUS 99
Pigeon chest

62 Cist Sk2208, Elaborate Coffin Sk3945, Bone Only Sk5378
63 Bone Only Sk10457, Elaborate Coffin Sk4641
64 5/434 of individuals with a femoral head (or 5/767 total femur heads)
65 CPR 3.7%

SKELETON	BURIAL GROUP	SEX	AGE CATEGORY	TUMOUR TYPE & LOCATION
Sk1790	Cist	M	18+	Osteoma, right mandible
Sk4934	Cist	M	O AD	Osteoma, frontal bone
Sk2227	Bone Only	M	O–M AD	Two osteomas, frontal bone
Sk3150	Bone Only	M	O AD	Multiple osteomas (*c* 29), frontal bone
Sk4566	Bone Only	F	O AD	Osteoma, frontal bone
Sk4602	Bone Only	F	O–M AD	Osteoma, mandible
Sk5186	Bone Only	F	O–M AD	Probable osteoblastoma, frontal bone
Sk10440	Bone Only	M	18+	Osteoma, right parietal
Sk10478	Bone Only	F	Y–M AD	Two osteomas, frontal bone
Sk10601	Bone Only	M	O–M AD	Multiple osteomas, both parietals (5) & mandible (1)
Sk11398	Bone Only	M	Y–M AD	Enchondroma, right humeral head
Sk12276	Bone Only	F	O–M AD	Bone cyst, left ilium
Sk12313	Bone Only	M	O AD	Bone cyst, left proximal humerus
Sk12383	Bone Only	F	18+	Bone cyst, right ilium
Sk30173	Bone Only	M	O–M AD	Two osteomas, frontal bone
Sk31232	Bone Only	F	Y–M AD	Osteoma, left parietal bone
Sk40300	Bone Only	F	Y–M AD	Two osteomas, frontal & left parietal bones
Sk40600	Bone Only	M	O–M AD	Osteoma, right parietal bone
Sk1834	Simple Coffin	M	Y–M AD	Ossifying fibroma filling left maxilla sinus and entire area between palatine process and orbital surface
Sk2087	Simple Coffin	F	O–M AD	Osteoma, frontal bone
Sk2999	Simple Coffin	F	O AD	Osteoma, zygomatic bone
Sk3508	Simple Coffin	M	O–M AD	Osteoma, mandible
Sk11969	Simple Coffin	M	O–M AD	Osteoma, left parietal bone
Sk30066	Simple Coffin	F	O–M AD	Osteoma, right parietal bone
Sk30602	Simple Coffin	M	18+	Multiple osteomas (5), left & right parietals
Sk11408	Elaborate Coffin	M	O–M AD	Bone cyst, left acromion process of scapula
Sk11548	Elaborate Coffin	M	Y–M AD	Enchondroma, left femoral head

TABLE 48

Cases of benign tumours

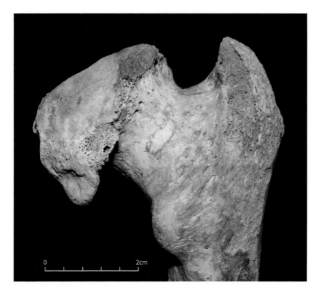

ILLUS 100
Slipped femoral capital epiphysis

present in the pelvis (ilium), and two males with the upper arm (proximal humerus) and shoulder (acromion process of the scapula) being affected. These may not have been so obvious to outside observers, unlike the following case.

Possibly the most disfiguring case of benign tumour affected a 30–35 year old male from a Simple Coffin burial[70]. A globular mass called an **ossifying fibroma** filled the area behind the left central part of his face (Illus 103). He must have had a considerable disfigurement of the face as well as problems with breathing through his nose.

At Hereford 19 individuals, 5.3%[66] of adults with observable facial or vault bones of the skull, exhibited *osteomas*. Interestingly, although the majority of individuals affected had only one or two *osteomas*, three adult males (all from medieval burials) exhibited more[67]. Multiple *osteomas* on the forehead can lead to facial disfigurement.

An older-middle female[68], exhibited a localised subcortical bone-forming lesion on the right front part of her skull measuring 4cm by 3cm and most likely represents an **osteoblastoma** which may have caused localized pain[69] (Illus 101).

Two younger adult males had growths within their upper arm and leg, called *enchondromas* (Illus 102).

There were four cases of fluid filled spaces called **bone cysts**, two females with cysts

Perhaps the most interesting point that comes out of the above catalogue of ailments is the number of individuals with quite debilitating or disfiguring conditions who survived into adulthood. It is perhaps difficult to determine whether there was any discrimination against these individuals and the numbers under consideration probably wouldn't withstand robust statistical analysis. However, of those mentioned above with numerous *osteomas* (possibly resulting in some facial disfigurement) they all exhibited some signs of poor diet through (*porotic hyperstosis* either active or healed). There was little indication from the teeth that this occurred during childhood (*dental enamel hypoplasia*) with only one individual exhibiting one tooth affected. There is no real pattern to the remaining indications of poor diet and notably the individual with *Erb's palsy* shows no signs of not being well cared for.

66   19/356
67   Sk30602 having five *osteomas*, Sk10601 a total of six, and Sk3150 had a profuse scattering of *osteomas*, approximately 29 in total, all on his frontal bone
68   Sk5186
69   Aufderheide & Rodriguez-Martin 1998, 376

70   Sk1834

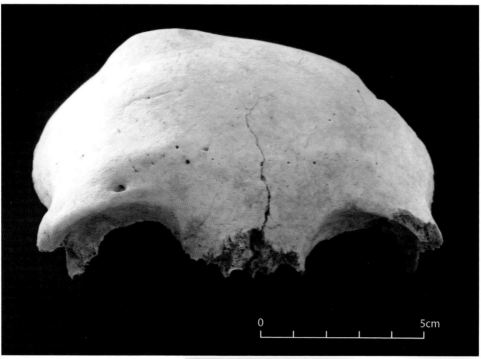

0   5cm

INJURIES AND VIOLENCE

Given the turbulent history that surrounds Hereford and its strained relationship with its Welsh neighbours as well as later battles such as those during the English Civil War, it might be expected that occupants of the city's main burial ground would exhibit the markers and reminders of these many violent events. However, for this to be the case, it would have been necessary in many instances for the individual to survive their injuries (and therefore be living back in the city when they died). It is also difficult in many cases to distinguish the cause of the injury, ie did they have an accident or was violence involved?

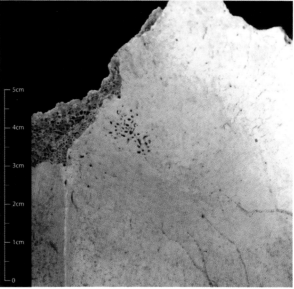

ILLUS 101
Probable osteoblastoma

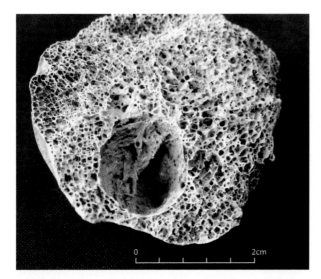

ILLUS 102
Enchondroma

onto an outstretched arm, and one older child[73] with a fracture to the *styloid process of the temporal bone* of the skull. The latter is most often caused by an intense blunt impact possibly of quite a serious nature[74].

Seven adult individuals exhibited injuries to the skull (Illus 104); with four towards the front and three towards the side. With the exception of one, all these were caused by a blunt force. The exception[75] had a healed linear wound on his right frontal bone which was most likely caused by an edged weapon of some kind. Only one individual[76] had more than one injury with a depression fracture on his left frontal and right parietal bones.

A wide range of traumatic pathological conditions can be observed in the skeleton. Fractures are by far the most frequent and the Hereford assemblage is no exception in this respect. Soft tissue injuries, by contrast, are relatively rarely detected but occur more frequently in living populations. Such conditions are important in the study of past populations as the types of *trauma* suffered will be related to lifestyle and occupation. Equally, a fracture may be due to an underlying pathological condition which highlights the health of the individual.

A total of 162 individuals had **fractured bones**. The relatively small number of fractures observed in children may be due to particularly good remodelling of young bones[71] also implying a relatively good level of immediate after care (Table 49). As such only two sub-adult individuals exhibited fractures, both from Bone Only burials and both of which had healed by the time of death. They include an adolescent[72] with a *Colles' fracture* of the lower arm (radius) usually caused by a fall

The majority of individuals with skull injuries were males, interestingly, however, an older-middle female from a Simple Coffin[77] also exhibited multiple *trauma* in other areas than just the head including two parry fractures and multiple haematomas some of these showed signs of having healed whilst others were in the process of doing so implying sustained and regular injury over a period of time (Table 50). The parry fracture of the upper arm (ulna) is usually associated with a defensive movement of raising the arm to fend off a blow[78] but it may occur when someone falls on the arm or tries to protect the body against a falling

---

71   Roberts 2000, 345; Wakely 1996, 81
72   Sk40248

---

73   Sk10302
74   McCorkell 1985
75   Sk10601
76   Sk10440
77   Sk3251
78   Merbs, 1989; Jurmain, 1991; Webb, 1995

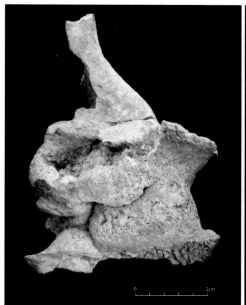
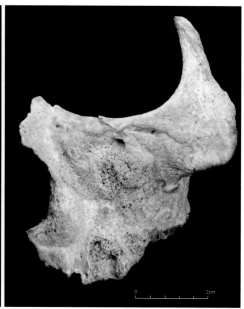

ILLUS 103
Ossifying fibroma, Sk1834

AGE	NO.	%
F	0/5	0.0
N	0/17	0.0
I	0/13	0.0
YC	0/95	0.0
OC	1/68	1.5
AO	1/38	2.6
All sub–adults	**2/236**	**0.8**
Y AD male	2/21	9.5
Y AD female	1/14	7.1
Y AD unsexed	0/1	0.0
Y–M male	22/57	38.6

AGE	NO.	%
Y–M female	9/51	7.6
O–M AD male	40/116	34.5
O–M AD female	30/81	37.9
O–M AD unsexed	0/2	0.0
O AD male	31/57	54.4
O AD female	15/47	31.9
O AD unsexed	1/1	100.0
AD male	8/20	40.0
AD female	1/6	16.7
All adults	160/474	33.8
Total	**162/710**	**22.8**

TABLE 49
Prevalence of all fractures by age and sex

147

SKELETON	SEX	AGE CATEGORY	BURIAL GROUP	DESCRIPTION
Sk2098	M?	O AD	Pre-Cist	Blunt force trauma to left frontal bone; oval depression measuring 10.8 x 7.0mm with edges well-remodelled but porosity and woven bone within central region. Two Rib fractures.
Sk5336	M	O–M AD	Cist	Blunt force trauma to left parietal boss region; well-healed circular depression measuring 8.4 x 7.1mm. Fracture of MC5; rotator cuff disease.
Sk10440	M	AD	Cist	Blunt force trauma to central-left frontal bone; 28.1 x 14.8mm in size, well-healed, exhibiting some porosity at base of depression. Blunt force trauma to right parietal; superior to parietal boss, 8 x 9mm, well- healed. Clay-shoveler's fracture.
Sk10601	M	O–M AD	Cist	Sharp force trauma on right frontal boss ; linear depressed area measuring 17.4 x 6.8mm, well-healed. Two rib fractures.
Sk30173	M	O–M AD	Bone Only	Blunt force trauma to left frontal; oval lesion 19.0 x 13.9mm. Two vertebral fractures and OD lesion.
Sk31558	F	Y–M AD	Bone Only	Blunt force trauma to left parietal?; anterior to parietal foramen close to sagittal suture, semi-circular depression broken post-mortem so extent unknown, healed. One vertebral fracture.
Sk3251	F	O–M AD	Simple Coffin	Right parietal, blunt force trauma; posterior to parietal boss, partial depression but broken post-mortem so extent unknown, on the endocranial surface vascular impressions are located around site of trauma. Bilateral ulna parry fractures; two vertebral fractures; haematomas bilateral femora and right tibial shaft.

TABLE 50
Cranial injuries with notes of other injuries to the same individuals

ILLUS 104
Cranial blunt and sharp trauma

heavy object. The presence of cranial *trauma*, parry fractures and multiple haematomas indicating blunt force *trauma* may indicate this individual was a victim of violence. Butler's[79] study of later-medieval ecclesiastical and criminal court records (from Essex and York) found that domestic violence was considered justified but there were efforts to limit it. The court employed strategies ranging from public humiliation, floggings, and fines to involving the community to correct the abusive spouse while preserving the marriage.

The most common location, by far, for a fracture in the adults was in the spine (Table 51). In total there were 160 vertebral fractures in 85 individuals, with all but three, being compression fractures to the vertebral bodies (Illus 105). Vertebral compression fractures usually result from a fall on the buttocks or downward blow to the head (Illus 106). They were more common in males than females in Hereford and both sexes were affected to a greater extent in the lower (lumbar and thoracic) regions of the spine (Table 52). It is likely that some of these fractures in older adults are secondary to the vertebrae being weakened by *osteoporosis* and in one individual[80], by cancer. In ten individuals compression fractures were severe and/or numerous enough to produce a spinal deformity (nine exhibited mild to moderate

ANATOMICAL SITE	MALE	FEMALE	UNSEXED	SUB-ADULT	TOTAL	% OF TOTAL
Skull	6	2	0	1	9	4.2%
Spine	54*	31*	0	0	85	39.9%
Rib	35	8*	1	0	44	20.7%
Clavicle	3	1	0	0	4	1.9%
Scapula	1	3*	0	0	4	1.9%
Humerus	1	1	0	0	2	0.9%
Radius	9	8	0	1	18	8.5%
Ulna	7	6	0	0	13	6.1%
Carpals	2	0	0	0	2	0.9%
Metacarpals	7	0	0	0	7	2.3%
Phalanges	1	0	0	0	1	0.5%
Acetabulum	1	0	0	0	1	0.5%
Patella	1	0	0	0	1	0.5%
Tibia	1	5	0	0	6	2.8%
Fibula	5	8	0	0	13	6.1%
Metatarsals	3	0	0	0	3	1.4%
Total	137	73	1	2	213	100%

+Fractures of the ribs and vertebrae have been counted as a single occurrence, irrespective of how many bones were broken; *Three scapula and one rib are a result of *osteomalacia* and in the spine seven females and one male had fractures associated with *osteoporosis*

TABLE 51
Distribution of fractures by anatomical site

kyphosis, a forward bending of the spine, and one had *scoliosis*, a lateral curvature).

The second most commonly fractured bones were the ribs and it is here that evidence for violent *trauma* becomes more obvious and easier to interpret. In total 35 males and eight females (and one unsexed individual) had fractured ribs and out of all the locations where breaks occurred this was the only one

---

79   Butler 2007
80   Sk4486

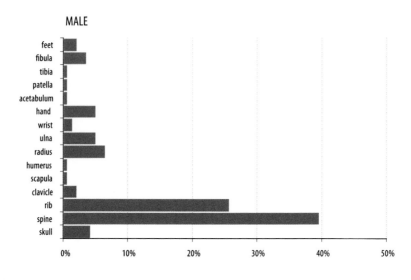

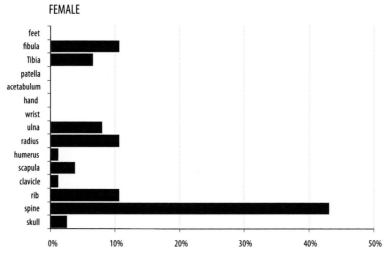

ILLUS 105
Distribution of fractures by anatomical site and sex

to demonstrate a statistically significantly difference between the sexes[81]. Of the men, 19 had more than one rib broken, the maximum being nine. Rib fractures are generally caused by a direct impact, such as a fall against a hard object, or, in the case of multiple rib fractures, by a crushing injury to the chest. They may also be a result of brawling, usually from a kick when the individual is on the floor which is more likely to involve male individuals[82]. Interestingly there were three males (four fractures) in the assemblage who exhibited boxer's fractures, that is to the proximal or distal extremity of a metacarpal bone of the hand.

---

81   $x^2 = 8.90$, p= 0.003

82   Sirmali et al 2003

ILLUS 106
Vertebral compression fracture

The majority of rib fractures were well-healed at the time of death, however four male individuals, including two with nine rib fractures each[83], exhibited ribs at differing stages of healing indicating that more than one episode of *trauma* had occurred. Also, these four men plus two women exhibited rib fractures which were in the early stages of healing implying the injuries had occurred relatively shortly before death[84].

Of the two women, one from a Bone Only burial[85] had a rib fracture possibly associated with weakened bones (*osteomalacia*). The other, buried in a Simple Coffin[86], was the only individual with a *comminuted fracture* to the rib, where the bone breaks into multiple fragments, most likely due to direct impact (Illus 107). One of her mid-ribs exhibited a rectangular 'hole' (6.9mm by 3.8mm) on its ventral surface. A small amount of woven bone was present around its edges, and radiating fracture lines indicated a *comminuted fracture* in which fragment/s had been lost post-mortem. This individual died approximately one week after the injury occurred. It is quite likely the result of a projectile of some description such as a crossbow bolt or arrow.

Of particular note is one of the men with nine rib fractures[87] (Illus 108). This was an older adult

83   Sk10457 and Sk5347
84   Un-united ends with callus or woven bone spicules present
85   Sk31645
86   Sk11116
87   Sk5347

	CERVICAL VERTEBRAE		THORACIC VERTEBRAE		LUMBAR VERTEBRAE		TOTAL	
	No.	%	No.	%	No.	%	No.	%
Male	2/858	0.2	66/2196	3.0	29/968	3.0	97/4022	2.4
Female	4/615	0.7	38/1671	2.3	18/741	2.4	60/3027	2.0
Total adults*	6/1480	0.4	104/3883	2.7	47/1715	2.7	157/7078	2.2

*figures for total adults includes data from unsexed adults

TABLE 52
Adult prevalence of vertebral compression fractures in differing regions of the spine

man from a Cist burial. Along with his nine dorsally located rib fractures, he also sustained a *comminuted fracture* to the right shoulder as well as a lower leg (fibular) fracture. The scapula (shoulder blade) had been pushed forwards and an irregular 'hole' that had subsequently healed was present close to the edge of the bone. The hole itself measured 20mm in one direction although its extent in the other had been lost through damage to the bone after burial. The fracture to the lower right leg was also healed by time of death. The location of the rib fractures and the scapula fracture could represent a backwards fall from height with penetration of the scapula by a hard object which pushed it forward at the same time.

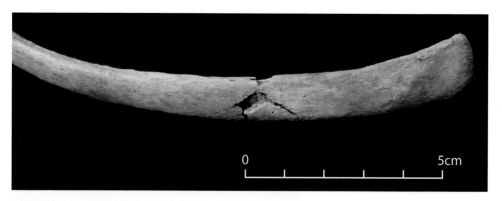

ILLUS 107
Comminuted fracture of rib, Sk11116

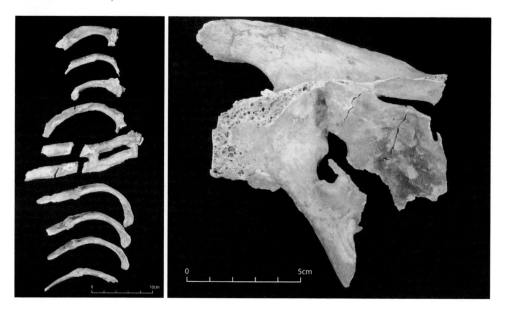

ILLUS 108
Fractured ribs and scapula, Sk5347

Another male, an older adult from an Elaborate Coffin[88], exhibited the only fracture to the pelvic bone consisting of a *comminuted fracture* to the left hip socket (acetabulum). A large central triangular fragment of the acetabulum was missing and the remaining hole had irregular but well-healed margins.

This fracture resulted in infection (*osteomyelitis*) around the fracture site, plus secondary osteoarthritic changes to the hip joint (both acetabulum and femoral head exhibited excessive degeneration or eburnation). Acetabular fractures either occur with high-velocity *trauma* eg auto collisions in modern populations or falls when the head of the femur is driven into the pelvis or as an

88 Sk5615

insufficiency fracture due to weakened bone as a result of *osteoporosis* in older adults.

Overall, males exhibited fractures at a wider range of anatomical sites compared to females. Females had more fractures to their forearms and lower legs than males. The most common arm fracture in both sexes was a *Colles' fracture*, a fracture at the wrist. The fracture is most probably caused by people putting their arms out to protect themselves from a fall and people with *osteoporosis* may be particularly susceptible to breaks of this kind. In the lower arm (ulna) parry fractures (mid-shaft) were the most common type with three females[89] and three males[90] exhibiting this. In one Bone Only female[91] and one Simple Coffin male[92] both the forearm bones were fractured at the mid-shaft position exhibiting spiral fractures indicating a twisting force was involved (Illus 109). This could have resulted from operating machinery that had a rotary action such as milling apparatus.

Breaks of the lower leg affected females near the ankle (distal fibula) whilst in males was more common nearer the knee (proximal fibula). Breaks in the larger of the lower leg bones (tibia) occurred as a compression fracture in a male[93] and female[94] Bone Only burial at a point just below the knee (tibial plateau) (Illus 110). Fractures of the tibial plateau are frequently associated with soft tissue injuries including the ligaments within and without the knee joint[95].

In total, 38% of males and 28% of females suffered fractures, suggesting that men

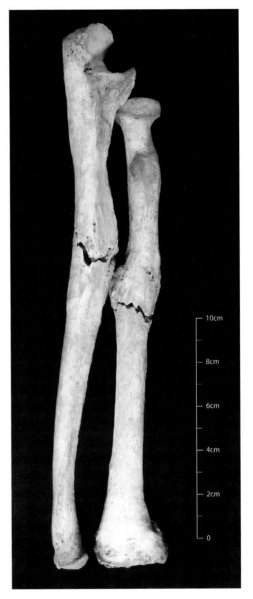

ILLUS 109
Radial and ulna fractures

---

89   Sk5133, Sk5186, Sk3251
90   Sk4237, Sk2609, Sk3053
91   Sk5186
92   Sk2533
93   Sk3032
94   Sk5017
95   Bennett & Browner 1994

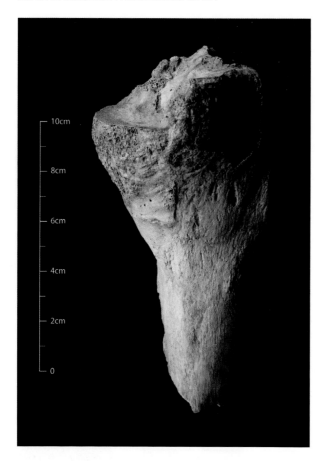

- 10cm
- 8cm
- 6cm
- 4cm
- 2cm
- 0

ILLUS 110
Tibial plateau fracture

through time with a significant[98] difference between the medieval (Pre-Cist, Cist and Bone Only) and later post-medieval (Elaborate Coffin) periods.

At Hereford 33.8% of adults showed one or more fracture, and in total 0.9% of bones were fractured. The occurrence is higher than the canons and wealthy lay folk at St Andrews Fishergate (21%), and the rural populations from Wharram Percy (19%; 0.6% of bones) and Barton-on-Humber (8% of individuals 15 years or older). At St-Helens-on-the-Walls the prevalence of individuals with one or more long bone shaft fracture (excluding clavicles) was recorded resulting in a prevalence of 4.4% for adults[99]. The comparable prevalence at Hereford is 9.6% so individuals at Hereford also sustained more fractures than low status urban dwellers.

It has been found that long-bone fractures were more frequent in rural medieval populations compared to their urban counterparts[100]. The study used a denominator including all complete bones plus any incomplete ones that show fractures. The Hereford prevalence recalculated using this denominator is 12% of individuals affected and 3% of bones. This is higher than the range given for urban sites of 4.7% to 5.5%, and fits between the prevalences for the two rural sites being used

were more at risk of fracture in the past (Table 53). At Hereford the difference is more pronounced in the Cist and Elaborate Coffin groups, but only in the later group was there a statistically significant difference between the sexes[96]. Within the burials groups, those in Cist burials most frequently suffered from fractures. Through time there is a significant[97] drop in fracture prevalence in males from the medieval groups (Pre-Cist, Cist and Bone Only) to the late-medieval/early post-medieval period (Simple Coffins). In the females, when the medieval groups are combined there is a decline in fracture rate

---

96 $x^2 = 6.54$, p= 0.01
97 $x^2 = 8.64$, p= 0.003

98 $x^2 = 6.65$, p= 0.009
99 Grauer & Roberts 1996
100 Judd & Roberts 1999

as a comparison including Jarrow Abbey, with a 10.7% by individual and a 2.2% by bone, and Raunds at 19.4% and 3.5% respectively. Overall, the comparison suggests that Hereford adults exhibited a relatively high rate of fractures in general especially if it is to be considered as an urban centre.

There were two instances of injuries caused by **edged weapons**. The first is noted above under cranial injuries, an older middle adult man[101] from a Cist burial with a well healed cut to the head (Table 50). The second is an older-middle adult female from a Bone Only burial[102]. The end of her right arm displayed evidence of angular cut-marks indicating that her forearm had been severed just above the wrist (Illus 111). The ends of both bones were healed by the time of death, but there is evidence that the wound was repeatedly infected with both healed and active infection (*periostitis*) present around the distal bone shafts. The humerus also exhibited active infection which was possibly related, as well as a healed fracture to her left tibial plateau.

There are eight identified cases of **dislocation**: seven individuals with evidence of a dislocated joint; and one partial dislocation (subluxation) (Table 54). As most cases of dislocation are almost immediately repaired there would not be any trace on the skeleton so only cases of untreated prolonged dislocation where a new joint surface is formed can be identified. Therefore although dislocation is relatively common in living populations it tends to be quite rare in skeletal ones.

101 Sk10601
102 Sk10400

BURIAL GROUP	MALES		FEMALES		TOTAL NO. AFFECTED (ADULTS & SUB-ADULTS)	
	No.	%	No.	%	No.	%
Pre-Cist	0/1	0.0	1/5	20.0	1/8	12.5
Cist	11/27	40.7	2/8	25.0	13/44	29.5
Bone Only	59/132	44.7	36/98	36.7	98*/409	24.0
Simple Coffin	13/59	22.0	13/56	23.2	26/153	17.0
Elaborate Coffin	20/52	38.5	4/32	12.5	24/96	25.0
Total	103/271	38.0	56/199	28.1	162/710	22.8

*includes one unsexed adult and the two sub-adults affected

TABLE 53
Prevalence of fractures by sex and burial group

Three individuals[103] showed evidence of a type of dislocation of the jaw[104] termed anterior dislocation, which results from excessive mouth opening such as from yawning, laughing, taking a large bite, seizure, or intraoral procedures such as tooth extraction[105].

There was also one dislocated hip[106] (Illus 112) and two dislocated elbows (radii)[107]. The latter is one of the most frequently recorded dislocations in later-medieval assemblages[108], though in one case here[109] it is associated with *Erb's palsy* (see Chapter 6).

Occasionally there can be exuberant bone growth (*ossification*) in muscle tissue where it joins the bone due to muscle *trauma* (technically called *myositis ossificans traumatica* – although as

103 Sk11805, Sk5151, Sk2204
104 TMJ = temporomandibular joint
105 Ardehali et al 2009
106 Sk3085
107 Sk30141, Sk2874
108 Roberts & Cox 2003, 238
109 Sk2874

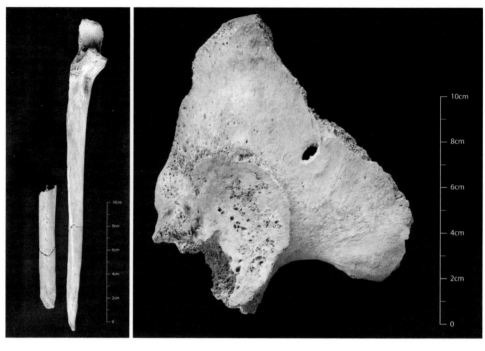

ILLUS 111
Severed hand, Sk10400

ILLUS 112
Hip dislocation, Sk3085

SKELETON	SEX	AGE	BURIAL GROUP	DESCRIPTION
Sk11805	M	O–M AD	Cist	Left
Sk2874	M	O AD	Bone Only	Left radial head – new joint surface formed superior
Sk3032	M	O–M AD	Bone Only	Right talus – medial subluxation with secondary OA
Sk3085	F	O–M AD	Bone Only	Left hip joint – left ilium has a new joint surface
Sk3213	M	Y AD	Bone Only	Right distal radius – new joint surface on anterior of
Sk5151	F	Y–M AD	Bone Only	Right
Sk30141	M	Y AD	Bone Only	Left radial head – small oval depression present
Sk2204	M	O–M AD	Simple Coffin	Right

TABLE 54

Dislocation cases

in the case of Hereford burials it affects ligaments heterotopy is a more relevant term)[110], thus giving a rare glimpse of **soft tissue injuries** (Illus 113). Twenty-four adults at Hereford exhibited this[111] with the vast majority showing *trauma* to the muscles or ligaments of their legs (Table 55). One of the more common injuries affected the ligament responsible for stabilisation of the knee (medial collateral ligament). This ligament is usually injured when the outside of the knee is struck causing it to buckle, the inside to widen, overstretching and resulting in tearing and injury[112]. The other

110   Ortner 2003, 134
111   CPR = 3.38%
112   Singhal et al 2009

SKELETON	BURIAL GROUP	AGE CATEGORY	SEX	SITE	SIDE
SK 11785	Cist	O—M AD	M	Femur – vastus lateralis	L
SK 31344	Cist	O AD	M	Femur – short head of triceps	R
SK 2501	Bone Only	O—M AD	M	Femur – vastus medialis	L
SK 3032	Bone Only	O—M AD	M	Tibia + fibulae – posterior + anterior tibiofibular lig. Tibia – tibialis posterior	L+R
SK 3749	Bone Only	O—M AD	M	Femur – gluteus maximus	L
SK 3897	Bone Only	O AD	M	Fibula – flexor hallicus longus	R
SK 4242	Bone Only	O—M AD	M	Tibia – medial collateral ligament	R
SK 11479	Bone Only	O—M AD	M	Femur – distal medial adductor tubercle	R
SK 11850	Bone Only	O—M AD	M	Tibiae – proximal postero-superior tibio-fibular ligament, pseudoarthrosis with left fibula	R+L
SK 30390	Bone Only	O—M AD	F	Clavicle – deltoid	R
SK 31571	Bone Only	O—M AD	M	Tibia – distal anterior tibiofibular ligament	R
SK 40303	Bone Only	O—M AD	M	Tibia – soleal	L
SK 40318	Bone Only	Y—M AD	M?	Femur – gluteus maximus	R
SK 40612	Bone Only	O—M AD	F	Fibula – distal anterior tibiofibular ligament	R
SK 2181	Simple Coffin	O—M AD	F	Tibia – distal anterior tibiofibular ligament	R
SK 2310	Simple Coffin	Y—M A	M	Tibia – medial collateral lig.	L
SK 3622	Simple Coffin	O—M AD	M	Tibia – distal posterior tibiofibular ligament	R
SK 11713	Simple Coffin	O—M AD	M	Femur – gluteus maximus	R
SK 40104	Simple Coffin	Y—M AD	M	Rib – intercostal muscle (assos. rib fracture)	L
SK 40656	Simple Coffin	O—M AD	M?	Tibia – distal anterior tibiofibular ligament	L
SK 1386	Elaborate Coffin	Y—M AD	M	Femur – medial collateral ligament	R
SK 1544	Elaborate Coffin	O—M AD	M	Fibula – proximal postero-superior tibiofibular ligament, with ankylosis of the tibia and fibula	L
SK 1549	Elaborate Coffin	Y—M AD	M	Tibia – medial collateral ligament	R
SK 12590	Elaborate Coffin	Y—M AD	F	Tibia– vastus medialis	R

TABLE 55

Cases of myositis ossificans traumatica

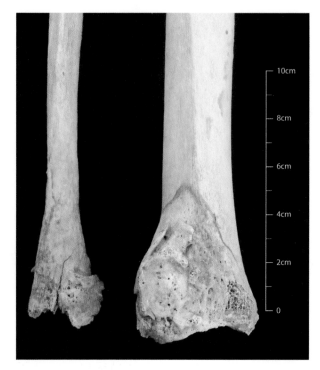

ILLUS 113
Myositis ossificans traumatica

apart from having one on both femurs and one on the right tibia also had multiple fractures (Table 50).

INFECTIOUS DISEASE & HEALTH

During the excavations for the New Library Building in 1993, a probable plague pit containing the bodies of about 180 people was discovered. There were no such indications within the current excavations, although grave cuts were impossible to identify, and burial density very high. The Black Death hit Herefordshire in 1348–9 and the Episcopal registers state 'It swept away half the population; land was untilled, and the supply of clergy (and their incomes) was lamentably reduced'[116]. A second outbreak occurred within Hereford in 1361–2 and spread with the same devastating effect. In addition early 14th century famines killed one third of the population[117]. The result was a greatly reduced population size recorded in the poll tax of 1377 (Table 56).

ligament affected within the assemblage is the one responsible for stabilizing the lower leg bones (fibula and tibia) at the ankle joint (anterior inferior tibiofibular ligament) and is the most commonly injured ligament in a sprained ankle[113].

Severe bruising, most commonly to the shin (anterior tibial surface), will frequently generate a localized collection of blood that subsequently is almost invariably ossified by the overlying membrane (periosteum) covering the bone[114]. Seven individuals exhibited localized sharply demarcated oval bone lesions which best fit the above diagnosis. Lesions were observed on both the lower and upper leg (tibiae and femur). Whilst it was usual for only one lesion to be visible on an individual it is worth drawing attention to a female in a Simple Coffin[115] who

Poor living conditions during the medieval and post-medieval periods were a major cause of outbreaks of infectious disease. In Hereford shortly after the Civil War the grand jury recorded that 'all the streets and back lanes within ye City be very foull and nastye for want of skvengers to keep it clean and hollsom.' Also acute overcrowding occurred within the city as for more than five centuries much of the

113 Takao et al 2003
114 Aufderheide & Rodriguez-Martin 1998, 27
115 Sk3251

116 Langford 1956, 147
117 Roseff 2003

158

increased population had been concentrated into the 93 acres enclosed by the 13th century walled defences. In the maps by John Speede (1610) and Isaac Taylor (1757) there are signs of overcrowding and a consequent outward movement, many places between the market place and the six gates were severely congested and run-down with poor hygiene and sanitation. Slaughter-houses were situated in the centre of town on Butchers Row and the streets were frequently blocked by cattle being sold. The bacteria-carrying dust from the excrement of livestock and all the transport horses must have caused many respiratory problems. Living in close quarters and working with animals is also believed to promote diseases such as tuberculosis.

Some infections are thought to be genetic but could also be triggered by ailments such as measles. The changes seen in one adult female[118] skeleton from a Simple Coffin represent a probable case of *Paget's disease* which is potentially measles-related.

Most of the infections that affected the population would have left no skeletal evidence, either because the infection was of the soft tissue or the gut, or because the individual died early in the course of the disease before skeletal manifestations occurred. Where it does affect the bones this is usually because it affects the membranes adjacent to them. In the Hereford assemblage there were two key membranes affected: that surrounding the outside surfaces of bones themselves (called the periosteum); and those surrounding the central nervous system (called meninges). In most cases although the evidence for this type of infection can be seen the thing that caused it is not known and is referred to as non-specific. However, in some cases the morphology and distribution of

YEAR	POPULATION	URBAN	RURAL	URBAN
1086	32,556	558	32,075	2%
c 1300	81,696	–	–	0.0%
1377	30,636	6,568	24,068	21%
1664	65,505	9145	56,360	14%
1801	88,436	19,831	68,605	22%

*Figures estimated from the Doomsday Survey of 1086, c 1300 from articles cited above, the poll tax in 1377, the Hearth Tax of 1664 and in 1801 the first official national census.

TABLE 56
Herefordshire population statistics (from Roseff 2003)

lesions in the skeleton permits identification of a particular disease such as *leprosy* (thus termed specific).

Inflammation of the membrane surrounding the bone, **periostitis**, can cause new bone formation on the surface of the bone. Whilst it is generally taken as an indication of bone infection in archaeological material[119] conditions other than bone infection such as *trauma*, bleeding and some forms of bone cancer may produce similar manifestations. Clearly disease was quite rampant within Hereford as 213 individuals showed non-specific infection on the bone surface[120] (Table 57). Of the bones affected 36%[121] exhibited active infection and the rest showed healed (remodelled) lesions.

In four bones (a right ulna, a right radius, and two left fibulae) *periostitis* was secondary to fracture and in one case it occurred as a result of a blade injury (the woman with a severed hand[122] described above), illustrating that diagnosis can be reliable.

---

118 Sk1823

119 Ortner 2003
120 96 males, 67 females, and 45 sub-adults
121 175/484
122 Sk10400

BONE	MALE			FEMALE			SUB-ADULT			TOTAL	
	No.	%	Individuals	No.	%	Individuals	No.	%	Individuals	No.	%
Maxilla	1/148	0.7	1	0/111	0.0	0	2/92	2.2	2	3/351	0.9
Mandible	1/189	0.5	1	0/144	0.0	0	0/2,142	0.0	0	1/476	0.2
Z	2/254	0.8	1	0/188	0.0	0	4/126	1.6	2	6/568	1.1
Scapula	0/428	0.0	0	1/322	0.3	1	3/282	1.1	3	4/1,037	0.4
Clavicle	0/384	0.0	0	2/303	0.7	2	1/268	0.4	1	3/960	0.3
Humerus	4/440	0.9	5	0/328	0.0	0	2/301	0.7	2	6/1,075	0.6
Radius	2/445	0.4	2	5/332	1.5	4	2/196	1.0	2	9/1,100	0.8
Ulna	1/447	0.2	1	4/337	1.2	3	2/311	0.6	2	7/1,101	0.6
Ribs	30/3,361	0.9	8^	33/2,343	1.4	8^	39/2,899	1.3	9^	102/8,636	1.2
Sacrum	0/219	0.0	0	0/173	0.0	0	1/144	0.7	1	1/539	0.2
Pelvis	3/469	0.6	3	3/353	0.8	3	2/353	0.6	2	8/1,182	0.7
Femur	32/463	6.9	23	17/341	5.0	11	19/342	5.6	14	68/1,154	5.9
Tibia	88/349	25.2	57	68/284	23.9	45	15/252	6.0	12	175+/891	19.6
Fibula	41/175	23.4	29	29/144	20.1	24	9/277	3.2	7	79/860	9.2
Calcaneous	0/255	0.0	0	1/224	0.4	1	1/115	0.9	1	2/599	0.3
Metatarsals	3/872	0.3	2^	5/1,009	0.5	1^	0/512	0.0	0^	10/2,401	0.4

*Unsexed adults are included in the total prevalence; + includes two unsexed individuals with 4 bones affected; ^ number of individuals with more than one bone affected

TABLE 57
Prevalence of non-specific periostitis by bone, showing numbers of individuals represented

The most frequent site of non-specific infection was the lower leg, with 137 of the 215 individuals showing *periostitis* (63.4%) having lesions on either of the two lower leg bones. The larger of these (tibia or shin bone) lying close to the skin surface is vulnerable to infection, ulceration and undergoes minor injury more frequently[123].

Forty-seven individuals had *periostitis* on the inside (visceral) surface of the ribs, and although there are a number of differential diagnoses[124], the lesions in these individuals are likely to represent a bony response to underlying (pleuro-pulmonary) infection relating to the lungs[125] (Illus 114). Such rib lesions have been found to be more frequent in tuberculosis than in other respiratory diseases[126].

123 Roberts & Manchester 1995

124 Matos & Santos 2006
125 Roberts et al 1998
126 Ibid; Roberts et al. 1994

ILLUS 114
Rib periostitis

Overall, non-specific *periostitis* affected 29.9% of the population at Hereford. This prevalence was higher than the vast majority of comparative sites, and lay closest to and in between the prevalences of St-Helens-on-the-Walls at 21.5%[127], St Andrew's Fishergate at 24.0% and Fishergate House at 41.8%, the latter assemblage having the only prevalence higher than that found at Hereford. This suggests that non-specific infection in Hereford is consistent with other contemporaneous urban centres, although at the higher end of the scale. A greater pathogen load in urban environments (versus rural eg Wharram Percy 8.4%) no doubt reflects the unhygienic and crowded conditions of medieval towns and cities. Looking at the medieval versus the post-medieval population there appears to be a slight decrease over time, 32% to 27% respectively. However, a large proportion of the later assemblage derives from higher status burials which could skew the picture somewhat.

A total of 20 individuals exhibited endocranial lesions. These are the result of inflammation or haemorrhage of the meninges though what caused them is unknown. They have been associated with *trauma*, primary and secondary infections of the meninges, tumours, tuberculosis, syphilis and vitamin deficiencies[128].

Three individuals[129] found in Bone Only burials may represent possible cases of clubbing (**hypertrophic osteoarthropathy**) (Illus 115). This is manifested by clubbing of the hands and feet, joint inflammation, and diffuse bone deposition beneath the surface of the bone[130]. In the skeleton, however, only the latter criterion usually manifests itself and it is only this therefore that is observable for diagnosis. All three individuals had a disease that was active at the time of death. The adolescent age (16–18 years) of the youngest man[131] may indicate a primary case. The older ages of the other man[132] (30–34 years) and woman[133] (48–55 years) suggests a secondary form of the disease as a more likely diagnosis. Interestingly, tuberculosis caused 22% of secondary infection of this type in the mid-20th century[134] and new bone formation is present on the ribs of both the adolescent and older man[135] suggestive of a chronic pulmonary infection (as noted above).

127 Grauer 1993
128 Lewis 2004
129 Sk2323, Sk2654 and Sk5286

130 Mays 2002
131 Sk2654
132 Sk5286
133 Sk2323
134 Locke 1915
135 Sk5286 and Sk2654

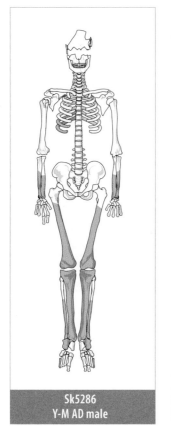
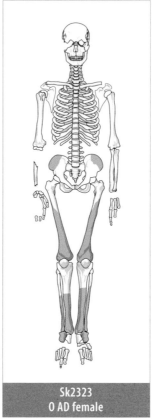
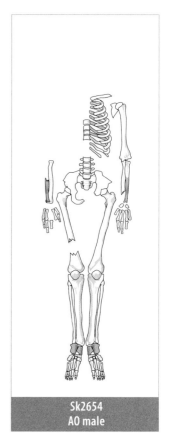

Sk5286
Y-M AD male

Sk2323
O AD female

Sk2654
AO male

ILLUS 115
Distribution of pathological changes in three possible cases of hypertrophic osteoarthropathy

However, none of these three individuals showed any skeletal lesions associated with a diagnosis of tuberculosis. There are very few reported cases of *hypertrophic osteoarthropathy* in skeletal assemblages, although five individuals from Wharram Percy were diagnosed with it.

Three cases[136] within the assemblage showed infection deeper into the bone, the compact bone (cortex) of skeletal elements being involved in the infection (**ostitis**)[137]. These

were a Bone Only adolescent[138] with the right ulna affected, the left radius of an adult female[139] from a Simple Coffin and the right tibia of older-middle female[140] also from a Bone Only burial.

In the Hereford assemblage seven individuals exhibited skeletal changes diagnostic of **osteomyelitis**, an inflammatory destruction of the bone. In five cases the long bones were affected and in the remaining two it was

---

136 CPR of 0.4%.
137 Roberts & Manchester 1995, 168

138 Sk30949
139 Sk3189
140 Sk4602

ILLUS 116
Osteomyelitis, Sk11031, Thomas Skyrme

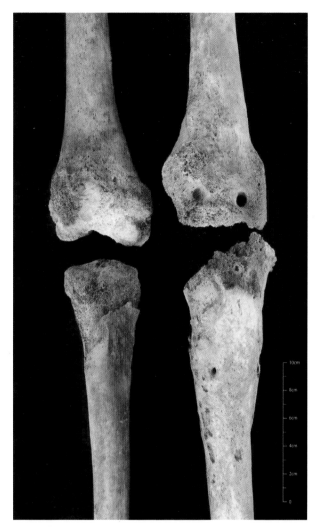

sited in the ribs[141] and pelvis[142]. All individuals affected were adults and it did not noticeably affect one sex more than the other. In two individuals[143], osteomyelitic infection was probably a result of compound (open) fractures which allowed direct contamination of the bone by bacteria. One man[144] exhibited *osteomyelitis* in his left leg about the knee (distal femur and proximal tibia) (Illus 116). This was the only named individual in the assemblage, Thomas Skyrme. His death notice in the Hereford Journal[145] records that he died 'after a long and painful illness'. This may infer that he suffered from a more generalized bacterial infection which spread to the bone.

A similar type of infection can occur in the spine (**discitis***)* and an older adult female from a Bone Only burial[146], exhibited focal erosions and bone growth that might be attributed to this condition although the vertebrae were not well preserved and diagnosis is tentative.

A child aged 9–12 years at death[147] from a Simple Coffin, had marked inequality in the

lower limbs which fitted best with a diagnosis of **polio**, compared to alternative diagnoses such as *trauma* or cerebral palsy (Illus 117). The right leg and feet bones are shorter and more gracile than those on the left side. Also the right side of the pelvis (ischium) is slightly smaller than the left and there are a lack of significant muscle attachments on the lower limbs of the right side compared to left. The paralysis of these muscles would clearly impact on the ability of this individual to walk normally. There are relatively few cases of *polio*

---

141 Sk4993
142 Sk5615
143 the pelvis of Sk5615 and the right lower leg (tibia) of Sk30722
144 Sk11031
145 Hereford Journal 1831
146 Sk4622
147 Sk11860

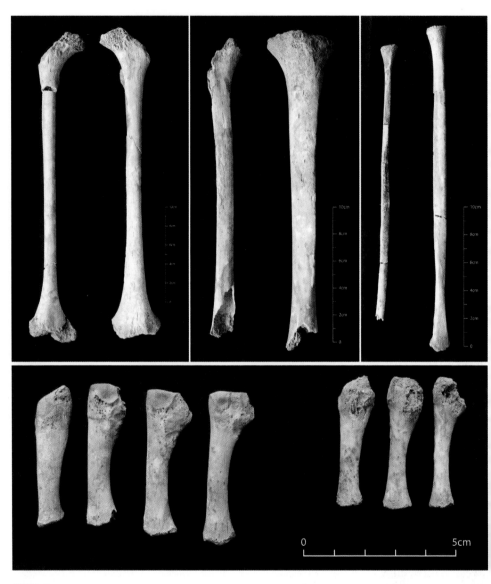

ILLUS 117
Polio, Sk11860

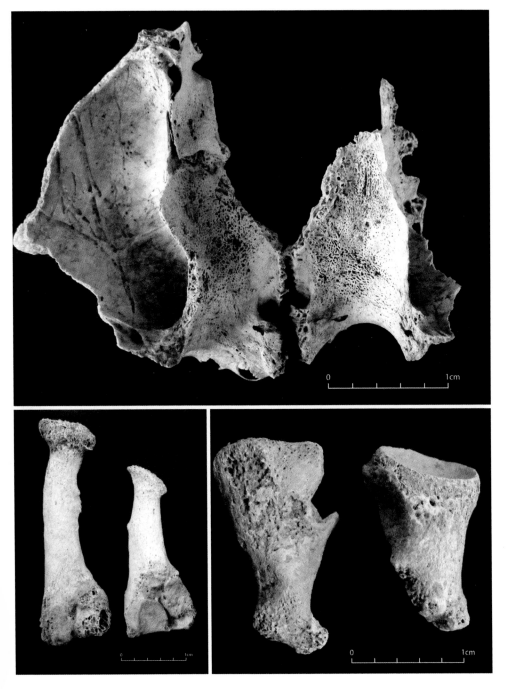

ILLUS 118
Leprosy, Sk2971

in the archaeological record despite the fact that it is thought to have great antiquity and was epidemic in historic times[148]. This may be because very few individuals survived the initial stages of infection.

Leprosy was possibly brought from eastern Asia to the Mediterranean by the troops of Alexander the Great and it spread on a large scale to Europe during the 4th century BC[149]. During the medieval period, as the disease became endemic in Europe, the awareness of the disorder increased. By the 12th and 13th centuries leper hospitals, as a means of isolation, were established with patients being interred in the hospital cemetery when they died. The hospital of St Giles (founded 1290) and the Lazarus hospital of Hereford were for lepers. There was apparently another St Giles Hospital in St Owen Street (founded 1150) which may also have been for lepers, and the Corporation manuscripts of Hereford contain a notification in 1547 of the appointment of collectors for 'the house of leprous persons founded in the worship of St Anne and St Loye'[150]. Due to the slow progress of the disease it has been known almost throughout time as the living death; 'Mundo mortuis sis, sed Deo vivas' – be thou dead to the world but alive unto God – was the medieval pronouncement to those diagnosed with *leprosy*[151].

The disease was diagnosed in one skeleton from the assemblage, a young adult male in a Bone Only burial[152] (Illus 72, 118). Clinically, the

resulting erosion of bones in the central part of the face results in 'saddle nose' with the sinking and widening of overlying skin and other soft tissues. The extremely obvious soft tissue deformity constitutes one of the major features of a *leprosy*-sufferer's facial alterations[153]. Changes to the remainder of the skeleton are the result of sensory loss due to nerve damage resulting in anaesthesia, circulatory disturbances and local pressure leading to resorption of feet and toe bones as well as the individual being prone to injury and secondary infection with ulcerations, thrombosis and gangrene[154]. The Hereford skeleton exhibited chronic infection in the bones (*periostitis*) of the lower leg as well as resorption (and tapering) of the ends of the right toes and feet bones some of which had enlarged proximal ends (cupped). This would result in changing the feet into club-shaped stubs[155].

Segregation of *leprosy* sufferers was routine in the 12th century[156], however, despite the fact that skeletal changes indicate that facial signs of *leprosy* would have been clearly visible this man was buried centrally within St Johns Quad. He was one of only two individuals to be buried in a crouched position although the other[157] did not show any signs of *leprosy* or any other infectious disease in their skeleton.

The finding of benign tumours in archaeological skeletons is relatively common and occurrences have been noted above (Table 48), however, since **malignant tumours** become common

---

148 Major 1954, 43
149 Kjellström 2012
150 Clay 1909
151 Roberts & Manchester 1995, 194
152 Sk2971 exhibits rhinomaxillary bone changes pathognomic of *leprosy* (lepromatous form; Auf 150). He has inflammation and destruction of the hard palate which has an extensive pitted and porous appearance. The margins of the pyriform aperture show resorption and remodelling – with the distance between the

aperture margins widened and the margins are thickened and rounded. Resorption of the anterior nasal spine and central part of the alveolar bone of the maxilla is present; minor pitting in both areas is indicative of superficial inflammation (Andersen & Manchester 1992).
153 Aufderheide & Rodriguez-Martin 1998, 144
154 Aufderheide & Rodriguez-Martin 1998, 152
155 Aufderheide & Rodriguez-Martin 1998, 145
156 Clay 1909
157 Sk30544

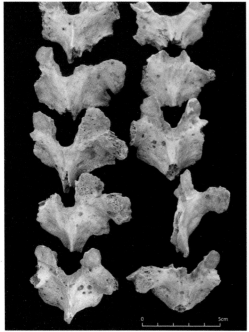
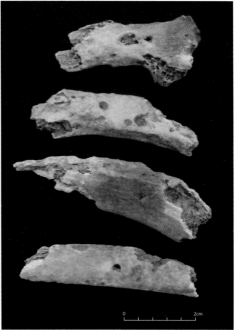

ILLUS 119
Multiple myeloma

only in the elderly the frequency of cancer in archaeological populations is less than that of modern populations as much fewer people survived to an older age. Five individuals exhibited skeletal changes associated with a malignant tumours[158].

Four individuals were diagnosed with **multiple myeloma** including a female of 48 years or more in a Simple Coffin burial[159] and a male in an Elaborate Coffin aged 35–44 years at death[160] (Illus 119). The disease is meant to be more common in males and usually occurs in individuals over 40 years of age. It represents a malignant transformation of plasma cells in bone marrow[161]. In later stages, sufficient bone

destruction can cause vertebral collapse and pathological fractures in long bones. The affected woman[162] exhibited profuse small lytic lesions (c 2mm diameter) on both pelvic bones (ilium and ischium), on two middle (lumbar) vertebral bodies and on the outer (endocranial) surface of the bone. The man[163] again exhibited characteristic lesions (1.5–4 mm diameter) on the upper and middle (thoracic and lumbar) vertebral bodies and arches, on the ribs, left collar bone (clavicle) and both shoulders (scapulae). The other two cases were younger women[164]. Because many organs can be affected by *myeloma*, the symptoms and signs vary greatly, although bone pain affects almost 70% of patients and is the most common symptom.

158 5/474 adults – CPR 1.0%

159 Sk4486

160 Sk1767

161 Roberts & Manchester 1995

162 Sk4486

163 Sk1767

164 Sk5771 Simple Coffin, and 3375 Elaborate Coffin

The other diagnoses of cancer identified was a possible case of **osteosarcoma** (a rare form of cancer in younger people) seen in an older child from a Bone Only burial[165].

OVERVIEW

The human skeletal remains provide a tantalising glimpse into early Hereford life. The old adage that perhaps more questions were raised than answered in many respects remains true, although there is nothing wrong with establishing new lines of enquiry. Looking back at what the project aimed to achieve this is a good point to remeasure the aspirations that were set at the outset and the level to which they were achieved. Can we see a difference in health or lifestyle between the earlier and later burials in the assemblage? Certainly the medieval population appears to have had a shorter life expectancy (Chapter 5). There appears to be a significant difference between how males and females were treated during the early medieval period, with Cist burials exhibiting a greater than three to one ratio in favour of males. A less pronounced but still notably similar trend was observed in the Elaborate Coffin burials. There is a general consideration that these two classes of burial are likely to be of higher status with respect to others on the site, and if this were the case then they could reflect a very real bias towards higher status males in society than females.

Another area where there appears to have been a clear distinction between male and females across the whole assemblage is the location of fractures. Men appear to experience breaks in the extremities (hands, wrists and feet) where women had none, whilst broken legs and arms were much more

common in women than men. The other significant bias occurred in a marked increase in broken ribs in men. This may go some way to identifying variations in occupational risk between the sexes (although there are other better indicators of this), or might relate to higher levels of violence in men with the ribs hands and feet more likely to be broken in brawls than other limbs. The coincidence of squatting facets and *osteoarthritis* of the knee in women does tent to suggest females were undertaking tasks nearer to the ground than men. In general *osteoarthritis* seems to affect the upper parts of the body more in men and lower parts in women. Whilst the onset of the condition is potentially more related to hereditary or dietary factors, the locations where it manifests itself in many cases could well indicate occupational stress and thus such distinctions may well be demonstrating variations in activities between the different sexes.

In terms of the dietary health of the population there are hints that childhood illness may have been prevalent, both through the presence of *dental enamel hypoplasia* on the teeth as well as the rare cases of *rickets* and *scurvy* in very young children possibly implying they were bed ridden for a period before dying at a very young age. *Dental enamel hypoplasia* could also indicate periods of malnutrition and other indications for iron or vitamin B12 deficiency were also observed within the population indicating dietary deficiency at various stages in life. Regarding the former it is more than 90% prevalent in the main bulk of the Bone Only burial groups implying that the general population from Hereford suffered some levels of stress such as malnutrition at some point in their life. This does appear to have improved a bit in the post-medieval period and those burials that might be classed as being higher in status have much lower percentage of occurrences.

165 Sk11988

Regarding the iron deficiency in some cases individuals can be seen to recover from this whilst in others the deficiencies seem to continue through to death. In terms of *cribra orbitalia* this seems to reduce in prevalence with age whilst the other indicator, *porotic hyperstosis*, peaks in the younger to middle adult age band. If the coincidence of *caries* in teeth and sugar in diet are to be believed then the increase in *caries* from the early medieval period through to the later burials could well imply that more refined sugar was finding its way into the diet of individuals during the later periods represented.

Many illnesses will not leave a trace in the skeletal record. Documentarily there is some indication of the severity and rapid progress of some diseases or afflictions such as in 1251 when the Sherriff of Herefordshire was taken ill at Hereford, so ill in fact that John de Neville (marshall of the exchequer) was directed by the treasurer and barons to receive his oath and appoint Robert de Trillet (Clerk) and Reginald de Rode to adjust and pass his accounts[166]. Alongside this many were long drawn out affairs such as the case of Sir Thomas Coningsby whose affliction was summed up in the following text: "to the honour of God, the father of every good and perfect gift, in thankfulness to him for his defence and protection, as well as in foreign travels as by sea and land, as also for his preservation against malice and evil practices at home; in submission to his chastisements upon the person of Sir Thomas, which have disabled his body in this world and enabled his mind and thoughts to the expectation of a world to come"[167]. The archaeological record above does indicate that many disabled or otherwise afflicted individuals were integrated into society, the above

---

166 Duncomb 1804, 347
167 Duncomb 1804, 405

documentary account seems to support this. One exception in the archaeological record seems to be where the result was a disfigurement to facial features.

There were very few instances of violent *trauma* within the excavated population. The instance of a female adult from a Bone Only medieval burial who had a completely severed hand is interesting. She was buried on the north side of the Cathedral but very close to it. Had she been a thief, it would seem unlikely that she would have been afforded such a prominent burial location. One female within the post-medieval population could have been a victim of domestic violence. She exhibited blunt force *trauma* to her skull and has parry fractures, which can occur when the arms are raised to protect the head from blows, on both arms. Given the turbulent history surrounding Hereford it is notable that there are very few injuries that might be classed as battle wounds. Perhaps one blade injury to a skull and a projectile wound in another instance. One s burial stands out with multiple wounds to various locations of his anatomy, and he will be discussed in more detail in the following chapter.

Regarding whether this assemblage is more like rural or urban ones recorded elsewhere then the first challenge is to find reliably consistent indicators from other populations. Certainly stature does not appear to hold any clues here as there is too much variability across both types of population. The Hereford assemblage appears to be slightly taller with respect to the comparative assemblages considered and also the medieval burials at Hereford are slightly taller than their later counterparts in the same burial ground. The number of fractures present within the assemblage could be more indicative of manual rural type activities, or simply a function of a rougher urban lifestyle.

The difficulties in interpreting the skeletal record are all too clear from the above few paragraphs. Once consideration as to the representativeness of the burial ground with respect to its living population is thrown into the mix then the problems that this raises for understanding the assemblage and comparing it to others becomes considerably magnified.

DELIBERATING THE VERDICT

In any forensic examination it is necessary to weigh up the physical evidence against the statements of witnesses, a similar case lies between archaeological and historical accounts. In the first instance the physical evidence might seem to be incontrovertible, but under cross examination it soon becomes clear that it is not so much the evidence but its subsequent interpretation that comes under scrutiny. Similarly the accounts of witnesses become blurred by time and this too applies to accounts of historic events where the interpretation of future commentators distorts and changes original accounts, the text for which has since been lost alongside potential original inaccuracies. So standing before the mass of evidence accumulated as part of the work undertaken during the excavation of the Cathedral Close between 2009–11 there is a great risk that, whilst on the one hand such a volume of data can be manipulated to support historic theories, on the other no further theories might be advanced for fear of producing inaccurate or at best blurred accounts of the past history of the city. The philosophy of science suggests it is better to put forward theories for future testing than to hold back and simply accumulate data in the hope that at some point the interpretation will become self-evident. The following pages progress on this basis.

Whilst the work on the Close has still only focused on a small proportion of the whole city it adds to an increasing volume of data and can't help but intersect previous models relating to the history and development of the city.

Although there does not appear to be any substantial Roman settlement prior to the foundation of the Saxon occupation there is increasing evidence for some activity of this date. Significantly finds of Roman date increase in concentration towards Broad Street with only occasional pot of this date being located on other sites further afield. One notable instance is the road side ditch originally located in the excavations for the New Library Building, another the discovery of opus signinum sealed beneath a soil deposit in a rubble layer beneath Broad Street during water mains work in 1998. This could well suggest a fording point of the Wye there in the Roman period with some associated structures such as shrines (the altars may not have been brought from Kenchester to build the 8th century corn driers beneath Berrington Street) and perhaps some other buildings. Finds from the 2009–11 excavations include a sherd of box flue tile and a possible pilae, both parts of hypocaust systems, implying a bathhouse or structure of some status. Larger quantities of Roman finds were recovered from the New Library Building excavations[1] and thus it seems more and more likely that there was a nearby structure of this date.

Topographically, to the west of Broad Street archaeological evidence has confirmed the location of a north-south running stream and associated boggy channel dating back as far as the Bronze Age, with upper peat deposits dated to just prior to the Norman Conquest. To the west of this is the earliest evidence for secular occupation in the city with a rectilinear pattern of roads around dwellings, post-dating an early 8th century corn drier. At some distance to the east lies the site of St Guthlacs Priory, clearly ecclesiastical and with burials dated as early as the late 7th century. Regarding this latter point Duncomb's reference[2] that in AD 736 Bishop Cuthbert 'also obtained from the pope a disposition for allowing burials within towns and cities, a practice not allowed before this time' is quite pertinent. The current thought about how the city developed do not seem to consider that either the priory or secular settlement at Berrington Street were enclosed before the 9th century, but they do propose that urban conurbation joined the two.

This seems to be at odds with the reasonably well supported idea that secular occupation of early and middle Saxon date in many cases occupied naturally defended locations, such as areas of dry land enclosed by marshy

environments with London being a prime example. Occupation in Hereford seems to follow this pattern with Widemarsh to the north, and a marshy stream following the line of Aubrey Street. It would therefore seem unlikely that the early settlement extended to the east of this stream. The monastic cell on Castle Green, from which St Guthlacs later grew, appears quite isolated and the archaeological evidence from the recent spate of excavations has failed to identify any features that definitively pre-date the early 9th century. As the whole of the Cathedral Close lies between the two aforementioned sites and would otherwise seem to be an ideal location for settlement, the body of evidence implies two entirely separate settlements, one ecclesiastical, the other enclosed by marshy ground, and secular. This could also explain why evidence for the earliest phase of the defensive circuit, a 2m high gravel and clay rampart, has only been found at the north-west corner of the city; it may have bounded a much smaller area. The decision during the early stages of Saxon settlement to avoid this central area might possibly have been affected by the remains of some earlier Roman activity there.

What appears to be a large blacksmiths' complex located to the north of All Saints Church could represent activity extending to the north-east of the early settlement later in the 8th century. This is however, rather tentatively dated by a worn coin of Offa and the aceramic (no pottery) nature of the deposits there. Aceramic deposits could imply, in Hereford, any date after the end of the Roman period and prior to the last quarter of the 9th century. The earliest evidence, residual Roman pottery aside, for archaeological activity within the Cathedral Close are two radiocarbon dates associated

---

1   Vince 1994
2   Duncomb 1804, 449

with a large timber structure[3] identified on the north side of St Johns Quad. As previously discussed this has more in common with Saxon palaces than other structures and the presence of a burial beneath its foundation appears more than a coincidence and seems to be unheard of with respect to ecclesiastical buildings. The presence of eagle bones in associated deposits infers relatively high status to this structure too. In terms of interpreting the development and nature of this building too little was exposed to draw definitive conclusions. On the basis of the radiocarbon dates then the burial beneath the palisade trench is indistinguishable from the date of the grass seed in the post hole. This together with the alignment of the burial matching that of the foundation trench overwhelmingly stacks in favour of the burial being some form of dedication or votive burial. It is likely that the seed was introduced when the lower part of the large upright timber was being charred, possibly fuel contamination or just material used in the bonfire. The most likely date for construction, combining the highest probability of the two radiocarbon dates, falls between AD 859 and AD 968. The earliest likely date for the industrial phase that occurs following this is AD 987, again, based on radiocarbon evidence, although it could begin as late as 1023. On this basis, whilst there is an outside chance that the building could date from as early as the documented AD 825 construction of the second Saxon Cathedral, this was reputedly built of stone to replace an earlier timber cathedral on the same site and thus is unlikely to match the timber structure exposed during the excavations. The identified building is therefore at odds with both historically acknowledged dates and construction methods for a cathedral in Hereford, and yet is clearly of relatively high status. It also post-dates the period when burial was accepted in towns and there are no contemporary burials within the areas of the site investigated. If this structure was a palace then it is questionable how long it retained such a status as significant industrial activity took place to its south and appears to respect the building meaning it probably still stood at this point in time. Given the range of radiocarbon dates it is clear that this building must have stood in excess of two decades and possibly up to a century. Perhaps at this time ironworking went hand in hand with power, and segregations in society were not so well established in the 10th and 11th centuries. The range of dates for this large timber building may well place it at the time of burgh building towards the end of the 9th century and around the time of Hereford's first major defensive circuit.

The extensive evidence for metalworking across the close sits uncomfortably alongside an ecclesiastical use for the site. The latest date in the date range for the industry only just overlaps the currently acknowledged window for the construction of Aethelstan's cathedral. In fact it lies only eight years after his ordination in 1015. One suggestion is that the work was associated with the construction of his cathedral. In practice the types of industry present appear to fit this, with evidence for possible glass and lead working. It would however place a much earlier date on the cathedral and doesn't explain the multiple phases of workshops and overlying activities that imply they occurred over a much longer period of time. Indeed if the footing discovered in the southern part of St Johns Quad was part of this early 11th-century cathedral, then it clearly postdates the industrial activity in the area.

Of the total ironworking debris from the site, 42% was recovered from St John's Quad the

---

3   Building 1

south-western part of which contained burnt areas associated with slag. The majority of the slag was non-diagnostic, or was indicative of blacksmithing. However, one deposit contained three extremely dense fragments of a type more usually associated with iron smelting suggesting this was taking place in the vicinity, as seems to have been the case in other parts of Hereford during the 11th and 12th centuries[4]. Burnt or vitrified furnace lining was found in a number of deposits but in insufficient quantities to be used to establish the proximity of hearths. The presence of two 'hearth bases' redeposited in a cobbled surface and in the fill of a cut for a possible industrial hearth with stone floor and wooden walls also indicates smithing. In addition, a 'smithing pan' (a conglomeration of slag and anvil debris) was found redeposited in the fill of a grave.

Hammerscale was also concentrated in the south-west part of the St John's Quad excavation. This can indicate what type of process was taking place with spherical fragments usually resulting from welding or small particles of slag squeezed out from a bloom during initial refining. Flake hammerscale results when the hot iron is struck with the hammer, the glossy type indicating a high temperature process such as might be associated with the edging of tools.

Metalworking in the northern and western parts of the close also appears to date from the 11th to 12th century with a number of burnt patches to the north of the Cathedral almost certainly being associated with smithing hearths. The burnt, sooty fill of a shallow bowl-shaped feature contained smithing slag and a high density of hammerscale as well as a fragment of iron

sheet. The area around it had been subjected to considerable heat and thus it seems certain that the feature was directly involved in smithing. Unfortunately there was no associated dating evidence, but the cutting of this feature by a stone burial Cist indicates a pre-13th century date at the latest. An area of apparently more mixed deposits at the western end of the Cathedral contained burnt patches which may have resulted from the raking out of hearths or ovens including glossy hammerscale with a high proportion of spherical fragments.

The fact dues paid by the smiths in Hereford were specifically mentioned in the Domesday survey[5] is unusual. The large scale of ironworking in the town during this period has also been noted from excavations at Bewell Street, Wye Street and St Martin's Street on the southern bank of the river[6]. It is becoming apparent that Hereford was a significant ironworking community just before the conquest.

Other evidence associated with the industrial activity implied occupation of a more domestic nature and certainly finds relating to other cottage-type industries were present. The spindle whorls provide evidence for this. These were used to weight the ends of drop spindles to sustain rotary momentum. They would have been regularly used by most women and girls during this period and the whorls would have been familiar personal possessions, possibly being handed down from mothers to daughters. Three whorls were recovered from amongst the industrial deposits (Illus 120). One was made from the proximal end of a cattle femur[7]. A second found with it, of clay, was the most decorative[8],

4   Crooks 2005; Crooks 2009

5   Williams & Martin 2000, 493
6   Crooks 2005; Crooks 2009
7   SF855b, similar to the more complete SF1169, illustrated
8   SF855a

ILLUS 120

Spindle whorls (Top row left to right: SF855a, clay, 11th century; SF883, oolitic limestone, early 10th to early 11th century; SF1169, bone, 10th to 12th century. Bottom row left to right: SF800, siltstone, 7th to 11th century, found in Simple Coffin of middle-aged woman; SF2012, 11th-century reuse of Roman pot sherd)

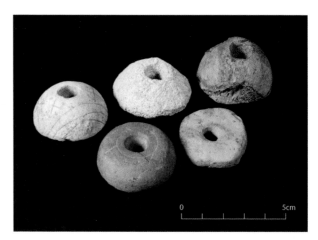

incised with three crosses and three triple arcs, possibly a reference to the holy trinity. The third[9] is quite plain and crudely made but has a story to tell geologically. It is made of a Jurassic oolitic limestone the nearest source for which is the Cotswolds. The stone, termed 'Cotswold stone' is soft and easily carved and was widely used for architectural details and sculpture, and is known to have been used in the Cathedral at Hereford. However, this whorl predates the construction of the Cathedral and thus may suggest that its owner hailed from the Cotswold area. Two further whorls are of note. The first[10] represents Saxon reuse of a Roman pot sherd, implying these were available locally at the time, and has clearly been well used. The second, of stone[11], while of a form that can be typologically dated to the 7th to 11th centuries, was found in Simple Coffin burial of a middle aged woman[12]. It could represent a personal possession buried with her but given the date range of this type of burial might have been some centuries old when interred.

One of two flat pin-beaters or picker-cum-beaters[13] from the site was found in the same industrial deposit as the two spindle whorls

above[14] and is yet another piece of evidence indicating textile working in the vicinity (Illus 121). This type of tool was in use between the late 9th or 10th centuries and the 13th or 14th centuries. Observation of the wear patterns on excavated examples and experimental work with reconstructed looms has led to the theory that these were used with two-beamed looms to pick out small groups of warp threads in order to pass the weft behind them for patterned weaves. The flat end may have been used to beat down the weft threads after they had been threaded through, which would explain the concave wear sometimes seen on these ends. Two-beamed looms became popular after the introduction of the horizontal loom had made the vertical warp-weighted loom obsolete. The horizontal loom was used by professional weavers for making cloth in quantity, while the two-beamed loom was used for making tapestries and other patterned weaves, probably by women in the home[15].

Given the above evidence it seems unlikely that the rubbish deposits filling the features of this phase of activity came from far afield, particularly given the incorporation of industrial waste that

---

9   SF883
10   SF2012
11   SF800
12   Sk1815
13   SF1050

---

14   SF855a, SF855b
15   Rogers 1997, 1755; Brown 1990, 227–228

was obviously locally derived. Therefore the area appears to be more broadly artesan, the industrial nature of the activity perhaps overemphasised through the nature of the residues it creates rather than any overriding dominance.

So what about the later robbed out wall footing[16]? Certainly the rubble and worked stone filling it, and its vertical-sided, flat-bottomed profile is suggestive that it served as a foundation trench for a stone-built structure. All that can now be deduced is the span of use of the building. Its foundation post-dates the industrial activity on the site (1023 being the latest date for this activity, see above). Its robbing out occurring in the 12th century on the basis of chevron decorated architectural masonry recovered from its fills. This sits comfortably with the postulated life-span of Aethelstan's cathedral.

Does the orientation of the structure fit this theory? The varying orientation of buildings within the Close was originally identified by Alfred Watkins in the 1920s. The three surviving significant ecclesiastical Norman buildings – the cathedral, the Losinga Chapel and the Bishop's Palace – all have slightly different orientations[17] (Illus 122, Table 58).

Prior to the 1993 New Library Building excavations, the orientation of the Bishop's

0   2.5cm

ILLUS 121
Flat pin beater (SF1050)

Palace could well have been considered to be the latest of these, as the earliest parts of the building are dated to the 1180s and therefore post-date the Cathedral and Losinga Chapel. The 1993 discovery of a Saxon road heading through the Close to join with Widemarsh Street and the basement of a Saxon building matching the orientation of the Bishop's Palace imply that the road line and structures associated with it have a considerable degree of longevity. The 9th to 10th century post-in-trench structure[18] excavated during the 2009–11 excavations is also on the same orientation (within a tolerance of 1°). This orientation underlines the planned nature of Saxon settlements and probably relates more to secular layout than ecclesiastical, particularly as, of the three orientations, it is the one furthest from true east-west.

Considering that the Losinga Chapel is at variance with the orientation of the later Norman Cathedral and the possible earlier secular layout mentioned above then there is a strong possibility that it was instead aligned to Aethelstan's minster. It is logical to assume that Aethelstan's 11th century minster was still standing when Bishop Robert built the Losinga Chapel as there is no record of any replacement for the late Saxon Cathedral until the early 12th century when work on the Norman building starts.

16   Building 6
17   Stone & Appleton-Fox 1996

18   Building 1

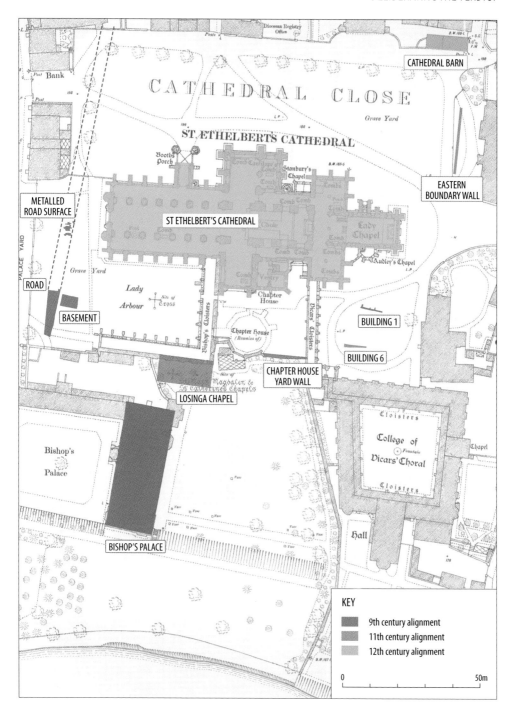

ILLUS 122
Orientation of structures within the Cathedral Close (see Illus 12, 18, 36, 46 for details)

DATE	ORIENTATION	STRUCTURES
9th century	Tending to SW-NE from true N-S by 12.5°	Bishops Palace N-S road, 1993 excavation Saxon basement, 1993 excavation 9th – 10th century timber building on north side of St John's Quad (Building 1)
11th century	Tending to SW-NE from true N-S by 7.5°	Losinga Chapel (founded 1079–95) Chapter House yard south wall Eastern boundary wall (H17) 11th – 12th century foundation trench on south side of St John's Quad (Building 6)
12th century	Tending to SW-NE from true N-S by 2.8°	Norman Cathedral Cathedral Barn, 2009 excavation 13th century wall beneath the barn

TABLE 58

Changes in orientation of structures within the Cathedral Close

The robbed out foundation trench[19] on the south side of St John's Quad is on an identical orientation to the remaining north wall of the Losinga Chapel and fits the time window that Aethelstan's cathedral might be expected to occupy.

The same orientation can also be seen in a wall, partly still standing and partly traced as footings underneath the ruined 14th-century chapter house (suggested by some to be the foundation of an earlier chapter house). An examination of the wall by the Royal Commission reported that 'it continued up to and probably beneath the wall of the Vicar's cloister; near this point was found the west splay of a doorway dating from the 12th or 13th century'[20]. It seems unlikely that the wall running through the chapter house yard directly relates to the foundation trench discovered in the 2009–11 excavations. Although on the same orientation, the walls are on different alignments and yet

are too closely spaced to form opposing walls of the same building. If the 12th or 13th century date established by the Royal Commission is correct, then the wall is unlikely to be contemporary with the early 11th century foundation trench. Instead it may belong to a later structure which referenced the same orientation as the Losinga Chapel. Despite the vagaries of orientation it is also more closely aligned to east-west and this orientation would appear to be more ecclesiastical in origin. So is this what is left of Aethelstan's cathedral? As ever the size and location of the excavation confound the archaeologist but the presence of worked masonry strongly leans towards this argument.

One further feature matching the Losinga Chapel's orientation is the wall discovered to the west of the Old Deanery[21] that is believed to have surrounded the Close by the time Speede produced his map of 1606. The wall itself is likely to date to the late 14th century when a royal charter was granted for the enclosure of the graveyard. It would seem likely however, that a formalised enclosure would be built on the line of an already established boundary. Taylor's map of 1757 shows the 'square' area previously defined by the wall but the enclosure is not in fact square at all. The east and west boundaries to the Close are parallel and match the orientation of the Losinga Chapel. The northern boundary to the Close, and the wall revealed beneath the Cathedral Barn are not, however, at 90° to the east and west walls, but instead match the orientation of the later Norman cathedral.

---

19   Building 6
20   RCHME 1931, Herefordshire, i, p.116

21   H17

If the second orientation was established by the construction of Aethelstan's minster church in the early 11th century and subsequently adopted by Bishop Robert during the transitionary period prior to the construction of the Norman cathedral, then it was relatively short lived. However, the matching orientations of the Losinga Chapel and the Close boundaries suggest that Bishop Robert's contribution to the layout of the Close extended beyond the construction of his chapel, and he got some way towards establishing the 'site boundaries' in advance of Bishop Reinhelm's construction work.

However, if this is the case then it was truly a precinct and not a burial ground as there is only one burial definitively predating the construction of the Norman Cathedral identified within the Cathedral Close to date[22]. Where was its associated burial ground then? Observations within a water pipe trench excavated north-south across the southern part of the Vicars Choral did not find any evidence for burial in this area[23] and south of the complex only stone sills for timber structures of medieval or later date were recorded[24]. On the other hand the date range for burial within Castle Green spans from the 7th to 12th centuries. If Castle Green was the site of the earlier Saxon churches then did Aethelstan clear the area now occupied by the Close to construct his new work, but with burial rites continuing on the existing Castle Green?

With the construction of the Romanesque cathedral, Bishop Reinhelm disregarded the orientation of the Losinga Chapel and presumably the orientation of Aethelstan's minster. This suggests an entire disregard for the past and establishment of a new order

in contrast to an earlier need for continuity between the Saxon and the Norman during Robert's transition period.

The evidence from the 2009 excavation at the Cathedral Barn and analysis of Taylor's map of 1757 suggest that the Norman boundary to the Close was established with reference to the orientation of the Norman cathedral.

The story so far for the wider development of this part of the city is more complex and appears to be different to that originally proposed in 1982[25]. No. evidence for an east-west road through the close was found, this undermining the early theory for a cross roads and settlement focus at the west end of the Cathedral. In fact the road forming the east side of this route has subsequently been shown to be 11th century at its earliest and potentially as late as the 12th century[26].

So what evidence was there associated with the construction of the current cathedral? Construction began in the early 12th century and was probably finished by the time Robert de Betun died in 1148 as he is recorded as either adding to or repairing it[27].

With the exception of a few pieces of worked masonry evidence is probably restricted to the 62 fragments of medieval window glass which give tantalising glimpses of the cathedral's former glazing schemes (Illus 123). The earliest date from the 13th and 14th centuries, and measure up to 3.8mm thick with later medieval glass being 15th or 16th century in date and generally a little thinner. The medieval glass shows evidence of later 13th- and 14th-century grisaille stiff-leaf foliage and other 14th-century painted designs as well as some unpainted

22   SK 5061, the 'foundation trench burial'
23   Vyce 1999
24   Stone 1991; Thomas 1993

25   Shoesmith 1982
26   Thomas & Boucher 2002, 24
27   Duncomb 1804, 521–3

0   2.5cm

ILLUS 123
Decorative grisaille window glass (top: probable Victorian copy, SF0851; bottom: 13th- to 14th-century shards, SF2200, SF2203, SF2213)

late medieval glass. Later glass of interest includes an enamel-painted star no earlier than the 17th century, and a probable Victorian replication of a grisaille-style fleur-de-lys. Most of the glass was recovered from around St John's Quad, to the east end of the Cathedral outside the Lady Chapel and south-east transept. However, as most of the glass derived from grave fills and graveyard soils, it is likely to have been redeposited a number of times and thus may not relate to its original position in the windows. The circumstances of deposition likewise are unknown. The medieval window glass in

Hereford Cathedral has had an unfortunate history, of vandalism and architectural disaster. For example, a letter from Henry VIII in 1547 required the removal of all images including stained glass[28], and in 1786 the west front of the Cathedral collapsed. It is perhaps remarkable that any medieval glass is left installed in the cathedral. The late 13th-century windows in the south side of the Lady Chapel are imports from St Peter's church in Hereford, installed in the 1850s[29]

---

28   Whitehead 2000, 243
29   Iles 2000, 316

180

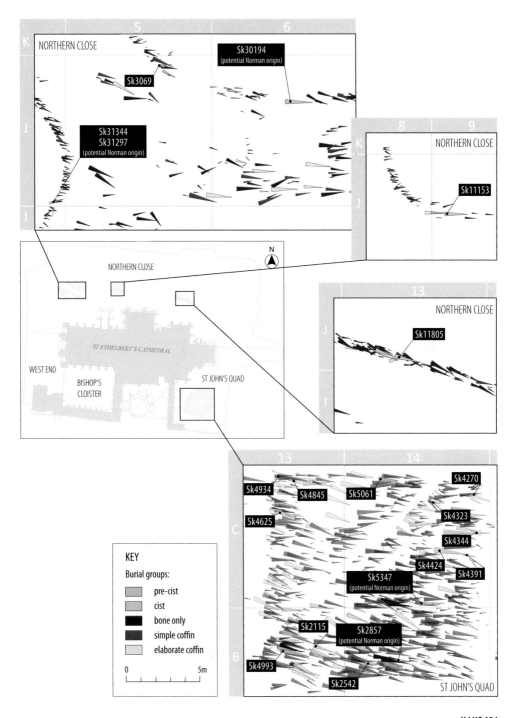

ILLUS 124
Skeletons selected for isotope analysis.

SKELETON	SEX	AGE	BURIAL GROUP	POTENTIAL ORIGIN	RADIOCARBON DATE
Sk5061	–	8–10	Pre-Cist 'foundation trench burial'	Northern or western Britain	AD 830–968
Sk2542	–	9–11	Pre-Cist	East of Hereford	–
Sk4344	F	20–35	Pre-Cist	Local	–
Sk4993	F	18–23	Pre-Cist	Local	1044–1159
Sk2115	F	18+	Cist	Local	–
Sk2857	M	35–44	Cist	Normandy	1171–1221
Sk4270	M	21–24	Cist	Local	–
Sk4323	F	40–44	Cist	Local	–
Sk4391	F	16–17	Cist	Local	–
Sk4424	M	25–30	Cist	Northern or western Britain	–
Sk4625	F	24–30	Cist	East of Hereford	–
Sk4845	F	20–35	Cist	Local	–
Sk4934	M	45–49	Cist	Northern or western Britain	–
Sk5347	M	35–39	Cist	Normandy	–
Sk11153	F	25–35	Cist	Local	–
Sk11805	M	40–45	Cist	Northern or western Britain	–
Sk30194	M	35–39	Cist	Normandy	–
Sk30690	M	25–34	Cist	Local	–
Sk31297	F	18–25	Cist	Normandy	–
Sk31344	M	45–49	Cist	Northern or western Britain	–

*Radiocarbon dates calibrated

TABLE 59
Skeletons selected for isotope analysis

and a Victorian glazier, William Warrington, found several boxes of 14th-century glass in the cathedral, which he incorporated with new glass in his glazing schemes in the south choir aisle and north-east transept[30].

The greatest mass of evidence associated with the cathedral comes from the establishment of the cemetery and the stories that its occupants tell. Stratigraphically the earliest burials consistently comprised Cist burials and with Pre-Cist Bone Only burials cut by these. In each case where Cists cut earlier burials, there was only one burial earlier. This interesting relationship

---

30   Iles 2000, 314

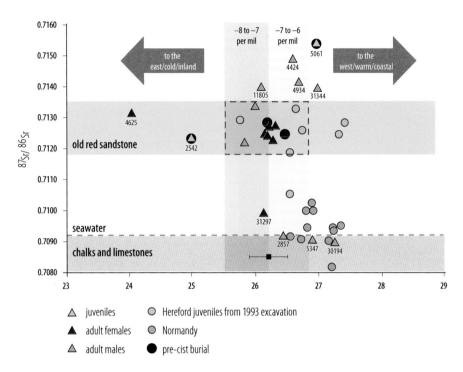

The horizontal red band denotes the expected strontium isotope values for inhabitants of Hereford and its environs located on Old Red Sandstone. The vertical coloured bands indicate the range of oxygen isotope ratios which are consistent with Hereford (green) and adjacent areas to the south and west (yellow). Given the large uncertainty on oxygen isotope measurements and the possibility that medieval people were altering the oxygen isotope ratios of their drinking water by brewing and boiling or drinking milk (Brettell et al 2012), it is probable that people living in Hereford would have values within the range enclosed by the dashed box. The grey band shows strontium isotope ratios consistent with areas of chalk and limestone. For comparative purposes, results are shown with seven 14th century juveniles from the 1993 New Library Building excavations and 11 individuals from early medieval contexts in Sannerville and Giberville, Normandy.

ILLUS 125
Results of isotope analysis

between the Pre-Cist and Cist burials raised the question as to why two distinctly different forms of burial should be taking place during the same period. Osteological analysis showed that the choice of one form over the other was not based on age, although there does appear to be a disproportionate number of males to females in the Cist burials. If status or wealth was the determining factor different burial groups might have been expected to be buried at different locations within the graveyard.

It was considered possible that the burial traditions represented two different cultural groups and isotope analysis was employed to test this theory. Chemical elements from ingested food and water are incorporated into teeth. Tooth enamel is highly resistant to change during life and subsequent burial and therefore can be related to childhood diet. The isotope ratios of elements such as strontium and oxygen vary geographically, and hence these differences can be used to draw conclusions about whether individuals were of local or non-local origin. Twenty teeth drawn from skeletons were submitted for analysis with results as follows (Illus 124–125, Table 59.

ILLUS 126
An 18–23 year old adult woman of local origin showing signs of a poor diet, Sk4993

All bar one of the children tested from the New Library Building excavation appear to be of local origin (if measurement uncertainty is taken into account) and they are comparable with the majority of the women tested from the 2009–11 excavations. In a cemetery, it is generally assumed that the young children will be predominantly of local origin given

that they have had far less time in their shorter lives to relocate[31] and thus they form a useful control group.

Most of the women (seven out of nine) have remarkably similar values and appear to be of local origin whilst most of the men (seven out of nine) appear to have originated elsewhere.

Four men[32] and the Pre-Cist juvenile 'foundation trench burial'[33] have higher strontium ratios than would be expected from regions of Old Red Sandstone. Such values are usually indicative of origins on granites or ancient Palaeozoic rocks which can only be found in restricted regions of northern and western Britain.

Three men[34] have lower strontium ratios than would be expected locally and are consistent with origins on chalks and limestones. One of the females[35] also has low strontium ratios. It is interesting to note that the three men fall within the Normandy group. However, this is not proof that they have origins in Normandy only that the isotope data would support such a conclusion. Equally there are many other places in southern and central England where chalks and limestones occur, for example the nearby Mendips and the South Downs, as well as other parts of northern Europe.

The results, albeit from a small group, were certainly surprising and also quite thought provoking. There appears to be a pattern but what does it mean? Duncomb[36] quotes substantial tracts from an 1154 text 'A book

31 Montgomery et al 2005
32 Sk4424, Sk4934, Sk11805, Sk31344
33 Sk5061
34 Sk30197, Sk5347, Sk2857
35 Sk31297
36 Duncomb 1804, 330

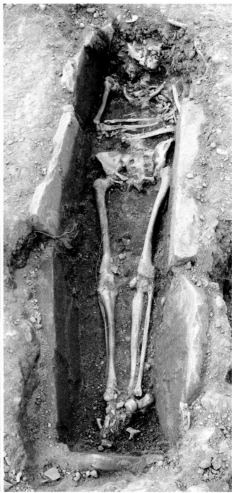

ILLUS 127
An older local woman who was suffering from a leg infection when she died, Sk4323

of the priviledges and bounds of the City of Hereford, extracted out of an ancient book of record'. One particular passage catches the eye 'If any forreyner shall espouse any one of ours or fellow citizens daughters, or any widow amongst us, which have tenements in any manner for term of life at least, that forreyner, by virtue of his liberty, may freely buy and sell amongst us without redemption to be made'. Also by 1295 the rights and privileges of widows and eldest daughters of freemen of Hereford gave anyone marrying them the right to elect a member of parliament[37]. The Cist burials span the early 12th to mid 13th centuries and are roughly contemporary with the first of these accounts. For whatever reason it appears that local statutes existed that encouraged men to come from outside the city and marry local women. Such an occurrence might

---

37   Duncomb 1804, 348

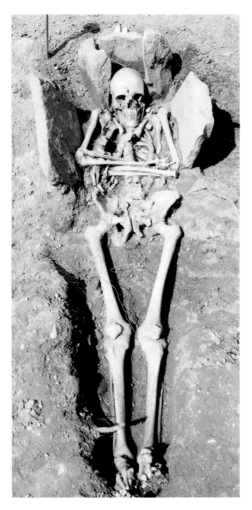

ILLUS 128

A man of Norman origin who's injuries might be consistent with violence or combat, Sk5347

be used to explain the apparent bias in the isotope results. Could this be the earliest scientific evidence for tax evasion?

It seems a shame to leave these individuals without at least looking at a little of what the study of their remains can tell us about them. Looking at the local women first we can compare a burial in a Cist with one without.

The burial of a young, local adult female[38] aged 18–23 years old was cut by a later Cist burial (Illus 26). She was suffering from active infection and iron deficiency anaemia at the time of death with evidence of previous stresses experienced during childhood. Dental evidence suggests poor dental health which may reflect a poor diet rich in carbohydrates but lacking other important nutrients.

A 40–44 year old local woman[39] buried in a Cist had indications of similar childhood malnutrition and iron deficiency to the younger women above (Illus 127). She showed indications that she had recovered from some form of infection in her lower legs although her upper right leg was suffering from infection (*periostitis*) at the time of her death. At some point she had fallen and broken her right wrist. The evidence suggests this individual lived an active lifestyle and had poor dental health.

Turning our attention to four of the male Cist burials it is interesting to consider whether there are any indications of status within the skeletal record.

An older male aged 45+ years old and possibly from Normandy[40] was buried within one of the Cists (Illus 128). He was quite tall for the period standing at 178cm. This individual exhibits multiple fractures throughout the skeleton. Nine of the ribs on the right side display evidence of fractures which subsequently healed and there is evidence that the individual continued an active life following his recovery although unhealed rib fractures at the time of his death indicate he may have suffered injuries later in life that he didn't survive. The right shoulder appears

38   Sk4993
39   Sk4323
40   Sk5347

ILLUS 129
A 25–35 year old man brought up in Normandy with congenital disorders including Pigeon chest, Sk30194

to have been broken by a blow to the back of the shoulder with some sort of pointed implement and he also has a well healed fracture to the mid-shaft of the left lower leg. Evidence suggests that it was an incomplete fracture and can occur due to a rolled ankle, a fall or a direct blow to the outer lower leg. He had also lost three front teeth. The fractures to the lower ribs are likely to have occurred at a different time to those higher up (including the shoulder) suggesting two separate violent events. Such trauma to the ribs and shoulder might suggest a fall from a height onto the right side of the body, perhaps from a horse. It could have occurred by accident but given this man travelled from Normandy it is possible that he was involved in military action, though this cannot be determined for certain. Despite his older age, he continued to live an active lifestyle and potentially quite a violent one. Given the lack of blade injuries one further possibility presents itself, that he was involved in jousting tournaments. His earlier injuries which had all healed include one fracture to the front of his top rib, a number of fractures to the upper ribs in his back, a broken left leg and a blow to the back of his shoulder. The breaks to his lower ribs were more towards his side and had only partially healed at the time of his death. The healed broken leg is a type of twisting wound that could have been caused by falling from a horse with the leg stuck in the stirrup. The fact that his upper body injuries are all focused on the right side of the body, the one most exposed during jousting, alongside the nature of the broken leg strongly suggests such an explanation. It seems improbable that so many injuries would be incurred so close to one another through different types of accidents.

It is tempting to identify this man as a Norman knight. An account in Duncomb's history of the city for 1241 states that Gilbert Marshal, Earl of Pembroke and Lord of Goodrich Castle undertook a tournament without license from the king and was thrown from an unruly horse and killed on the spot[41]. The injuries incurred by our elderly 'Norman' are potentially commensurate with those that might be expected from a similar jousting incident. The nearest tournament to Hereford was probably Chepstow where such an event was held in 1227[42]. Despite jousting having been endorsed under Richard the Lionheart's 1194 charter this latter tournament was held illicitly (ie did not pay the rather high dues to the Crown) and was organised by a certain William Marshall. The burial identified here could well be contemporary with this episode. In theory individuals killed in tournaments were

41   Duncomb 1804, 347
42   Maclean 1884

187

denied the right to burial in a churchyard. However, as in this case there is evidence that the gentleman survived for a period following receiving his final wounds, then it may be his death was not officially viewed as connected with the 'joust'.

Another possible Norman man buried in a Cist[43] was 25–35 years old when he died (Illus 129). This individual also had evidence of iron deficiency. He had suffered a partially dislocated left hip which would have resulted in an abnormal gait possibly resulting in damaged to his left ankle. He seems to have suffered from a number of congenital disorders including *pigeon chest* where the sternum is fused together giving a distinctive bowed out appearance and an unfused atlas (the vertebra that supports the skull). The spine also showed signs of *degenerative disc disease* and *Schmorl's nodes* which can form either as a result of occupational activity or an active lifestyle.

Another of the Cist burials was an older man[44] aged 40–45 years but this time from north-west Britain (Illus 130). Like the other burials mentioned above there were signs of malnutrition or stress in childhood, and anaemia. He had a healed infection in his left upper arm and a smooth area of bone on the right lower leg bone may indicate he suffered a blunt force injury. This skeleton represents the only identified case of *gout* within the Hereford assemblage which may suggest an individual who could afford a more luxurious lifestyle or was simply in poor health. *Osteoarthritis* which could result from occupational activities was also present in the right ankle and parts of the spine. The individual displayed evidence for dislocation of the left side of the jaw with tooth wear reflecting this. Such an occurrence can be

ILLUS 130

An older man who came to Hereford from the north-west of the country and showed signs of gout, Sk11805

43 Sk30194
44 Sk11805

linked with occupational activity involving the use of teeth as a tool to grip items in the mouth. Three skeletons at Wharram Percy, North Yorkshire displayed signs of tooth wear caused by being used as tools[45]. He had particularly poor dental health possibly reflecting abuse of the teeth alongside a diet high in carbohydrates and protein. He seems to have been an active and possibly quite wealthy man.

Another Cist burial from northern or western Britain[46] was of a male aged 25–30 years old (Illus 131). The individual displayed a number of genetic conditions which can go unnoticed throughout life. However, he probably had a noticeably 'hunch-back' appearance.

If there was a status distinction in burials within the Cists then it is clear that neither illness nor malnutrition in early life respected such a distinction. The presence of *gout* implies that at least one of these individuals may have had a relatively rich diet in later life. Certainly the account of Bishop Raynelm (consecrated 1107) who apparently practiced his duty of hospitality to the degree which was thought by some to border on intemperance and apparently died from an attack of *gout* on 28th October 1115, indicates that the disease was associated with status, although the diagnosis might not be 100% reliable here. Clearly not all Bishops were guilty of such indulgences in some ways illustrated by the latter days of the early 18th century bishop Benjamin Hoadley. In an act of kindness after he was Bishop of Hereford he took a French priest under his wing, a charleton by all accounts. 'In return for this act of humanity, the priest found an opportunity of getting the Bishop's name written by his own hand and causing a note of some thousand pounds to be placed

ILLUS 131
A 25–30 year old man with a possible hunch-back, Sk4424

---

45   Mays 2007a
46   Sk4424

0   2.5cm

ILLUS 132
Padlock slide key, 12th century (SF0867)

above it, offered it for payment. A court of justice found for the bishop. The French priest produced a pamphlet charging the Bishop of being a drunkard and that he had received the note when he was drunk. The Bishop claimed to have never been intoxicated in his whole life and was acquitted'[47].

Given the disproportionate treatment of sexes and hints of higher status occupational and leisure activities of the incumbents of the Cist burials there does appear to be some degree of selection of individuals, and this may reflect status in one form or another.

One burial that stands out within the cemetery was that of a leper[48]. This was one of only two individuals buried in a crouched position (Illus 72). However, it is unusual for lepers to be found in community burial grounds. Duncomb[49] notes that Peter de Aquablanca was afflicted by *leprosy* in 1263 dying in 1268, and it is worth consideration that the leprous burial could be from around that time. There is also a reference to lepers in the miracles of Thomas Cantilupe where

60+ people were raised to life and 21 lepers healed along with 23 blind and dumb men[50].

One final thought relating to the burials is the fate of the lady whose hand had been severed[51] (Illus 111). Initial thoughts relate to the severing of thieves' hands although archaeological evidence is quite sparse regarding this. Clearly citizens felt that there was some risk to their possessions given the find of a slide key (Illus 132). This was for use with a barrel padlock, a type of lock working on a completely different principle to the later case padlocks that we are familiar with today and an ingenious medieval solution to one of the problems of urban living. They could be used to secure chests, doors, shutters or gates. The bit was inserted into a key hole at one end of the barrel and slid along, compressing the springs of the bolt and allowing it to be drawn out of the bolt hole on the opposing end[52]. This example is of the most common type of medieval slide key[53]. At Winchester they were found in

47 Duncomb 1804, 493–5
48 Sk2971
49 Duncomb 1804, 461–3

50 Duncomb 1804, 468
51 Sk10400
52 See Ottaway & Rogers 2002, 2866–7 for diagram of the working of a similar padlock and key
53 Type A, Goodall 1990, 1005–6; 1020–2; fig.322–3

contexts from the 10th to the 15th centuries. This one was found associated pottery of 12th century date and a knife which was possibly a little earlier.

Certainly for citizens of Hereford a fine for stealing was more likely than severance of limbs. Even that was limited such as under the decree by John of Gaunt for a 12p limit of fine for those in the liberty. Notably anyone persisting in not accepting punishment would be extradited and on returning without permission would have their goods and tenements seized back[54], no mention of physical injury. By the early post-medieval period in 1620 the only mention of physical punishment was for gallows to be erected for the execution of felons. Interestingly in the same entry it was a crime to refuse to take up a position on the council and this carried a gaol sentence[55]. The above would tend to suggest she was more likely the victim of an accident or interpersonal violence.

Historical and archaeological evidence highlights the fact that in Hereford, like in many other medieval towns and cities, individuals were involved in a variety of industrial processes; each often being nucleated and having related street names. Such industries would have taken place in both rural and urban locations, only differing in scale of activity.

It is considered that 'a specific (skeletal) modification…may not be attributed to a single activity pattern, but rather a wide range of habitual behaviours. Thus, a proper diagnosis may be limited to stating that an individual had engaged in strenuous labour'[56]. It should be remembered that in the past physical labour was not the confine of adults and involved children of both sexes – strenuous activities that commence early in the lifetime of the individual (before skeletal maturity) will present the greatest change in the skeleton[57].

Historical evidence indicates that Herefordshire has remained a largely rural county throughout its history; the townspeople would also have had common meadows and backyard plots to grow food and rear animals. During the medieval period Herefordshire was synonymous with the wool trade, although it declined in the 17th century due to competition from the north of England. Wool was largely exported to north-west Europe and was the main nationally exported commodity in terms of value in this period[58]. Fulling was the process of treating wool for use in the cloth industry and such mills were situated along the Rivers Wye and Lugg. Two fulling mills were located at Hereford in 1527 and six mills present near Hereford by 1690[59]. It is likely that there were many more mills in the county, over 100 mills in medieval Herefordshire, many of which cannot now be located[60]. A couple of individuals in the burials from the Cathedral had injuries commensurate with twisting, as if they had been caught in machinery, and this could relate to working mills as very few other activities of the period involve machinery that would be robust enough to cause such injuries. Many small rural industries employed carders (people who combed the wool), staplers (who graded and sold the wool), spinners, weavers and dyers who sprang up alongside these watermills. Hemp and flax retting creates pollutants, as did other aspects of textile production[61] such as dying and fixing. In 1594–6 fines were

54 Duncomb 1804, 339–41
55 Duncomb 1804, 357–8
56 Capasso et al. 1998, 5

57 Knusel 2000
58 Hurst 2012
59 Greene 2005
60 Hurst 2012
61 Walton 1991

imposed for washing flax and hemp in the river Wye at Welsh Bicknor, and at Hereford in 1700 an order was issued restricting the dressing or drying of flax and hemp within the walls of the city[62]. These orders were presumably made to counteract the pollution of the water supply that would have occurred as a result of these processes. Environmental pollution from leather production through the by-products resulting from soaking and heating would have also been detrimental to health[63]. Evidence for tanneries just outside the city walls have been uncovered, most notably at the site of Hereford Magistrates Court dating to the 12th – 14th century[64].

Evidence of intensive ironworking, including smithing and smelting, dating to the 10th to 12th centuries was uncovered during the Cathedral Close excavation. The fact that dues paid by the smiths in Hereford were specifically mentioned in the Domesday survey appears to be representative of the scale of the industry in the city[65]. Further, medieval ironworking sites in Hereford include that at Gaol Street/Bath Street[66], Bewell Street[67] and that on Wye Street and St Martin's Street on the southern bank of the river[68]. A further site at Commercial Street/Union Street[69] uncovered copper or bronze-smithing waste at the rear of medieval tenements although the quantities found did not suggest large-scale industrial activity. Back plot industry was a normal feature of medieval towns and might sometimes have been on a fairly small scale and carried on in conjunction with normal household activities[70].

Furthermore, constant building and decoration on the Cathedral provided employment for many craftsmen and its liturgical needs, in wax, vestments, incense and wine sustained trade and industry. A variety of work was undertaken by the inhabitants of the city and its liberty and in the latter part of the 16th century a new market hall was built, with the ground floor used for a market and the above rooms for 14 city guilds including bakers, barbers, butchers, clothiers, coopers, glovers, tanners and weavers.

In 1777, downward traffic on the Wye from Hereford included 9,000 tons of corn and 26 tons of cider[71]. Cider was, and still is, one of the main products of Hereford and the neighbouring areas and it reached its peak production in the 17th century. Evidence of the popularity and profitability of early cider-making within Hereford is present within the Cathedral where a tomb and carved effigy, dating to the 14th century, depicts Andrew Jones a prominent and rich cider-maker with a large money purse and a barrel of cider at his feet. Defoe in the early 18th century wrote 'we could get no beer or ale in their publick houses, only cider, and that so very good, so fine, and so cheap…great quantities of this cider are sent to London, even by land carriage tho' so very remote, which is evidence for the goodness of it, beyond contradiction'[72].

The manufacture and trade of gloves also became important in 17th century Hereford, though no evidence for this trade survived archaeologically. However, regarding clothing and fashion in general, some evidence as to what the occupants of Hereford might have worn was recovered during the

---

62   Jenkins 1936
63   Cherry 1991
64   Vyce 2001
65   Crooks 2012
66   Crooks 2009a
67   Crooks 2005
68   Crooks 2009b
69   Crooks 2007
70   Schofield & Vince 1994

71   Shoesmith 1992, 78
72   Defoe 1724

excavations. Perhaps the earliest was in the form of hooked tags whose exact function is uncertain (Illus 31). They are of relatively flimsy construction and as no rivets have ever been found in the plate perforations, it is assumed they were sewn into place. Some sort of light weight dress fastening is then implied and the current consensus of opinion is that they were probably fasteners for purses[73]. The use of these tags was dated in Winchester to between the 7th and 11th centuries, and seems to have died out around the time of the Norman Conquest[74]. They can be found with triangular or round plates, most frequently with two holes in the plate but sometimes three and occasionally one, and are sometimes decorated, though there seems to be no significance in terms of dating to these variations.

Five tags were found during the excavations. They range from the small[75] to the rather more substantial[76]. The most ornate[77] is simply decorated with incised rings around the perforations. The best stratified example[78] was found in an early- to mid-11th century layer in St John's Quad (see Chapter 3), while another was also found associated with 11th century pottery[79]. The decorative example[80] was found in a poorly preserved Bone Only adult burial[81] in the Northern Close. It is likely that this find was residual in the grave particularly as, given that burials did not appear to begin in the graveyard until the 12th century, had it been deliberately interred with the body, it must have been

somewhat outdated at the time. Other finds were found in the general graveyard soil in St John's Quad and are likely to relate to the Saxon activity in this area. Similar tags were found in 11th century contexts at Berrington Street, Hereford[82] but examples from St Guthlac's, Cinema, Trinity Almshouses and Wall Street all appeared to be residual in 13th century deposits[83].

Other dress accessories include three beads, two of glass, and one humbler version made from a fish vertebra. Potentially the earliest was a blue-green annular bead[84] found in a gully dug through an abandoned industrial phase building[85] (Illus 26). Annular beads were a long-lived type, from Roman times through to the medieval period[86], though are most common between the 5th and 10th centuries[87]. The second glass bead is yellow and globular[88]. It is not closely datable and was found in the general graveyard soil.

The fish vertebra needed no shaping to fashion it into a bead, only a hole drilled through the narrow centre. The finished effect is not particularly decorative but this was probably not its intended function. Fish vertebra beads have been noted at several sites in Britain and Europe, including a 13th or 14th century chapel site in Northumberland[89], a late medieval monastery in Iceland[90] and a Saxon context in Southampton[91]. While these sites are all notably close to the sea, the salmon which provided the raw material

73   Rogers 2007, 134
74   Hinton 1990, 548–52; Mainman & Rogers 2000, 2576
75   SF0903
76   SF0596
77   SF1045
78   SF0903
79   SF2191
80   SF1045
81   Sk11788

82   Shoesmith 1985, 9–10, fiche M4.G3
83   Thomas 2002, 155
84   SF0909
85   Building 2 (Illus 23)
86   Mainman & Rogers 2000, 2591–6
87   Biddle & Creasey 1990, 659
88   SF1134
89   Stallibrass 2002; 2005
90   Hamilton-Dyer 2010, 48–51
91   Hamilton-Dyer 1997

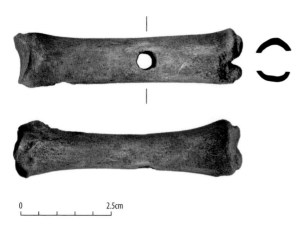

0 ⊢⊣⊢⊣⊢⊣⊢⊣⊢⊣ 2.5cm

ILLUS 133
Buzz bone, 12th century (SF2007)

repair during the lifetime of the garment. It is likely then that this garment was used to dress the body for burial. Though highly unusual for bodies to be buried wearing regular clothing, it was known on occasions during the 18th and 19th centuries[95].

There is some evidence for leisure activities, in the form of toys or gaming items, showing that life was not all toil and hardship. Pierced pig metapodials are regular finds in medieval contexts and have at various times been interpreted as bobbins for thread or toggles for fastening clothing[96]. However, it has been argued convincingly that they are in fact toys or primitive musical instruments[97]. A cord would be passed twice through the hole in a large figure-of-eight shape. It could then be twisted, and when pulled and released would send the bone spinning, making a whirring sound. Pierced discs could be used in the same way and can still be found as children's toys today. This use is consistent with the slight wear around the hole but complete lack of it on the ends. An example[98] was found during the excavations in a pit at the West End with some 12th century pottery (Illus 133).

for this bead would have been available locally and was probably fished out of the River Wye. Fish bone necklaces have been associated with fertility and with warding off evil[92] and are known to have been used for rosaries. The very humility of the material may have made it attractive to the more ascetic Christians of the age, as would the symbolism of Christ as 'fisher of men'.

A number of buttons, mostly of copper alloy, were found Simple Coffin and Elaborate Coffin graves, though as only single examples were found in each grave, it seems unlikely that they were attached to deliberately interred garments. These were probably accidental losses in the graveyard, though conceivably they may have been used as shroud fastenings. The exception is a Simple Coffin adult burial[93] where five buttons[94] all of the same type, and all probably deriving from the same garment were found. Their size and weight suggests a coat or waistcoat. Interestingly, one of the buttons is slightly mismatched, though appearing identical from the front, and was probably a replacement used for a

Two gaming counters were also found, one purpose made in white pipeclay, the other fashioned from a sherd of a possible Willow pattern plate. Both are unlikely to be earlier than the 19th century. Being found in the graveyard soil, might be indicative

---

92 Hamilton-Dyer 2010, 51
93 Sk1952
94 SF1293

95 Reeve & Adams 1993, 110–1
96 MacGregor 1985, 102–3
97 Lawson 1995; MacGregor et al 1999
98 SF2007

of games played within graveyard. Three ceramic marbles were also recovered from the graveyard soil. Again these are made of pipeclay and are likely to be 19th century.

It is clear from the excavations that life in medieval and post-medieval Hereford was not easy for its occupants. Life expectancy was short and what glimpses of the effects of disease we can glean from the archaeological evidence suggests this was common affecting many in childhood. Amongst the hustle and bustle of the city, apart from the daily occupations of its residents, these being physically demanding and in some cases dangerous, there are indications of violence. There is evidence suggesting domestic assault of women, blade wounds perhaps from battles as well as possible sporting injuries including from jousting tournaments and bare fist fighting.

The way in which the dead were treated in their burial rites suggests that the burial ground contained the poorer end of society alongside its more prestigious elements. It is, however, the archaeological evidence of activity pre-dating the burial ground that is arguably of greatest interest. One burial in particular perhaps sheds more light on our understanding of Hereford than any other of the massive number of burials uncovered during the work of 2009–11. This is the earliest burial, the only one to predate the Norman Conquest, and is that of a child[99] buried beneath the footings of a large, prestigious timber building[100]. It is in many respects the presence of this burial that implies the building in question was not ecclesiastical in function, this and the absence of any other earlier identified burials.

No. firm evidence for Saxon burials around the Cathedral has ever been uncovered. Purported Saxon burials found during the New Library Building excavations are not securely dated, the original dating resting largely on the presence of two barrel padlocks which are in fact more likely to be of medieval date. The only known Hereford Saxon burial ground is that on Castle Green, so if the Saxon Cathedral was not on the Close, could it have been there?

The Castle Green site is monastic in origin. Could it be occupied simultaneously by the mainstream ecclesiastical community? Sarah Foot, in her comprehensive treatise on monasticism during this period[101] identifies early religious philosophical stand points that suggest it would not be untoward for minster and monastery to occupy the same site. Lindisfarne was both the seat of a bishop and home of abbot and monks. The bishop lived with his clergy, with the monks being part of the bishop's household[102]. Nor was this situation unique; Augustine was bishop at Canterbury just as Aidan was bishop at Lindisfarne. In fact Bede seems to have positively encouraged such cohabitation as in a letter from Bishop Eccgberht of York in AD 734, he suggested the sites of minsters in Northumbria be adapted as dwelling places for bishops.

Did all this change in the early AD 970s when the rule of Benedict became the sole system imposed by the council of Winchester under King Edgar[103]? Even if this were the case and the footings for the mid-11th century building[104] were in fact part of a new ecclesiastical centre away from the monastery, there still does not appear to be any burial within the close until the late 11th or early 12th century. On present

99   Sk5061
100 Building 1

101 Foot 2006
102 Foot 2006, 65–6
103 Foot 2006, 68
104 Building 6

evidence it does appear that burial rights continued on Castle Green within St Guthlac's. They may only have moved to the Close following the sacking of the burial ground in 1139 during the Anarchy[105]. In the later campaign King Stephen's men occupied the castle with Matilda's forces attacking it from two fronts, Geoffrey Talbot from the Cathedral, which he turned into a place of war, and Miles of Gloucester from the other side. During this there is a record made by Robert de Bec, one of Stephen's adherents, that 'the citizens in tears, uttering loud cries, either because the burial place of their friends was thrown up against the ramparts of the castle, and they saw the bodies of their relations, some half putrified, others very lately buried, drawn without remorse from their graves; or because on the tower, whence they used to hear the sweet and peaceful summons of the bells, they now saw engines erected and missiles thrown against the king's men'[106]. In the end the King's forces who were occupying the castle were forced to surrender. It is tempting to consider David Whitehead's suggestion[107] that were this the case, the charnel pits at the west end of the cathedral might contain the remains of those burials disturbed during the raising of earthworks across Castle Green as part of that conflict, rather than burials that once occupied the site of the current Cathedral.

All of which leaves our child from the foundation trench, a 'medieval mystery', lying removed by centuries from these later events and by some distance from the nearest contemporary burial. Perhaps it is fitting that we give this youngster the final, but rather sad, word.

They probably died between AD 868 and AD 968, an older child (c 8–10 years old) of unknown sex. They had clearly suffered from malnutrition and their leg bones indicated some evidence for disease or soft tissue injury. They also appear to have suffered from haemorrhaging (tuberculosis is one possible cause of this). The one remaining tooth showed signs of childhood stress. The presence of both active and healed *periostitis* may indicate a chronic or long term infection which began early in childhood. Healing suggests a degree of recovery with a subsequent re-emergence of illness again later in childhood. The presence of *dental enamel hypoplasia* suggests there were stresses placed on the individual during early childhood as a result of illness or malnutrition. The *periostitis* and the *dental enamel hypoplasia* together may suggest a recurring illness from early up to later childhood. They were not local but probably from the north or west of Britain. It is tempting to speculate, but what circumstances led to their unusual interment here we will probably never know.

---

105 The war of succession between Matilda and Stephen 1135–54
106 Shoesmith 1992, 22–23
107 Pers comm

GLOSSARY

Abscess

See *dental abscess*

Ankylosing spondylitis

A chronic inflammatory disease of the axial skeleton, mainly affecting the spine and sacroiliac joint in the pelvis. It has a strong genetic predisposition and tends to occur more commonly males. Typically beginning in the second or third decade of a person's life, with symptoms appearing gradually. The most common symptom is chronic dull pain and stiffness in the lower back, particularly in the morning, easing with physical activity (Sieper et al 2009; Jiménez-Balderas and Mintz G 1993).

Anterior vertebral erosions

They are considered most likely to be the result of anterior herniation of the intervertebral disc due to trauma, termed limbus vertebra (Schmorl and Junghanns 1971). These lesions have been observed more frequently in athletes than non-athletes (Hellström et al 1990; Swärd et al 1993) and most consider that overload of the spine in flexion is the most probable cause (Greene et al 1985; Mandell et al 1993).

Bone cysts

Fluid-filled spaces within the medullary cavity, which are most commonly located in the proximal humerus and proximal femur (Aufderheide & Rodriguez-Martin 1998, 390). Children are most commonly affected but the lesion may persist into adulthood and they are frequently asymptomatic; some resolving spontaneously (Murray et al 1990), however, others may respond to fluid pressure by expanding and thinning the cortex, which may lead to pathological fracture (Violas et al 2004).

Bunions

Hallux abducto valgus, a deformity characterised by medial deviation of the first metatarsal and lateral deviation of the hallux (big toe). They are commonly associated with wearing shoes, particularly tight-fitting shoes with pointed toes. The side of the big toe is forced inwards and sometimes under other toes. Tissues surrounding the joint can become swollen and tender (Howell 2010).

Calculus

Calculus or tartar is mineralised plaque and forms concretions around the crowns or roots of teeth.

Caries

This is the medical term for tooth decay (Moore and Corbett 1978).

Clay-shoveller's fracture

A stable fracture through the spinous process of a vertebra, classically at C6 or C7. The condition was named in 1930s Australia where men digging deep ditches, tossing clay 10 or 15 feet above their heads, suffered from this kind of injury when the clay stuck to their shovels. It was characterised by an audible pop and sudden pain between the shoulder blades and rendered them unable to keep working (Mckellar Hall 1940).

Colles' fracture

A fracture of the distal radius with dorsal posterior displacement of the wrist and hand.

Comminuted fracture

A fracture where the bone shatters into many fragments or splinters, usually the result of a high-impact injury to the bone. Modern causes include vehicle accidents, falls from height and gun shots.

Craniosynostoses

The premature closure of one or more cranial sutures which limits growth in the direction perpendicular to the involved suture which is compensated for by increased growth in other directions, resulting in an abnormal head shape (Aufderheide & Rodriguez-Martin 1998, 52). Premature cranial fusion is relatively rare with a crude prevalence rate of 0.8% recorded at Blackfriars Friary in Ipswich and 1.33% at the Franciscan Church, Hartlepool (Roberts and Cox 2003, 277).

Cribra orbitalia

This consists of pitting in the roof of the orbits and *porotic hyperostosis* pitting on the parietal and/or occipital bones. These conditions are indicators of general stress in childhood and are the result of iron deficiency anaemia (Stuart-Macadam, 1992) due to a diet deficient in vitamin B12 (in animal products) and/or folic acid but can also be caused by chronic disease, particularly gastro-intestinal parasites or other gut infections (Walker et al 2009; Ibid). The porosity is a result of the thinning of the outer table of the cranium due to the expansion of the dipole (trabecular bone between the cranial tables) produced by the body's expansion of the marrow to increase production of red blood and iron levels (Roberts and Manchester 1995). When cribra orbitalia was present, lesions were classified as porotic, cribriotic or trabecular, according to the scheme of Brothwell (1981, fig. 6.17) and remodelled lesions were also distinguished from those which were active using the criteria of Mensforth et al (1978).

Degenerative disc disease

Degeneration of one or more discs of the spine. A disease of aging, it can cause severe chronic pain and can greatly affect quality of life. Symptoms include chronic lower back pain, sometimes radiating to the hips, or pain in the buttocks or thighs while walking as well as sporadic tingling or weakness Lawrence, J S 1969.

Dental abscess

There are a wide range of abscesses that can affect the mouth and teeth. Those that only soft tissue such as gums will not normally be recordable in the archaeological record. This can be caused by bacterial infection in the pulp cavity of the tooth, usually because of tooth decay or damage.

Dental enamel hypoplasia

This is a tooth enamel defect that results in a tooth or teeth having less than the normal amount of enamel. It could be the result of a poor diet or infections during tooth development in childhood. Dental enamel hypoplasias were recorded by the number of observable teeth including partially erupted teeth.

Discitis

A special form of *osteomyelitis* with *S. aureus* again the most common infectious agent, however, others include Streptococus viridans (IVDU & immunocompromised), Gram negative organisms and Mycobacterium tuberculosis (Jevtic 2004; Hopkinson et al 2001). This is primarily a disease of adults, with most patients being over 50 years of age at diagnosis, and presenting with severe localised pain at the spinal level (Ibid).

DISH (diffuse idiopathic skeletal hyperostosis)

DISH is a progressive ossification of the spinal ligaments, particularly in the thoracic region, which leads to fusion (ankylosis) of the vertebrae body; the intervertebral disc space and facet joints are not affected. The changes have a 'melted candle-wax' appearance and are found only down the right-hand side of the thoracic vertebrae because of the presence of the descending aorta on the left side. Extra-spinal ligaments and tendon insertions also ossify producing spurs and spicules of bone at the sites of entheses. Clinical investigations have demonstrated that the condition is often painless and frequently no symptoms are apparent during the life of an individual affected (Aufderheide and Rodriguez-Martin 1998, 97). The causes of DISH are unknown, however, it had been found in association with a number of other conditions, most notably obesity and late onset (type II) diabetes (Julkunen et al 1971); a degree of inherited predisposition and abnormalities in vitamin A metabolism have also been associated with DISH (Oxenham et al 2006; Abiteboul and Arlet 1985). The current thinking is that DISH is a multi-system hormonal disorder (Denko et al 1994; Rogers and Waldron 2001) and recent studies have established DISH's association with risk factors for stroke and cardiovascular disease, which are similarly related to metabolism (Mader et al 2009; Nobuhiko and Akiyama 2006). In the assemblage, DISH was diagnosed by the presence of three or more fused vertebrae with a characteristic DISH morphology (Rogers et al 1987; Julkunen et al 1971).

Enchondroma

An osteochondroma or cartilaginous exostosis is a tumour that forms cartilage; it starts to develop during growth and it is commonly located near the growth plate of long bones (Ortner 2003, 508). The condition only really has an adverse effect on the individual if the swelling is very large or inconveniently located (Roberts and Manchester 1995, 187). These are called enchondromas if they had developed within the substance of the bone.

Erb's palsy

Also known as brachial plexus palsy. This is an injury most often caused to a child during the birth process where nerves passing across the shoulder from the spinal cord are damaged resulting in a lack of muscle control and limpness or paralysis in the arm, hand or wrist.

Gout

Gout is a condition which can affect the skeleton as a result of high levels of uric acid in the blood allowing deposition of uric acid crystals within joints and associated tissues and initiating an inflammatory response (Rogers and Waldron 1995, 78). This leads to erosions with a punched-out appearance, sclerotic border and overhanging edges (Aufderheide and Rodriguez-Martin 1998, 108).

Kyphosis

An anterior curvature of the spine so the affected individual bends forwards (Ortner 2003, 463).

Klippel-Fiel syndrome

Characterised by the congenital fusion of two or more cervical vertebrae due to a segmentation failure of the spine between the 3rd and 8th weeks of embryogenesis (Aufderheide & Rodriguez-Martin 1998, 60). This defect results in a 'short neck, low posterior hair line, and limited movement of the neck' (Barnes 1994, 67).

Legg-Calvé-Perthes disease

A childhood affliction that affects the development of the femoral head. Caused by a lack of blood supply and bone death resulting in reduced bone density and associated problems. Sometimes there can be a disruption of the blood supply to the growing femoral head (where the upper part of the leg joins the pelvis at the hip in a ball and socket joint), which is probably initiated by trauma, resulting in bone death (osteonecrosis) of the femoral head (Legg-Calvé-Perthes disease). The normal ball shaped end of the femur instead exhibits a 'mushroom-shaped' appearance as it becomes increasingly deformed and severe osteoarthritis is common (Aufderheide and Rodriguez-Martin 1998, 84). It will usually only affect one side of the body, occurring between the ages of five and nine (Jaffe 1972, 566; Resnick 1995, 3561).

Leprosy

Leprosy (or Hansen's disease) is a chronic infectious disease caused by the bacteria *Mycobacterium leprae*. The disease is not highly infectious, but is believed to spread mainly through respiratory droplets or possibly via prolonged direct contact with ulcers or open wounds in a person with leprosy (Resnick and Niwayama 1998, 2688). Leprosy is the only bacterium that can infect nerves – however, the skin, eyes, bone and testes may also be involved in the disease process (Ibid). Leprosy is often acquired in childhood and has a long incubation period of *c* 2–5 years before symptoms occur and there seems to be a sex-specific prevalence where men are affected more often than females (Roberts & Manchester 2005, 194).

Maxillary sinusitis

The maxillary sinuses are located in the area of the upper jaw below the eye sockets and behind the cheekbone. Inflammation occurs as a result of infection in the throat, ear, chest or sinuses themselves (Roberts and Manchester 1995) and can cause pain and pressure in the upper jaw and cheeks, mucus formation and headaches (Melen et al 1986). In the skeleton chronic sinusitis can be inferred by the presence of new bone formation within the sinus cavities. Smoke, dust and environmental pollution can lead to sinusitis; urban sites have a higher incidence of the disease and it is thought to be due to atmospheric pollution in industrial cities and towns (Roberts et al 1998). The true prevalence of such infections is difficult to calculate as new bone will only be visible if the facial bones and sinuses are broken or if radiography or endoscopy are used; neither of the later two investigative techniques were undertaken on the Hereford assemblage. The maxillary sinuses may become infected by dental disease, and more specifically, by the perforation of the sinus by a dental abscess of the upper jaw (Roberts and Manchester 1995, 176).

Ochondrosis

Also known as alkaptonuria. An inherited error of metabolism, permitting the accumulation of homogentistic acid (HA) in connective tissues. HA is deposited in joint cartilage causing a black discolouration and sclerosis of the vertebral end-plates followed by ankylosis (Aufderheide and Rodriguez-Martin 1998, 111).

Os acromiale

The term given to a condition where a small bone at the front of the shoulder fails to fuse, and can result in shoulder pain particularly when carrying out above shoulder height arm actions.

Ossification

The term used to describe bone growth which can be normal such as in developing children or due to conditions (eg DISH) or trauma. See also *myositis ossificans traumatica*.

Ossifying fibroma (OF)

This is classified as, and behaves like a benign bone neoplasm. It affects the jaw in 20–40 year olds and produces large masses (up to 5cm) of osteolytic bone that expand and thin the cortex – the lesion may involve and distort the cortex but seldom penetrates it (Aufderheide & Rodriguez-Martin 1998, 377). The origin of OF is thought to be the periodontal membrane and some OFs do, in fact, contain prevalent cementum-like calcifications while others show only bony material, but a mixture of the two types of calcification is commonly seen in a single lesion (Liu et al 2010).

Osteoarthritis

Osteoarthritis (OA) involves deterioration of the cartilage between synovial joints, and the clearest diagnostic feature of osteoarthritis in bone is eburnation; when a polished surface is created from bone-to-bone contact. Further features of OA include osteophytes on or around the joint margin, porosity on the surfaces, and subchondral cysts (Rogers 2000). OA is characterised by the presence of at least two of these latter features or eburnation even if it occurs alone (Ibid). Individuals suffering from OA can experience stiffness and pain in the affected joint, which may become swollen, and in some cases can cause disability and a reduction in the quality of life (Kean et al 2004). Symptoms are not constant in this disease but instead flare up unpredictably and studies have shown no correlation between severity of pain experienced by the individual and the expression of OA (Cockburn et al 1979). Osteoarthritis can develop due to acute joint trauma including articular surface fractures, joint dislocations, and ligament and meniscal ruptures which increase joint instability (Buckwalter and Lane 1997; Honkonen 1995; Hadley et al 1990). Five individuals in the assemblage, including three females and two males exhibited secondary osteoarthritis due to *Legg-Calvé-Perthes disease* or *slipped capital femoral epiphysis*.

Osteoblastoma

A benign bone growth usually greater than 2cm in size.

Osteochondritis dissecans

A benign, non-inflammatory condition of young adults characterized by a small area of focal necrosis on the epiphyseal surface, resulting in partial or complete detachment of a segment of bone on the convex articular surface.

Osteoma

A bone-forming lesion which is usually small and commonly termed 'button osteomas'. The frequency of lesions peaks in individuals in their 30s and 40s and generally occurs on the ectocranial surface of the skull or facial bones. Multiple osteomas of the skull may be associated with an inherited syndrome termed Gardener's syndrome (also known as familial colorectal polyposis) characterized by the presence of multiple polyps in the colon together with tumors outside the colon (Lee et al 2011).

Osteomalacia

This is the adult form of vitamin D deficiency. In osteomalacia the accumulation of unmineralized osteoid replacing bone mineral leads to a generalized softening and weakening of the skeleton (Brickley et al 2007). This weakening leads to 'pseudofractures' (or Looser's zones) which are streaks of decreased density, possibly the result of stress fractures that have failed to heal which can progress to full fractures with minimal trauma. They occur symmetrically at specific locations throughout the skeleton; the scapula and ribs are two of the predilect areas affected by this disease (Ibid).

Osteomyelitis

An infection of the bone and the bone marrow resulting in inflammatory destruction of the bone. Many organisms may cause osteomyelitis but the majority of cases are caused by a pus-producing bacterium (*Staphylococcus aureus*) which predominately causes localized skin infections such as boils (Ortner 2003, 181; Waldron 2009, 85). There are three ways in which the infecting organisms can reach the skeleton: by spreading through the blood steam from an infection elsewhere (haematogenous spread), by direct extension from adjacent soft tissue, or by direct infection through traumatic wounds. The infected bone may swell and new bone is laid down by the periosteum. A thick collar around the bone may be formed which is known as an involucrum or pieces of the bone may suffer ischemic necrosis forming a sequestrum (an area of necrotic bone surrounded by living bone) that may separate from the rest of the bone. Furthermore, cloacae are formed in the bone; these are channels through which pus drains from the infected bone, with drainage continuing through sinuses which are formed in the overlying soft tissue. Osteomyelitis can persist for years as there was no cure for the disease until the advent of antibiotics; many

underwent amputation of the affected area as several complications could occur including malignant change in the tract of the sinus, deposition of amyloid in the kidney or the spread of infection to other organs eg the brain or meninges, which would all be fatal (Waldron 1999, 86).

Osteoporosis

An individual's maximum bone mass (MBM) is achieved at about 30–40 years of age, after which bone is lost with increasing age. Women lose bone at a faster rate than men at all ages and their rate of loss tends to increase further after menopause, when the protective effect of oestrogen is lost. Bone turnover and therefore potential bone loss is greater in the trabecular bone than cortical bone and therefore regions of the skeleton with a high proportion of trabecular bone are more susceptible to osteoporosis-related fractures (Brickley 2000 in Mays & Cox 2000). To date, there is no agreed way to diagnose osteoporosis in the skeleton – in macroscopic examination a number of factors should be taken into account when considering a diagnosis of osteoporosis, for example, location of the fracture and estimated age and sex of the individual. The regions of the skeleton with high trabecular bone content and where osteoporosis-related fractures are frequently recorded as having occurred include the proximal femur (hip), distal radius (wrist; also known as colles' fractures) and vertebral bodies (spine; crush fractures; Brickley 2002). Further, although more subjective, observations of reduced cortical thickness or thinning of the trabecular network within bones has been used to diagnose osteoporosis (Ibid).

Ostitis

Inflamation of the bone.

Paget's disease

The disease presents as a localized disruption of normal bone remodelling with an increase in osteoclast-mediated bone resorption and a compensatory increase in new bone formation. This process results in the increased formation of osteoid which is softer and weaker than normal, with the affected bone is often becoming enlarged and prone to bending or fracture under gravitational stress (Wade et al 2011). The cause of Paget's disease is, as yet, unclear but geographic distributions imply a genetic component; with as much as 6% of the population in areas of Great Britain affected (Monfort et al, 1999) and similarly common in Western Europe (Resnick, 1988), but rare in indigenous populations in China, Japan and Africa (Ibid; Ralston, 2002). Paramyxoviruses, such as measles and canine distemper virus (CDV), have also been suggested as activating factors (Meunier, 2002). The clinical, symptomatic form of the disease is one of older people; however, this is often preceded by a decades-long asymptomatic period by which it is found incidentally on radiographs obtained for other reasons (Aufderheide and Rodriguez-Martin 1998). Clinical symptoms of the disease include bone pain, fracture and deformity, and in a small proportion of cases, osteosarcoma may develop (Kaplan and Singer 1995).

Periodontal disease

The bacteria within accumulations of plaque and tartar can infect the gingival tissues and cause inflammation – gingivitis (Hillson 1996). In consequence, the bone around the tooth is resorbed (destroyed) creating an increasing distance between the bone and the cemento-enamel junction of the tooth, and the tooth is eventually lost. This process is largely painless although symptoms include swelling of the gums and halitosis (Scully and Cawson 1996).

Periostitis

Inflamation of the layer or membrane surrounding the bone (periosteum).

Pigeon chest

A condition where cartilage grown causes the sternum to jut out creating a protruding chest.

Polio

Poliomyelitis. Caused by an RNA virus and most often spread through fecal-oral transmission (Smallman-Raynor and Cliff 2006). The virus implants itself and multiplies in the epithelial lining of the gastrointestinal or respiratory tract. It is characterised in its mild form by flu-like symptoms however if the disease progresses

and the infection spreads to the central nervous system paralysis can occur. The motor cells in the spinal cord may be destroyed and the muscles supplied by these nerves become paralysed. The virus can also destroy motor nuclei in the brainstem and cause fatal complications involving breathing and respiration (Pritchard and Alloway 1999). Early descriptions of polio cited a much higher incidence in children, hence the alternative name of infantile paralysis. Paralysis most often occurs in M. *tibialis anterior*, M. *tibialis posterior*, and other long muscles of the toes (Sharrard 1955; Ferguson 1933). In children with paralysed limbs, the bones will fail to develop normally and will be shorter and more slender than those of the unaffected limb.

Porotic hyperostosis

Similar to *cribra orbitalia* but affects all bones of the cranial vault.

Psoriatic arthritis

A skin disease which affects about 1% of the population of which around 5% develop joint disease (Manchester and Roberts 1995, 159). The causes of the disease are unknown, although like AS it has a genetic factor; 60+% have antigen HLA-B27 (Aufderheide and Rodriguez-Martin 1998, 104). The disease can affect any of the synovial joints, singly or multiply, and usually asymmetrically (Manchester and Roberts 1995, 159). In the severe form of the disease lytic destruction of the fingers and toes, produces a 'cup-and-pencil' deformity and fusion can occur. In 25% of cases sacroiliac and vertebral lesions occur, which are also asymmetrical, including sacroiliitis and spinal syndesmophyte 'skip lesions' (intermittent bony growth attached to a ligament) – both of which cause ankylosis (Aufderheide and Rodriguez-Martin 1998, 104).

Reiter's syndrome (RS)

Also called reactive arthritis. Consists of non-specific urethritis, conjunctivitis and polyarthritis. RS may arise from gastro-intestinal infections such as Salmonella or Shigella dysentery, or from sexually-acquired infections related to the bacterium Chlamydia trachomatis causing urethritis (Rogers et al 1987; Aufderheide and Rodriguez-Martin 1998, 104). In London in the 19th century 3% of admissions in three of the largest hospitals were due to venereal disease with associated arthritis (Storey and Scott 1998). The skeletal manifestations of this disease in the sacroiliac joint and spinal are similar to PA. Furthermore, asymmetric erosions of joints are also present, however, in most cases few joints are affected and the arthritis is usually less destructive compared to that in PA. The peripheral joints affected are primarily the feet, ankle and knee and fluffy, periosteal, new bone growth may be present on the metacarpals, metatarsals and phalange shafts, around the knee and at tendons and ligaments (Rogers et al 1987).

Rickets

This is caused by a deficiency in vitamin D during infancy and childhood. The vitamin being obtained predominately by the action of ultra-violet light on precursors in the skin a lack of which causes softening of the bones and cessation in cartilage mineralisation. Subsequent skeletal manifestations most popularly include bowing of the weight-bearing long bones or arm bones in crawling infants, but also distortion of the pelvis, vertebrae and sacrum. Furthermore, porous and flared rib ends and long bone metaphyses, cranial porosity (Ortner and Mays 1998), coxa vara and flattening of the bone beneath the femoral head and medial tilting of the distal epiphysis of the tibia (Mays et al 2006). Retardation in growth may be apparent, however, bowing of long bones cannot occur if the growth is very retarded, as some bone growth needs to take place to cause bowing deformities (Stuart-Macadam 1989, 208). The number of cases of rickets is unlikely to represent the prevalence in the living population as once a child is exposed to the sun again the condition is rapidly reversible, although some bending deformity may still be evident in adulthood (Ibid, 209).

Rotator cuff disease

This is damage to the supraspinatus, infraspinatus, teres minor and subscapularis muscles; these four muscles act as rotators of the humerus and the combined tendinous structure around the shoulder joint is referred to as the rotator cuff. Of the inserts affected in the Hereford assemblage, the subscapularis muscle insertion most commonly showed diagnostic changes (21/24 inserts observed), followed by the suprascapularis (17/24),

with the infraspinatus (8/24) and the teres minor being the least affected (2/24).

Scoliosis

A lateral curvature of the spine with rotation of the vertebrae towards the concavity, usually exhibiting a double curve permitting the head to be located in the mid-sagittal plane (Aufderheide & Rodriguez-Martin 1998, 66). Scoliosis can be congenital or idiopathic; the latter is the most common (80%) and usually appears after birth or during childhood and although the aetiology remains obscure some population studies have shown that it is an inherited familial disease in 30% of cases (Ibid). The prognosis depends on the age of onset, and is worst if it appears early in life (Adams 1968).

Scheuermann's disease

This is a childhood affliction where one side of the vertebral body grows more than the other creating a curved spinal column (see *Kyphosis*).

Schmorl's node

A dent in the vertebral body possibly caused by heavy or repetitive lifting. The presence of a Schmorl's node may be associated with pain but is usually asymptomatic (Hamanishi et al 1994).

Scurvy

Scurvy is caused by a vitamin C deficiency. Vitamin C is required for collagen synthesis, which is the main protein component of connective tissue, including bone. Production of defective collagen leads to fragile blood vessels that rupture easily, leading to haemorrhages either spontaneously or following minor trauma/normal stress and strain. The inflammatory and hemorrhagic response to chronic bleeding on or near a bone surface is increased vascularity, causing an area of abnormal porosity in the cortical bone (Ortner and Ericksen 1997; Ortner 2003). Sub-periosteal haemorrhage may also result in the loosely attached periosteum becoming stripped from the underlying bone, activating bone formation and is commonly symmetrical (Aufderheide and Rodriguez-Martin 1998, 311). In adults these lesions are usually diaphyseal and restricted to a moderate size, however, in infants the periosteum is much more easily separated from the cortex and a sub-periosteal haemorrhage often involves a proportionately much greater area and volume (Ibid). Where chronic bleeding occurs at the joints of infants, widening of the long bone metaphysis (fusion sites near the long bone ends) and of the costo-cartilage junctions of the ribs occurs (Jaffe 1972, 449; Ibid). An expansion of the zone of calcification occurs as the osteoblastic activity (deposition of bone) is impaired however the osteoclastic phase (removal) of bone remodelling continues, producing a fragile region where fracturing can occur. Furthermore, the densely collegenous periodontal ligament, which anchors the teeth, loses its integrity and teeth become loosened with infection and haemorrhage around the roots resulting in exfoliation of the teeth (Aufderheide and Rodriguez-Martin 1998, 312).

Slipped femoral capital epiphysis

This occurs with rapid growth during adolescence, between 8 and 17 years of age (Aufderheide and Rodriguez-Martin 1998, 90). The primary pathology of this lesion is a stress fracture between the metaphyseal side of the growth plate and the neck of the femur, allowing medial posterior and downward displacement of the head of the femur (Ortner 2003, 347). In the skeleton, displacement, irregularities in the proximal end of the femoral neck due to the fracture and a short thick neck reflecting attrition in the fracture area and loss of endochondral growth for varying lengths of time, are diagnostic (Ibid). There is some evidence of an underlying genetic factor, but trauma and obesity are clear contributing factors (Resnick et al 1995, 2647). The most frequent complication of this condition is secondary degenerative joint disease whose severity depends on the degree of head displacement.

Spondylolysis

A defect of the vertebrae, most commonly found in lumbar vertebrae L5, but also found in other lumbar and thoracic vertebrae. There is a strong genetic component to the condition but it can also be caused, or exacerbated by repetitive strenuous activities. It can cause back and neck pain and nerve damage (Logrosino et al 2001).

Styloid process of the temporal bone

This is a slender projection attached to base of the skull that extends downwards and forwards deep in the wall of the pharynx or behind the upper part of the throat. Patients with fracture of the process may have a variety of signs and symptoms including pain and localised swelling, difficulty swallowing, problems with opening their mouth, pain on turning the head, pain in the ear, tinnitus, and headaches (Smith and Cherry 1988; Carro and Nunez 1995).

Tarsal coalition

Refers to a union between two or more tarsal bones and although such a fusion may be acquired (eg in rheumatoid arthritis or trauma) the term usually implies a developmental abnormality due to faulty segmentation during development. At Wharram Percy nine individuals exhibited tarsal coalition and the CPR for later-medieval sites is 0.34% (Roberts & Cox 2003, 277). SK11886 exhibited unilateral talocalcaneal coalition in her left foot.

Trauma

A term used to refer to actions on the body that result in the breaking of skin, flesh or bone. It is the latter that is most commonly diagnosed within archaeological assemblages.

BIBLIOGRAPHY

Abiteboul, M & Arlet, J 1985 'Retinol-related hyperostosis', *American Journal of Roentgenology* 44: 435–6.

Adams, C J 1968 *Manual de Ortopedia,* 4th edition, Toray, Barcelona.

Ali, A, Tetalman, M R, Fordham, E W, Turner, D A, Chiles, J T, Patel, S L & Schmidt, K D 1980 'Distribution of hypertrophic pulmonary osteoarthropathy', *American Journal of Roentgenology* 134: 771–80.

Andersen, J G & Manchester, K 1992 'The rhinomaxillary syndrome in leprosy: a clinical, radiological and palaeopathological study', *International Journal of Osteoarchaeology* 2: 121–129.

Anderson, T 2003 'The first evidence of brucellosis from British skeletal material', *Journal of Paleopathology* 15: 153–158.

Ardehali, M M, Kouhi, A, Meighani, A, Rad, F & Emami, H 2009 'Temporomandibular Joint Dislocation Reduction Technique: A New External Method vs the Traditional' *Annals of Plastic Surgery* 63 (2): 1–3.

Assefa, F, Jabarkhil, M Z, Salama, P & Spiegel, P 2001 'Malnutrition and mortality in Kohistan District, Afganistan, April 2001', *Journal of the American Medical Association* 286: 2723–8.

Aufderheide & Rodriguez-Martin 1998 *The Cambridge Encyclopaedia of Human Paleopathology,* Cambridge University Press, New York.

Barnes, E 1994 *Developmental Defects of the Axial Skeleton in Paleopathology,* University Press of Colorado, Niwot, Colorado.

Barrow, J 2000 'Athelstan to Aigueblanche, 1056–268', in Aylmer G E & Tiller J E (eds) *Hereford Cathedral: A History,* The Hambledon Press, London, 21–47.

Bashford, L & Sibun, L 2007 'Excavations at the Quaker Burial Ground, Kingston-upon-Thames, London', *Post-Medieval Archaeology* 41 (1): 100–54.

Bass, W M 2005 *Human Osteology; A Laboratory and Field Manual,* Special publication No. 2 of the Missouri Archaeological Society, 5th edition.

Becker, M H J, Lassner, F, Bahm, J, Ingianni, G & Pallua, N 2002 'The cervical rib: a predisposing factor for obstetric brachial plexus lesions', *Journal of Bone and Joint Surgery* 84-B (5): 740–3.

Bennett, W F & Browner, B 1994 'Tibial plateau fractures: A study of associated soft tissue injuries', *Journal of Orthopeadic Trauma,* 8 (3): 14.

Berry, A C 1974 'The use of non-metric variations of the cranium in a study of Scandinavian population movements', *American Journal of Physical Anthropology* 40: 345–58.

Berry, A C & Berry, R J 1967 'Epigenetic Variation in the Human Cranium', *Journal of Anatomy* 101: 361–79.

Biddle, M & Creasey, S 1990 'Beads', in Biddle, M (ed) *Object and Economy in Medieval Winchester,* Winchester Studies 7ii, Oxford, 659–65.

Black, R E, Morris, S S & Bryce, J 2003 'Where and why are 10 million children dying every year?' *The Lancet* 361: 2226–34.

Blair, J 2001 'The Anglo-Saxon Church in Herefordshire: Four Themes', in Malpas, J B, Butler, J, Davis, A, Davis, S, Malpas, T & Sanson, C *The Early Church in Herefordshire, Leominster History Study Group,* Leominster, 3–13.

Blair, J 2005 *The Church in Anglo-Saxon Society,* Oxford University Press, Oxford.

Bloodworth, A J, Cameron, D G, Harrison, D J, Highley, D E, Holloway, S & Warrington G 1999 'Mineral Resource Information for Development Plans: Phase 1 Herefordshire & Worcestershire: Resources and Constraints', *British Geological Survey Technical Report* WF/99/4.

Boston, C 2006 'Burial Practice and Material Culture', in Boston, C, Boyle, A & Witkin, A 'In The Vaults Beneath', *Archaeological Recording at St George's Church, Bloomsbury, Oxford Archaeology,* https://library.thehumanjourney.net/148/, 100–25.

Boston, C 2008 *Rycote Chapel, Coffins in the Crypt: Archaeological Watching Brief Report,* Oxford Archaeology, http://library the humanjourney net/118/.

Brettell, R, Montgomery, J & Evans, J 2012 'Brewing and stewing: the effect of culturally mediated behaviour on the oxygen isotope composition of ingested fluids and implications for human provenance studies', *Journal of Analytical Atomic Spectrometry* 27 (5): 778–85.

Brickley, M 2000 'The diagnosis of metabolic disease in archaeological bone', in Mays, S & Cox, M *Human Osteology in Archaeology and Forensic Science,* Cambridge University Press, New York, 183–98.

Brickley, M 2002 'An investigation of historical and archaeological evidence for age-related bone loss and osteoporosis', *International Journal of Osteoarchaeology* 12 (5): 364–71.

Brickley, M, Berry, H, & Western, G, 2006, 'The People: Physical Anthropology' in Brickley, M, Buteux, S, Adams, J, & Cherrington, R *St Martins Uncovered: Investigations into the churchyard of St Martins-in-the-Bull Ring, Birmingham, 2001,* Oxbow, Oxford, 90–151.

Brickley, M, Mays, S & Ives, R 2007 'An Investigation of Skeletal Indicators of Vitamin D Deficiency in Adults: Effective Markers for Interpreting Past Living Conditions and Pollution Levels in 18th and 19th Century Birmingham, England', *American Journal of Physical Anthropology* 132: 67–79.

Bridges, P S 1994 'Vertebral Arthritis and Physical Activities in the Prehistoric South-eastern United States', *American Journal of Physical Anthropology* 93: 83–93.

Brothwell, D & Zakrzewski, S 2004 'Metric and non-metric studies of archaeological human bone', in Brickley, M & McKinley, I J, *Guidelines to the Standard for Recording Human Remains,* BABAO and IFA paper No 7, 27–33.

Brothwell, D R 1981 *Digging up Bones,* Cornell University Press, New York.

Brown, D 1990 'Weaving tools', in Biddle, M (ed) *Object and Economy in Medieval Winchester,* Winchester Studies 7ii, Oxford, 225–32.

Buckwalter, J A & Lane, L E 1997 'Athletics and osteoarthritis', *American Journal of Sports Medicine* 25: 873–81.

Buikstra, J E & Ubelaker, D H (eds) 1994 *Standards for Data Collection from Human Skeletal Remains,* Fayetteville.

Butler, S M 2007 *The Language of Abuse: Marital Violence in Later Medieval England,* Brill, Leiden.

Buxton, L H D 1938 'Platymeria and Platycnemia', *Journal of Anatomy* 73: 31–6.

Caffell, A 1997 *A Comparison of Stature between British Skeletal Populations,* Bradford University, Unpublished Undergraduate Dissertation.

Capasso, L 1999 'Brucellosis at Herculaneum (79 AD)', *International Journal of Osteoarchaeology* 9: 277–288.

Capasso, L, Kennedy, K A R & Wilczak, C A 1998 *Atlas of Occupation Markers on Human Remains,* Journal of Paleontology – Monographic Publication 3, Edigrafital S p A Teramo, Italy.

Carro, L P & Nunez, N P 1995 'Fracture of the styloid process of the temporal bone', *International Orthopaedics* 19 (6): 359–60.

Chen L X, Schumacher H R 2008 'Gout: an evidence-based review', *Journal of Clinical Rheumatology* 14 (5 Suppl, October 2008): S55–62.

Cherry, J 1991 'Leather', in Blair, J & Ramsay, N (eds), *English Medieval Industries,* Hambledon Press, London, 295–318.

Clay, R M 1909 *The Mediaeval Hospitals of England,* (reprinted 1966), Cass, London.

Cockburn, A, Duncan, H & Riddle, J M 1979 'Arthritis, ancient and modern: guidelines for field workers', *Henry Ford Medical Journal* 27 (1): 74–7.

Coggon, D, Kellingray S, Inskip, H, Croft, P, Campbell, L & Cooper, C 1998 'Osteoarthritis of the hip and occupational lifting', *American Journal Epidemiology* 147: 523–8.

Cowgill, J, de Neergaard, M & Griffiths, N 1987 *Knives and Scabbards, Medieval finds from excavations in London: 1,* HMSO, London.

Craddock-Bennett, L 2012 *Cathedral Close Excavations 2009– 2011,* Unpublished report, Headland Archaeology (UK) Ltd, Hereford Archaeology Series 998.

Crawford, S 2008 'Special Burials, Special Buildings? An Anglo-Saxon Perspective on the Interpretation of Infant Burials in Association with Rural Settlement Structures', in Bacvarov, K (ed) *Babies Reborn: Infant/Child Burials in Pre- and Protohistory,* BAR International Series 1832.

Croft, P, Coggon, D, Cruddas, M & Cooper, C 1992 'Osteoarthritis of the Hip: An Occupational Disease in Farmers', *British Medical Journal* 304: 1269–72.

Crooks, K H 2000 *Toilets and Storage Area, Hereford Cathedral, Hereford Interim Report on an Archaeological watching brief,* Unpublished Report, Archaeological Investigations Ltd, Hereford Archaeology Series 926.

Crooks, K H 2000 *County Hospital, Hereford: Archaeological Evaluation in advance of Phase VI,* Unpublished Report, Archaeological Investigations Ltd, Hereford Archaeology Series 485.

Crooks, K H 2001 *Chapter House Yard, Hereford Archaeological Excavation and Survey,* Unpublished Report, Archaeological Investigations Ltd, Hereford Archaeology Series 490.

Crooks, K H 2005 *39–40 Bewell Street, Hereford: Archaeological excavation and watching brief,* Unpublished Report, Archaeological Investigations Ltd, Hereford Archaeology Series 683.

Crooks, K H 2007 *Land between Commercial Street and Union Street, Hereford: Archaeological evaluation, excavation and watching brief,* Unpublished Report, Archaeological Investigations Ltd, Hereford Archaeology Series 695.

Crooks, K H 2009a *Goal Street/Bath Street: Archaeological Evaluation,* Unpublished Report, Archaeological Investigations Ltd, Hereford Archaeology Series 782.

Crooks, K H 2009b *Hereford Flood Alleviation Scheme: Archaeological excavation and watching briefs,* Unpublished Report, Archaeological Investigations Ltd, Hereford Archaeology Series 827.

Crooks, K H 2012 'The High Temperature Residues' in Craddock-Bennett, L *Cathedral Close Excavations 2009–2011,* Unpublished report, Headland Archaeology (UK) Ltd, Hereford Archaeology Series 998.

Daniell, C 1997 *Death and Burial in Medieval England 1066–1550,* Routledge, London.

Dawes, J D & Magilton, J R 1980 *The Cemetery of St-Helen-on-the-Walls, Aldwalk, The Archaeology of York, The Medieval Cemeteries (York)* Vol 12/1, Council for British Archaeology, York.

Defoe, D 1724 'A Tour Through the Whole Island of Great Britain' quoted in Shoesmith, R 1992 *Hereford: History and Guide,* Alan Sutton, Cardiff.

Denko, C E, Boja, B & Moskowitz, R W 1994 'Growth promoting peptides in osteoarthritis and diffuse idiopathic skeletal hyperostosis – insulin, insulin-like growth factor-1, growth hormone', *Journal of Rheumatology* 21: 1725–30.

Duncumb, J 1804 *Collections towards the History and Antiquities of the County of Hereford* Merton Priory Press 1997, Cardiff.

Dyer, C 1989 *Standards of living in the Middle Ages: social change in England c 1200–1520,* Cambridge University Press, Cambridge.

English Heritage 2004 *Human Bones from Archaeological Sites: Guidelines for producing assessment documents and analytical reports,* Centre for Archaeology Guidelines, English Heritage, London.

Evans-Jones, G, Kay, S P J, Weindling, A M, Cranny, G, Ward, A, Bradshaw, A & Hernon, C 2003 'Congenital brachial palsy: incidence, causes, and outcome in the United Kingdom and Northern Ireland', *Archives of Diseases in Childhood, Foetal and Neonatal Edition* 88: 185–89.

Fazekas, I Gy & Kosa, F 1978 *Forensic Foetal Osteology,* Akadémiai Kiad ó, Budapest.

Felson, D T, Hannan, M T, Naimark, A, Berkeley, J, Gordon, G, Wilson, P W 1991 'Occupational physical demands, knee bending, and knee osteoarthritis: results from the Framingham Study', *Journal of Rheumatology* 18: 1587–92.

Ferguson, A B 1933 'Short metatarsal boxes and their relation to poliomyelitis', *Journal of Bone and Joint Surgery* 15: 98–100.

Finnegan, M 1978 'Non-metric variation of infracranial skeleton', *Journal of Anatomy* 125: 23–37.

Foot, S 2006 *Monastic Life in Anglo-Saxon England, c 600–900,* Cambridge University Press, Cambridge.

Garmonsway, G N (ed) 1953 *The Anglo Saxon Chronicle,* Littlehampton Book Services, Worthing.

Goodall, I H 1990 'Locks and Keys' in Biddle, M (ed) *Object and Economy in Medieval Winchester,* Winchester Studies 7ii, Oxford, 1001–36.

Grauer, A L 1993 'Patterns of anemia and infection from medieval York, England', *American Journal of Physical Anthropology* 91: 203–213.

Grauer, A L & Roberts, C A 1996 'Palaeoepidemiology, Healing and Possible Treatment of Trauma in the Medieval Cemetery Population of St Helen-on-the-Walls, York, England', *American Journal of Physical Anthropology,* 100: 531–44.

Greene, M 2005 Herefordshire Through Time, *Herefordshire Council,* accessed online Juky 2012: http://htt.herefordshire.gov.uk/767.aspx.

Greene, T L, Hensinger, R N & Hunter, L Y 1985 'Back pain and vertebral changes simulating Scheuermann's disease', *Journal of Pediatric Orthopaedics* 5: 1–7.

Gretton, F E 1889 *Memory's Harkback through Half-a-Century, 1808 to 1858,* Bentley and Son, London.

Hadley, N A, Brown, T D & Weinstein, S L 1990 'The effects of contact pressure elevations and aseptic necrosis on the long-term outcome of congenital hip dislocation', *Journal of Orthopaedic Research* 8: 504–13.

Hagberg, M & Wegman, D H 1987 'Prevalence rates and odds ratios of shoulder-neck diseases in different occupational groups', *British Journal of Industrial Medicine* 44(9): 602–10.

Hamanishi, C, Kawabata, T, Yosii, T & Tanaka, S 1994 'Schmorl's nodes on magnetic resonance imaging Their incidence and clinical relevance', *Spine* 19: 450–53.

Hamilton-Dyer S 1997 'The Animal Bones from Late Saxon and Medieval deposits', in Russel et al *The Lower High Street Project,* Unpublished report for Southampton City Archaeological Unit.

Hamilton-Dyer, S 2010 *Skriðuklaustur Monastery, Iceland, Animal Bones 2003 – 2007,* Skriðuklaustursrannsóknir Monograph XXVI, Reykjavik.

Hancox, E 2006 'Coffin and coffin furniture', in Brickley, M et al *St Martin's Uncovered Investigations in the churchyard of St Martin's-in-the-Bull Ring, Birmingham, 2001,* Oxbow Books, Oxford, 152–160.

Hanihara, T & Ishida, H 2001a 'Frequency variations of discrete cranial traits in major human populations I Supernumerary ossicle variations', *Journal of Anatomy* 198: 698–706.

Hanihara, T & Ishida, H 2001b 'Frequency variations of discrete cranial traits in major human populations II Hypostotic variations', *Journal of Anatomy* 198: 707–25.

Hanihara, T, Ishida, H & Dodo, Y 2003 'Characterization of biological diversity through analysis of discrete cranial traits', *American Journal of Physical Anthropology* 121: 241–51.

Harrison, W 1573 *The Great English Chronologie.*

Hellström, M, Jacobsson, B, Swärd, L & Peterson, L 1990 'Radiologic abnormalities of the thoraco-lumbar spine in athletes', *Acta Radiologica* 31: 127–132.

Hencken, H 1950 'Lagore Crannog: An Irish Residence of the 7th to 10th Centuries AD', *Proceedings of the Royal Irish Academy* 53C, 1–241.

Hengen, O P 1971 'Cribra Orbitalia: Pathogenesis and Possible Aetiology', *Homo* 22: 57–76.

Hereford Journal, Wed 23rd March 1831 Accessed October 2012, http://www britishnewspaperarchive co uk/viewer/bl/0000398/18310323/006/0003?browse=false

Hewlett, B S 1991 'Demography and Childcare in Pre-industrail Societies', *Journal of Anthropological Research* 47: 1–37.

Hill, P 1997 *Whithorn and St Ninian: the excavation of a monastic town 1984–91,* The Whithorn Trust and Sutton Publishing, Stroud.

Hillaby, J 2001 'The Early Church in Herefordshire: Columban and Roman', in Malpas, J B, Butler, J, Davis, A, Davis, S, Malpas, T & Sanson, C *The Early Church in Herefordshire, Leominster History Study Group,* Leominster, 41–76.

Hillson, S 1996 *Dental Anthropology,* Cambridge University Press, Cambridge.

Hinton, D 1990 'Hooked Tags', in Biddle, M (ed) *Object and Economy in Medieval Winchester,* Winchester Studies 7ii, Oxford, 548–52.

Holick, M F 2005 'The vitamin D epidemic and its health consequences', *Journal of Nutrition* 135: 2739S–2748S.

Holst, M 2005 'Artefacts & Environmental Evidence: The Human Bone', in Spall, C A & Toop, N J (eds), *Blue Bridge Lane & Fishergate House, York Report on Excavations: July 2000 to July 2002* accessed online October 2012 at: http://www archaeologicalplanningconsultancy.co.uk/mono/001/rep_bone_hum1a html

Honkonen, S E 1995 'Degenerative arthritis after tibial plateau fractures', *J Ortho Trauma* 9: 273–7.

Hooke, D 2006 *England's Landscape: The West Midlands,* English Heritage, London.

Hopkinson, N, Stevenson, J & Benjamin, S 2001 'A case ascertainment study of septic discitis: clinical, microbiological and radiological features' in *QJM* 94 (9): 465–470.

Hoverd, T 1998 *Cathedral Hole: A report on a trial hole,* Unpublished Report, Archaeological Investigations Ltd, Hereford Archaeology Series 359.

Howell, D 2010 *The Barefoot Book,* Hunter House, Alameda, California

Hurst, D 'Medieval industry in the West Midlands', in *West Midlands Regional Research Framework for Archaeology,* Seminar 5 Papers accessed online November 2012 at: http://www birmingham ac uk/schools/iaa/departments/archaeology/research/wmrrfa/seminar5 aspx

Iles, P 2000 'The Stained Glass', in Aylmer G E & Tiller J E (eds) *Hereford Cathedral: A History,* The Hambledon Press, London, 314–21.

International Myeloma Working Group 2003 'Criteria for the classification of monoclonal gammopathies, multiple myeloma and related disorders: a report of the International Myeloma Working Group', *British Journal of Haematology* 121 (5): 749–57.

Işcan, M Y, Loth, S R & Wright, R K 1984 'Age estimation from the rib phase analysis: white males', *Journal of Forensic Science* 29: 1094–110.

Işcan, M Y, Loth, S R & Wright, R K 1985 'Age estimation from the rib phase analysis: white females', *Journal of Forensic Science* 30: 853–863.

Ivens, R J, Busby, P & Shepherd, N 1995 *Tattenhoe and Westbury: two deserted medieval settlements in Milton Keynes,* Buckinghamshire Archaeological Society, Monograph No 8, Aylesbury.

Jaffe, H L 1972 *Metabolic, Degenerative and Inflammatory Disease of Bones and Joints,* Lea and Febiger, Philadelphia.

Jenkins, R 1936 'Industries of Herefordshire in Bygone Times', *Transactions of the Newcomen Society,* Vol 17: 175–189.

Jevtic, V (2004) 'Vertebral infection', *European Radiology Supplements* 14: E43–E52

Johnston, F E 1962 'The concept of skeletal age ', *Clinical Pediatrics* 1: 133–144,

Jiménez-Balderas, F J & Mintz, G 1993 'Ankylosing spondylitis: clinical course in women and men' *Journal of Rheumatology* 20 (12): 2069–72.

Judd, M A & Roberts, C A 1999 'Fracture Trauma in a Medieval British Farming Village', *American Journal of Physical Anthropology* 109: 229–43.

Julkunen, H, Heinonen, O P & Pyorala, K 1971 'Hyperostosis of the Spine in an adult population', *Annals of the Rheumatic Disease* 30: 605–12.

Jurmain, R D 1991 'Paleoepidemiology of trauma in a prehistoric Central California population', in Ortner, D J & Aufderheide, A C (eds) *Human Paleopathology: Current Synthesis and Future Options,* Smithsonian Institution Press, Washington.

Jurmain, R, Cardoso, F A, Henderson, C & Vilotte, 2011 'Bioarchaeology's Holy Grail: the reconstruction of activity', in Grauerm, A L (ed) *A Companion to Paleopathology,* Wiley-Blackwell, Oxford, 3–20.

Kaplan, F S & Singer, F R 1995 'Paget's Disease of Bone: Pathophysiology, Diagnosis, and Management', *Journal of the American Academy of Orthopaedic Surgeons* 3 (6): 336–44.

Kausmally, T 2004 *Report on the Human Remains from St Johns, Ousebridge, York,* Unpublished report, On-Site Archaeology, York.

Kean, W F, Kean, R, Buchanan, W W 2004 'Osteoarthritis: Symptoms, signs and sources of pain', *Inflammopharmacology* 12(1): 3–31.

Kelley, M A 1982 'Intervertebral osteochondrosis in ancient and modern populations', *American Journal of Physical Anthropology* 59(3): 271–79.

Keynes, S 2000 'Diocese and Cathedral before 1056', in Aylmer G E & Tiller J E (eds) *Hereford Cathedral: A History,* The Hambledon Press, London, 3–20.

Kjellström, A 2012 'Possible Cases of Leprosy and Tuberculosis in Medieval Sigtuna, Sweden', *International Journal of Osteoarchaeology* 22: 261–83.

Knusel, C 2000 Bone adaptation and its relationship to Physical activity in the past', in Mays, S & Cox, M **Human Osteology in Archaeology and Forensic Science,** Cambridge University Press, New York, 381–401.

Knusel, C J, Goggel, S & Lucy, D 1997 'Comparative Degenerative Joint Disease of the Vertebral Column in the Medieval Monastic Cemetery of the Gilbertine Priory of St Andrews, Fishergate, York, England', **American Journal of Physical Anthropology** 103: 481–95.

Knusel, C J, Roberts, C A & Boyleston, A 1996 'When Adam Delved…An Activity-Related Lesion in Three Human Skeletal Populations', American Journal of Physical Anthropology 100: 428–34.

Langford, A W 1956 'The Plague in Herefordshire' in **Transactions of the Woolhope Naturalists' Field Club** XXXV: 146–53.

Larsen, C S 1997 **Bioarchaeology: Interpreting Behaviour from the Human Skeleton,** Cambridge University Press, Cambridge.

Lawrence, J S 1969 'Disc Degeneration: its Frequency and Relationship to Symptoms', **Annals of the Rheumatic Diseases** 28: 121–38.

Lawson, G 1995 **Pig Metapodial 'Toggles' and Buzz-discs – Traditional Musical Instruments,** Unpublished report, Finds Research Group 700–1700, Datasheet 18.

Lee, H J, Shin, M S, Park, B Y, Lim, S Y, Pyon, J K, Bang, S I, Oh, K S & Mun, G H 2011 'Multiple Osteomas in the Skull Vault: Case Report', **Journal of Korean Society of Plastic Reconstructive Surgery** 38(4): 512–5.

Leonard, M A 1974 'The Inheritance of Tarsal Coalition and its Relationship to Spastic Flat Foot', **Journal of Bone and Joint Surgery** 56B (3), 520–6.

Lewis, M E 2004 'Endocranial Lesions in Non-adults Skeletons: Understanding their Aetiology', **International Journal of Osteoarchaeology** 14: 82–97.

Lewis, M E 2007 **The Bioarchaeology of Children,** Cambridge University Press, New York.

Litten, J 1991 **The English Way of Death: The Common Funeral Since 1450,** Robert Hale, London.

Liu, Y, Wang, H, You, M, Zang, Z, Miao, J, Shimisutani, K & Koseki, T 2010 'Ossifying fibromas of the jaw bone: 20 cases' in **Dentomaxillofacial Radiology** 39: 57–63.

Locke, E A 1915 'Secondary hypertrophic osteoarthropathy and its relation to simple club fingers', **Archives of Internal Medicine** 15: 659–713.

Logrosino, G, Mazza, O, Aulisa, G, Pitta, L, Pola, E & Aulisa, L 2001 'Spondylolysis and spondylolisthesis in the pediatric and adolescent population', **Child's Nervous System** 17: 644–55.

Lovejoy, C O, Meindl, R S, Pryzbeck, T R & Mensforth, R P 1985 'Chronological metamorphosis of the auricular surface of the ilium: a new method for the determination of adult skeletal age at death', **American Journal of Physical Anthropology** 68: 15–28.

Maclean, J F 1883 **Annals of Chepstow Castle or Six Centuries of the lords of Striguil from the Conquest to the revolution,** William Pollard, Exeter.

McCorkell, S J 1985 'Fractures of the styloid process and stylohyoid ligament: an uncommon injury', **The Journal of Trauma** 25 (10): 1010–2.

MacGregor, A 1985 **Bone Antler Ivory & Horn: the technology of skeletal materials since the Roman period,** Croom Helm, London.

MacGregor, A, Mainman, A J & Rogers, N S H 1999 'Craft, Industry and Everyday Life: Bone, Antler, Ivory and Horn from Anglo-Scandinavian and Medieval York', **The Archaeology of York: The Small Finds** Vol 17/12, Council for British Archaeology, York.

McKinley, J I & Roberts, C 1993 **Excavation and post-excavation treatment of cremated and inhumed human remains,** Institute for Archaeologists Technical paper No. 13.

Mader, R, Novofestovski, I, Adawi, M & Lavi, I 2009 'Metabolic syndrome and cardiovascular risk in patients with diffuse idiopathic skeletal hyperostosis', **Seminars in Arthritis and Rheumatism** 38: 361–5.

Mainman, A J & Rogers, N S H 2000 'Craft, Industry and Everyday Life: Finds from Anglo Scandinavian York', **The Archaeology of York** Vol 17/14, York Archaeological Trust, Council for British Archaeology, York.

Major, R H 1954 **A history of Medicine,** C C Thomas, Springfield.

Mandell, G A, Morales, R W, Harcke, H T & Bowen, J R 1993 'Bone scintigraphy in patients with atypical lumbar Scheuermann disease', **Journal of Pediatric Orthopedics** 13: 622–627.

Maresh, M M 1970 'Measurements from roentgenograms', in McCammon, R W (ed), *Human Growth and Development,* Springfield, Illinois, 157–200.

Marshall, G 1940 'The Defences of the City of Hereford', *Transactions of the Woolhope Naturalists' Field Club,* Vol XVI Part II: 67–70.

Matos, V & Santos, A L 2006 'On the trail of pulmonary tuberculosis based on rib lesions: results from the Human Identified Skeletal Collection from the Museu Bocage (Lisbon, Portugal)', *American Journal of Physical Anthropology* 130: 190–200.

Mays, S 1991a *The Medieval burials from Blackfriars, School Street, Ipswich, Suffolk,* Unpublished report, Ancient Monuments Laboratory Report, 16/91: Part 1, English Heritage

Mays, S 1991b 'Papers from the bone taphonomy workshop at York, September 1991: Taphonomic factors in a human skeletal assemblage', in *Circaea,* 9(2): 54–7.

Mays, S 2000 'Biodistance studies using craniometric variation in British archaeological skeletal material', in Mays, S & Cox, M *Human Osteology in Archaeology and Forensic Science,* Cambridge University Press, New York, 277–88.

Mays, S 2002 'Osteological and Biomolecular Study of Two Possible Cases of Hypertrophic Osteoarthropathy from Mediaeval England', *Journal of Archaeological Science* 29: 1267–76.

Mays, S 2007a 'Part Three The Human Remains', in Mays, S Harding, C & Heighway, C *Wharram XI: The Churchyard (A Study of Settlement on the Yorkshire Wolds),* York University Archaeological Publications 13, York, 77–192.

Mays, S 2007b 'Lysis at the Anterior Vertebral Body Margin: Evidence for Brucellar Spondylitis?', *International Journal of Osteoarchaeology* 17: 107–18.

Mays, S, Brickley, M & Ives, R 2006 'Skeletal Manifestations of Rickets in 'Infants and Young Children in a Historic Population from England', *American Journal of Physical Anthropology* 129: 362–74.

Mays, S & Cox, M 2000 *Human Osteology in Archaeology and Forensic Science,* Cambridge University Press, New York.

McKellar Hall, R D 1940 'Clay-Shoveler's Fracture', *Journal of Bone and Joint Surgery (American edition)* 22: 36–75.

Melen, I, Lindahl, L, Andreasson, L & Rundcrantz, H 1986 'Chronic maxillary sinusitis', *Acta Oto-laryngologica* Stockholm 101: 320–7.

Mensforth, R P, Lovejoy, C O, Lallo, J W & Armelagos, G J 1978 'The role of constitutional factors, diet, and infectious disease in the etiology of porotic hyperostosis and periosteal reactions in prehistoric infants and children', *Medical Anthropology Quarterly* 2(1): 1–59.

Merbs, C F 1989 'Trauma', in Iscan, M Y & Kennedy, K A R (eds) *Reconstruction of Life from the Skeleton,* Allan Liss, New York, 161–189.

Meunier, P J 2002 'The Pagetic lesion', *Clinical Review in Bone and Mineral Metabolism* 1(2): 103–7.

Miles, A, Powers, N, Wroe-Brown, R & Walker, D 2008 *St Marylebone Church and Burial Ground in the 18th to 19th Centuries: Excavations at St Marylebone School, 1992 and 2004–6,* MOLAS Monograph 46, London.

Millett, P J, Gobezie, R & Boykin, R E 2008 'Shoulder Osteoarthritis: Diagnosis and Management', *American Family Physician* 78 (5): 605–11.

Mittler, D M & van Gerven, D P 1994 'Developmental, Diachronic and Demographic Analysis of Cribra Orbitalia in the Medieval Christian Populations of Kulubnarti', *American Journal of Physical Anthropology* 93: 287–97.

Molleson, T & Cox, M 1993 *The Spitalfields Project Vol 2 The Anthropology: The Middling Sort,* CBA Research Report 86 Archaeology Data Service accessed online November 2012 at: http://archaeologydataservice acuk/archives/view/spitalfields_ var_2001/reports cfm?CFID=20848&CFTOKEN=8BCAA315-8D7E-4C53-8F

Monfort, J, Rotes Sala, D, Romero, A B, Duro, J C, Maymo, J & Carbonell, J 1999 'Epidemiological, clinical, biochemical, and imaging characteristics of monostotic and polyostotic Paget's disease', *Bone* 24(5): 13S–14S.

Montgomery, J, Evans, J, Powlesland, D & Roberts, C 2005 'Continuity or colonization in Anglo-Saxon England? Isotope evidence for mobility, subsistence practice, and status at West Heslerton', *American Journal of Physical Anthropology* 126(2), 123–38.

Moore, W J & Corbett, M E 1978 'Dental caries experience in man', in Rowe, N H (ed) *Diet, Nutrition and Dental Caries,* 3–19 University of Michigan School of Dentistry & the Dental Research Institute, Chicago.

Morgan, P 1976 *The Cathedral Close, Friends of Hereford Cathedral,* 42nd Annual Report.

Morris, R K 2000 'The Architectural History of the Medieval Cathedral Church', in Aylmer G E & Tiller J E (eds) *Hereford Cathedral: A History,* The Hambledon Press, London, 203–40.

Murray, R O, Jacobson, H G & Stocker, D J 1990 *The Radiology of Skeletal Disorders Vol 1; Fundamentals of Skeletal Radiology,* 3rd edition, Churchhill Livingstone, London.

Nobuhiko, M & Akiyama, I 2006 'Diffuse idiopathic skeletal hyperostosis associated with risk factors for stroke', *Spine* 31 (8): E225–9.

Ortner, D J 2003 *Identification of Pathological Conditions in Human Skeletal Remains,* 2nd edition, Academic Press, London.

Ortner, D J & Ericksen, M F 1997 'Bone Changes in the Human Skull Probably Resulting from Scurvy in Infancy and Childhood', *International Journal of Osteoarchaeology* 7: 212–20.

Ortner, D J & Mays, S 1998 'Dry-bone Manifestations of Rickets in Infancy and Early Childhood', *International Journal of Osteoarchaeology* 8: 45–55.

Ortner, D J, Butler, W, Cafarella, J & Milligan, L 2001 'Evidence of probable scurvy in subadults from archaeological sites in North America', *American Journal of Physical Anthropology* 114: 343–51.

Ottaway, P 1992 'Anglo-Scandinavian Ironwork from 16–22 Coppergate', *The Archaeology of York,* Vol 17/6, York Archaeological Trust, Council for British Archaeology, York.

Ottaway, P & Rogers, N 2002 'Craft, Industry and Everyday Life: Finds from Medieval York', *The Archaeology of York,* Vol 17/15, York Archaeological Trust, Council for British Archaeology, York

Ottaway, P, Wastling, L M, Rogers, N, Foreman, M, Starley, D 2009 'Domestic fittings and implements', in Evan, D H & Loveluck, C (eds) *Life and Economy at Early Medieval Flixborough, c AD 600–1000: Vol 2, The Artefact Evidence,* Oxbow Books, Oxford, 166–243.

Oxenham, M F, Matsumura, H & Nishimoto, T 2006 'Diffuse idiopathic skeletal hyperostosis in late Jomon Hokkaido, Japan', *International Journal of Osteoarchaeology* 16: 34–46.

Park, J G, Lee, J K & Phelps, C T 1994 'Os acromiale associated with rotator cuff impingement: MR imaging of the shoulder', *Radiology* 193: 255–7.

Pine, D S, Cohen, P & Brook, J 1996 'Emotional Problems During Youth as Predictors of Stature During Early Adulthood: Results From a Prospective Epidemiologic Study' *Pediatrics* 97: 6, 856–63.

Prentice, A 2003 'Pregnancy and lactation', in Gloriuex, F, Pettifor, J & Juppner, H (eds), *Pediatric bone biology and disease,* Academic Press, New York, 249–69.

Pritchard, T C & Alloway, K D 1999 *Medical Neuroscience,* Wiley-Blackwell, Malden.

Radin, E L, Paul, I L & Rose R M 1980 'Osteoarthritis as a Final Common Pathway', in Nuki, G (ed) *The Aetiopathogenesis of Osteoarthritis,* Pitman Medical, Tunbridge Wells, 84–9.

Rahtz, P 1976 'Buildings and Rural Settlement', in Wilson, D M (ed) 1976 *The Archaeology of Anglo-Saxon England,* University Press, Cambridge, 49–98.

Ralston, S H 2002 'Pathogenesis of Paget's disease of bone', *Clinical Review in Bone and Mineral Metabolism* 1(2): 109–14.

RCHME 1931 *An Inventory of the Historical Monuments in Herefordshire: Vol. 1 – South-West,* HMSO, Cardiff.

Reeve, J & Adams, M 1993 *The Spitalfields Project, Vol 1 – The Archaeology, Across the Styx,* CBA Research Report 85, Council for British Archaeology, York.

Resnick, D 1988 'Paget disease of bone: current status and a look back to 1943 and earlier', *American Journal of Roentgenology* 150: 249–56.

Resnick, D 1995 'Osteochondrosis', in Resnick, D (ed), *Diagnosis of Bone and Joint Disorders,* 3rd edition, Saunders, Philadelphia, 3559–610.

Resnick, D & Niwayama, G 1988 *Diagnosis of Bone and Joint Disorders,* 2nd Edition, WB Saunders, Philadelphia.

Resnick, D, Goergen, T & Niwayama, G 1995 'Physical Injury: Concepts and terminology', in Resnick, D (ed) *Diagnosis of Bone and Joint Disorders,* 3rd edition, Saunders, Philadelphia, 2561–692.

Richardson, R 1988 *Death, Dissection and the Destitute,* Phoenix Press, London.

Ring, M E 1985 *Dentistry: an illustrated history,* Abradale Press, New York.

Roberts, C A 2000 'Trauma in biocultural perspective: past, present and future work in Britain', in Mays, S & Cox, M *Human Osteology in Archaeology and Forensic Science,* Cambridge University Press, New York, 337–56.

Roberts, C A & Cox, M 2003 *Health and Disease in Britain: from prehistory to the present day,* Sutton Publishing, Gloucester.

Roberts, C A, Lewis, M E & Boocock, P 1998 'Infectious disease, sex and gender: the complexity of it all', in Grauer, A & Stuart-Macadam, P (eds), *Sex and gender in paleopathological perspective,* Cambridge University Press, Cambridge, 93–113.

Roberts, C A, Lucy, D & Manchester, K 1994 'Inflammatory Lesions of the Ribs: An Analysis of the Terry Collection', *American Journal of Physical Anthropology* 95: 169–82.

Roberts, C & Manchester, K 1995 *The Archaeology of Disease,* Sutton Publishing Ltd, Stroud.

Roberts, C & Manchester K 2012 *The Archaeology of Disease,* 3rd edition, The History Press, Stroud.

Roberts, G 2001 *The Shaping of Modern Hereford,* Logaston Press, Almeley.

Rogers, P W 1997 'Textile Production at 16–22 Coppergate', *The Archaeology of York: The Small Finds* Vol 17/11, Council for British Archaeology, York.

Rogers, J 2000 'The palaeopathology of joint disease', in Mays, S & Cox, M *Human Osteology in Archaeology and Forensic Science,* Cambridge University Press, New York, 163–82.

Rogers, J & Waldron, T 1995 *A Field Guide to Joint Diseases,* John Wiley & Sons, Chichester.

Rogers, J & Waldron, T 2001 'DISH and the monastic way of life', *International Journal of Osteoarchaeology* 11, 357–65.

Rogers, J, Waldron, T, Dieppe, P & Watt, I 1987 'Arthropathies in palaeopathology: the basis of classification according to most probable cause', *Journal of Archaeological Sciences* 14: 179–93.

Rogers, P W 2007 *Cloth and Clothing in Early Anglo-Saxon England, AD 450–700,* CBA Research Report 145, Council for British Archaeology, York.

Roseff, R 2003 'Hereford's Changing Population' in Hereford Through Time, *Herefordshire Council,* accessed online November 2012: http://www herefordshire gov uk/htt/1344 aspx

Rousham, E K & Humphrey, L T 2002 'The dynamics of child survival', in Macbeth, H & Collinson, P (eds), *Human population dynamics: cross-disciplinary perspectives,* Biosocial Society Symposium Series, Cambridge, 124–40.

Schaefer, M, Black, S & Scheuer, L 2009 *Juvenile Osteology: a laboratory and field manual,* Academic Press, Elsevier, USA.

Scheuer, L & Black, S 2000 *Developmental Juvenile Osteology,* London.

Scheuer, L & Black, S 2004 *The Juvenile Skeleton,* Elsevier Academic Press, London.

Schmorl, G & Junghanns, H 1971 *The Human Spine in Health and Disease,* 2nd American edition (transl E F Beseman), Grune & Stratton, New York.

Schofield, J & Vince, A 1994 *Medieval Towns,* Leicester University Press, Leicester.

Scully, C & Cawson, R A 1999 *Oral Disease: colour guide,* 2nd edition, Churchill Livingstone, Edinburgh.

Seah, Y H 1995 'Torus palatinus and torus mandibularis: a review of the literature', *Australian Dental Journal* 40: 318–21.

Shahar, S 1990 *Childhood in the Middle Ages,* Routledge, London.

Sharrard, W J W 1955 'The distribution of the permanent paralysis in the lower limb in poliomyelitis', *The Journal of Bone and Joint Surgery* 37B: 540–58.

Shoesmith, R 1980 *Hereford Cathedral Excavations, Vol 1 Excavations at Castle Green,* CBA Research Report 36, London.

Shoesmith, R 1982 *Hereford City Excavations Vol 2 Excavations on and close to the defences,* CBA Research Report 46, London.

Shoesmith, R 1984 'St Guthlac's Priory, Hereford: The skeletal remains', *Transactions of the Woolhope Naturalists' Field Club,* XLIV: III: 321–57.

Shoesmith, R 1985 *Hereford City Excavations, Vol 3, The Finds,* CBA Research Report No. 58, Council for British Archaeology.

Shoesmith, R 1992 *Hereford: History and Guide,* Alan Sutton, Stroud.

Shoesmith, R 2000 'The Close and its Buildings', in Aylmer G E & Tiller J E (eds) *Hereford Cathedral: A History,* The Hambledon Press, London, 293–310.

Shoesmith, R 2011 'Hereford Cathedral Barn', *Transactions of the Woolhope Naturalists' Field Club,* 59: 125–46.

Sieper J, van der Heijde D, Landewé R, Brandt J, Burgos-Vagas R, Collantes-Estevez E et al 2009 'New criteria for inflammatory back pain in patients with chronic back pain: a real patient exercise by experts from the Assessment of SpondyloArthritis international Society (ASAS)', *Annals of the Rheumatic Diseases* 68(6): 784–8.

Simon, S R, Radin, E L, Paul, I L & Rose R M 1972 'The Response of Joints to Impact Loading – II In Vivo Behaviour of Subchondral Bone', *Journal of Biomechanics* 5: 267–72.

Singhal, M, Patel, J & Johnson, D 2009 'Medical ligament injuries: 1 Medical collateral ligament injuries in adults', in DeLee, J C, Drez, D Jr & Miller, M D (eds), *DeLee and Dree's Orthopaedic Sports Medicine,* 3rd edition, Saunders Elsevier, Philadelphia, Chapter 23, Sect C.

Sirmali, M, Turut, H, Topcu, S, Gulham, E, Yazici, U, Kaya, S & Tastepe, L 2003 'A comprehensive analysis of traumatic rib fractures: morbidity, mortality and management', *European Journal of Cardiothoracic Surgery* 24: 133–8.

Smallman-Raynor, M R & Cliff, A D *Poliomyelitis: Emergence to Eradication,* Oxford University Press, New York.

Smith G R, Cherry J E 1988 'Traumatic Eagle's syndrome: report of a case and review of the literature', *Journal of Oral and Maxillofacial Surgery* 46: 606–9.

Sparks, C S & Jantz, R L 2002 'A reassessment of human cranial plasticity: Boas revisited', *Proceedings of the National Academy of Sciences of the United States of America* 99 (23): 14636–39.

Stallibrass, S 2002 *The possible use of fish and cattle bones as rosary beads,* Unpublished report, Finds Research Group 700–1700 Datasheet 29.

Stallibrass, S 2005 'Art, Archaeology, Religion and Dead Fish: A Medieval Case Study from Northern England' in Pluskowski, A *Just Skin and Bones? New Perspectives on Human-Animal Relations in the Historical Past,* BAR International Series 1410, Archaeopress, Oxford 105–12.

Stirland, A J 2000 *Raiding the Dead: The Skeleton Crew of King Henry VIII's Great Ship, the Mary Rose,* John Wiley & Sons, Chichester.

Stone, R 1991 *Watching Brief and Evaluation South of the Brewhouse of the Vicars' Choral,* Unpublished Report, Archaeological Investigations Ltd, Hereford Archaeology Series 105.

Stone, R & Appleton-Fox, N 1996 *A View from Hereford's Past: A report on the archaeological excavation of Hereford Cathedral Close 1993,* Logaston Press, Almeley

Storey, G O & Scott, D L 1998 'Arthritis associated with venereal disease in nineteenth century London', *Clinical Rheumatology* 17, 500–4.

Stroud, G & Kemp, R L 1993 'Cemeteries of the Church and Priory of St Andrew's, Fishergate, York', *The Archaeology of York: The Medieval Cemeteries (York)* Vol 12/2, Council for British Archaeology, York.

Stuart-Macadam, P 1985 'Porotic hyperostosis: representative of a childhood condition', *American Journal of Physical Anthropology* 66: 391–8.

Stuart-Macadam, P 1989 'Nutritional deficiency diseases: a survey of scurvy, rickets and iron-deficiency anemia', in Işcan, M Y & Kennedy K A R (eds), *Reconstruction of Life from the Skeleton,* 201–22 Allan Liss, New York.

Stuart-Macadam, P 1992 'Porotic hyperostosis: A new perspective', *American Journal of Physical Anthropology* 87: 39–47.

Suchey, J M & Brooks, S T 1990 'Skeletal age distribution based on the Os pubis: a comparison of the Acsadi-Nemeskeri and Suchey-Brooks Methods', *Human Evolution* 5: 227–38.

Swanson, R & Lepine, D 2000 'The Later Middle Ages, 1268–1535', in Aylmer G E & Tiller J E (eds) *Hereford Cathedral: A History,* The Hambledon Press, London, 48–86.

Swärd, L, Hellström, M, Jacobsson, B & Karlsson, L 1993 'Vertebral ring apophysis injury in athletes Is the etiology different in the thoracic and lumbar spine?' *American Journal of Sports Medicine* 21: 841–5.

Takao, M, Ochi, M, Oae, K, Naito, K & Uchio, Y 2003 'Diagnosis of a tear of the tibiofibular syndesmosis: the role of arthroscopy of the ankle' in *The Journal of Bone & Joint Surgery (British Vol)* 85-B: 324–9.

Talbott, J H & Lilienfeld, A 1959 'Longevity in gout', *Geriatrics* 14: 409–20.

Talbott, J H & Terplan, K L 1960 'The kidney in gout', *Medicine* (Baltimore) 36: 405–67.

Tamura, Y, Welch, D C, Zic, A J, Cooper, W O, Stein, S M & Hummell, D S 2000 'Scurvy presenting as a painful gait with bruising in a young boy', *Archives of Pediatrics & Adolescent Medicine* 154: 732–5.

Taylor, H M & Taylor, J 1965 *Anglo-Saxon Architecture,* Vol I, Cambridge University Press, Cambridge.

Thomas, A 1993 *The Vicars' Choral, Hereford: An interim report on an excavation at the Brewhouse,* Unpublished Report, Archaeological Investigations Ltd, Hereford Archaeology Series 181.

Thomas, A 2002 'Objects of copper alloy and iron', in Thomas, A & Boucher, A (eds) *Hereford City Excavations, Vol 4, Further Sites and Evolving Interpretations,* Logaston Press, Almeley, 155–62.

Thomas, A & Boucher, A (eds) 2002 *Hereford City Excavations, Vol 4, Further Sites and Evolving Interpretations,* Logaston Press, Almeley.

Trotter, M 1970 'Estimation of stature from intact long bones', in Stewart, T D (ed), *Personal Identification in Mass Disasters,* Washington, 71–83.

Ubelaker, D H 1989 *Human Skeletal Remains: Excavation, Analysis, Interpretation,* Taraxacum, Washington DC.

Ulrich-Bochsler, S 1997 'Jenseitsvorstellungen im Mittelalter: die Wiederbelebung von totgeborenen Kindern Archäologische und anthropologische Untersuchungen im Marienwallfahrtszentrum von Oberbüren im Kanton Bern/Schweiz', in De Boe, G & Verhaege, F (eds), *Death and Burial in Medieval Europe,* Papers of the 'Medieval Europe 1997' Conference: Vol II (Doornveld): 7–15.

Videman, T & Battie, M C 1999 'The influence of occupation on lumbar degeneration', *Spine* 24: 1164–8.

Violas, P, Salmeron, F, Chapuis, M, Sales de Gauzy, J, Bracq, H & Cahuzac, J P 2004 'Simple bone cysts of the proximal humerus complicated with growth arrest', *Acta Orthopedica Belgica* 70: 166–70.

Vince, A 1985 'The ceramic finds', in Shoesmith, R *Hereford City Excavations, Vol 3, The Finds,* CBA Research Report No. 58, Council for British Archaeology, 34–82, fiche M6 A2-M8 A4.

Vince, A 1994 *An Assessment of the pottery, brick and tile from the Mappa Mundi excavations at Hereford Cathedral,* Unpublished report, CLAU Archaeological Report No 85, Lincoln.

Vince, A 2002 'The pottery', in Thomas, A & Boucher, A (eds) *Hereford City Excavations, Vol 4, Further Sites and Evolving Interpretations,* Logaston Press, Almeley, 65–92

Vyce, D 1999 *The Vicars' Choral Hereford Cathedral: An Archaeological Watching brief,* Unpublished Report, Archaeological Investigations Ltd, Hereford Archaeology Series 402.

Vyce, D 2001 *Magistrates Court, Bath Street, Hereford: Assessment of Excavation,* Unpublished Report, Archaeological Investigations Ltd, Hereford Archaeology Series 495.

Wade, A D, Holdsworth, D W & Garvin, G J 2011 'CT and micro-CT analysis of a case of Paget's disease (osteitis deformans) in the Grant skeletal collection', *International Journal of Osteoarchaeology* 21(2): 127–35.

Wakely, J 1996 'Limits to interpretation of skeletal trauma – two case studies from medieval Abingdon, England', *International Journal of Osteoarchaeology* 6: 76–83.

Waldron, T 1999 *Palaeopathology,* Cambridge University Press, New York.

Waldron, T 2007 *St Peter's, Barton-upon-Humber, Lincolnshire: A Parish Church and its Community, Vol 2, The Human Remains,* Oxbow Books, Oxford.

Walker, P L, Bathurst, P R, Richman, R, Gjerdum, T & Andrushko, V A 2009 'The causes of porotic hyperostosis and cribra orbitalia: a reappraisal of the iron-deficiency-anaemia hypothesis', *American Journal of Physical Anthropology* 139: 109–25.

Walker, P L, Dean, G & Shapiro, P 1991 'Estimating age from tooth wear in archaeological populations', in Kelly, M A & Larsen, C S (eds), *Advances in Dental Anthropology,* Amsterdam, 145–79.

Walsh, J A 1989 'Disease problems in the Third World', *Annals of the New York Academy of Science* 569: 1–16.

Walton, P 1991 'Textiles', in Blair, J & Ramsay, N (eds), *English Medieval Industries,* London, Hambledon Press, 319–54.

Watkins, A 1920 'The Kings Ditch of the City of Hereford', *Transactions of the Woolhope Naturalists' Field Club,* Vol for 1920 Part III: 249–53.

Webb S 1995 *Paleopathology of Aboriginal Australians: Health and Disease Across a Hunter-gatherer Continent,* Cambridge University Press, London.

West, S 2001 *West Stow Revisited,* West Stow Anglo-Saxon Village Trust, Bury St Edmund's.

Whitehead, D 1980 'Historical Introduction' in Shoesmith, R *Hereford Cathedral Excavations, Vol 1 Excavations at Castle Green,* CBA Research Report 36, London.

Whitehead, D 1982 'The historical background to the city defences' in Shoesmith, R *Hereford City Excavations Vol 2 Excavations on and close to the defences,* CBA Research Report 46, London.

Whitehead, D 1986 'St Ethelbert's Hospital, Hereford: Its Architecture and Setting', *Transactions of the Woolhope Naturalists' Field Club,* Vol XLV Part II, 415–25.

Whitehead, D 2000 'The Architectural History of the Cathedral since the Reformation', in Aylmer, G E & Tiller, J E (eds) *Hereford Cathedral: A History,* The Hambledon Press, London, 241–86.

Whitehead, D 2007 *The Castle Green at Hereford: A Landscape of Ritual, Royalty and Recreation,* Logaston Press, Almeley.

Wiggins, R, Boylston, A & Roberts, C A 1993 *Report on Human Skeletal Remains from Blackfriars, Gloucester,* Unpublished report, Calvin Wells Laboratory, University of Bradford.

Williams, A & Martin, G (eds) 2000 *Domesday Book, A Complete Translation,* Penguin.

Wood, J G 1903 'Primary Roman Roads into Herefordshire and Monmouthshire and the Crossings of the Severn', *Transactions of the Woolhope Naturalists' Field Club,* 185–9.

Wyatt, H V 1976 'James Lind and the prevention of Scurvy', *Medical History* 20: 433–8.

INDEX